American Individualisms

CHILD REARING AND SOCIAL CLASS IN THREE NEIGHBORHOODS

Adrie S. Kusserow

palgrave
macmillan

For Naomi Quinn, Claudia Strauss,

Robert LeVine, and Charles Lindholm,

for all their insight and support on this book through

the years.

And for Ana and Will,

whose births unwittingly enriched this process.

American Individualisms
Copyright © Adrie S. Kusserow, 2004.
All rights reserved. No part of this book may be used or reproduced in any
manner whatsoever without written permission except in the case of brief
quotations embodied in critical articles or reviews.

First published 2004 by
PALGRAVE MACMILLAN™
175 Fifth Avenue, New York, N.Y. 10010 and
Houndmills, Basingstoke, Hampshire, England RG21 6XS.
Companies and representatives throughout the world.

PALGRAVE MACMILLAN is the global academic imprint of the Palgrave
Macmillan division of St. Martin's Press, LLC and of Palgrave Macmillan Ltd.
Macmillan® is a registered trademark in the United States, United Kingdom and
other countries. Palgrave is a registered trademark in the European Union and
other countries.

ISBN 1–4039-6480–7 hardback
ISBN 1–4039-6481–5 paperback

Library of Congress Cataloging-in-Publication Data Available from the Library of
Congress

A catalogue record for this book is available from the British Library.

Design by Autobookcomp.

First edition: July 2004
10 9 8 7 6 5 4 3 2 1

Printed in the United States of America.

Contents

Culture, Mind, and Society

THE BOOK SERIES OF THE SOCIETY FOR PSYCHOLOGICAL ANTHROPOLOGY

With its book series culture, mind, and society and journal *Ethos*, the Society for Psychological Anthropology publishes innovative research in culture and psychology now emerging from the discipline of anthropology and related fields. As anthropologists seek to bridge gaps between ideation and emotion or agency and structure—and as psychologists, psychiatrists, and medical anthropologists search for ways to engage with cultural meaning and difference—this interdisciplinary terrain is more active than ever.

This book series from the Society for Psychological Anthropology establishes a forum for the publication of books of the highest quality that illuminate the workings of the human mind, in all of its psychological and biological complexity, within the social, cultural, and political contexts that shape thought, emotion, and experience.

Introduction

For too long, social theorists have spoken of the genericized lump of "individualism" without reference to the varying styles, subtypes, subtleties, and nuances individualism inevitably takes on, especially in relation to one's social class. Social inequality has been left out of descriptions of individualism, as if both the poor and the wealthy practice and socialize the same monolithic and general meanings of individualism, as if like some Platonic form, the meanings of individualism float above one's local visions of the future, one's sense of hope or promise, danger, possibility, or caution. This book is primarily about class differences in socialization of individualism in three communities in Manhattan and Queens. It attempts to bring social class back into discussions of individualism in America. It attempts to dehomogenize the monolithic American "individualism" by describing the ways individualistic styles are conceptualized and socialized differently depending on the socioeconomic terrain (both conceptual and physical) one inhabits. This book is also about the ways parents and teachers from different class backgrounds conceptualize the self of the child in ways that are ultimately adaptive and reflective of the wealthy or poor environments the child inhabits. During my field work in the New York City area, I observed the ways in which children were socialized into *hard* and *soft* styles of individualism, within which various substyles of individualism (each with its projective and protective stances) also emerged. Hard individualism emphasized a tough, resilient self that was hardy enough either to protect itself from violence, poverty, and misfortune (as in Queenston) or to project itself into a higher social class (as in Kelley). Soft individualism, on the other hand, with its more psychologized conception of self, emphasized the delicacy of the child's self, the extreme care, resources, wide canvas, and gentle touch needed to help the unique self of the child flower and open up into her full potential. Both these general styles of hard and soft individualism are socialized in very different ways. By looking at the various strands of individualism that each community weaves into its own working-class or upper-middle-class concerns and life visions, we can better understand the subtle relationship between individualism and social inequality.

Throughout my years of writing this book, I have been asked what led me to do research on this particular topic. As an anthropologist, I am often asked why I once chose to do field work in America rather than some "exotic" tribe in New Guinea. What brought me to an interest in social class in America, the great "classless" society? Hence, it seems appropriate here to talk very briefly about the paths that led me to this topic.

Since childhood, I have been somewhat obsessively gnawing at the same question—why is suffering not distributed equally and how do humans make meaning out of social inequality? How do they weave their own prominent cultural symbols and models into explanations of their relative poverty or affluence? I grew up in rural Vermont, underneath the wings of an extremely selfless mother who continually emphasized the wealth my brothers and I shared by taking us to the poorer, less-fortunate subcultures in our own backyard. Visiting nursing homes, the sick, the lonely elderly man who lived on a deserted farm in the Northeast Kingdom, I kept stumbling over the huge gap between my incredible privilege and others' misfortune. I could not make sense of it, and still can't, and hence, I keep scratching at the same spot.

When I was nine, my own father died quite suddenly, and it was with these two key experiences that I arrived at Amherst College, gritting my teeth, hoping to make sense of inequality and random suffering. In many ways even though I was raised in a highly educated upper-middle-class family, I was in no way prepared for Amherst's boarding school–like campus and savvy white upper-middle-class students, and oddly enough, I felt a tremendous sense of alienation and disenchantment. In a sense, *still* recovering from my own father's sudden death, I was raw enough to feel like an outsider, to lack the social ease and take-it-for-granted attitude I felt was necessary to exist at a place like Amherst. Hence, my first foray into the "distance" so necessary in anthropological field work was an unknowing, awkward, and painful one, but it nonetheless established my first experiences of viewing my own culture, in fact, my own social class, as alien and exotic. One evening after dressing to go to dinner at the dining hall for the hundredth time, I panicked. In that moment it seemed to me that if I stayed in this environment, I might adopt the attitudes that I was increasingly growing to despise—the complacency, competitiveness, gossip, wealth, materialism, and good life of the preppies that filled the dining hall. I felt myself fall away into isolation as the college (which of course was more complex than my initial impression!) carried on with its rituals and activities. I did not want an easy life. Instead, I craved travel and shock, radical difference and challenge.

Hence, after my freshman year, I left Amherst and went to Nepal and northern India, where I studied and lived with Tibetan Buddhists in the Tibetan Refugee towns of Boudha (just outside Katmandu), Nepal, and later, Dharamsala, India. There I began first to study the Buddhist concept of suffering. It was this experience of witnessing such tremendous poverty and grace, coupled with my own sudden loss of my father, that led me to question further social inequality and the unequal "distribution" of suffering, especially in America, where the gap between rich and poor seemed widest. On coming home and stepping down from the plane at Kennedy Airport, I expected to be nicely shocked by American egalitarianism—to experience a sort of pleasant culture shock in which I noticed at least some of the unique ways Americans avoided the hierarchies that "burdened" caste-laden Nepal and India. And yet, in New York City, I watched as a woman with a Gucci purse politely stepped over a naked woman lying wrapped in a Hefty garbage bag, vomit draining from her mouth, and moved on, as all of us do in one way or another.

This discomfort and anger at the lack of acknowledgment of social class continued through graduate school at Harvard Divinity School, where I perhaps secretly hoped that in the process of studying comparative religion, one religion might give me a reasonable explanation for social inequality. Later on, as a Ph.D. student at Harvard interested in psychological and medical anthropology, my readings on varying cultural conceptions of mind, self, and body most often referred to the Western or American self as generically "individualistic," without reference to the subtle differences in class I saw every day of my life, especially between Cambridge and working-class Somerville, where I rented an apartment. For anthropologists to go into great depth and complexity about the sociocentric or collectivist "other" and then "come home" to describe Americans as all equally and similarly individualistic seemed naïve, sloppy, and theoretically irresponsible. I began to question whether there are certain kinds of individualism that "live" in a working-class household that might differ from those of a Park Avenue penthouse. How do communities filled with poverty and crime digest a cultural grand symbol such as individualism? How is such individualism socialized? What role does it possibly play in the perpetuation of social inequality?

Benjamin DeMott (1990) in *The Imperial Middle: Why Americans Can't Think Straight about Class* wrote that the reason class goes dismissed is in large part due to the assumptions Americans have concerning the nature and meaning of social class. If acknowledged at all, class is seen as epiphenomenal, the temporary and various icing on the cake that one can wipe off. He writes,

> At the center of this mythology stands a familiar binary opposition— appearance versus reality (hierarchy as the appearance, openness as the reality). Questers advance from blindness (the delusion that class matters) to light (recognition that class is immaterial). (1990:71)

DeMott feels we need to understand the ways in which social class is not simply shown and taken off in the manner of a Harvard degree or a gold wristwatch, but lived in the flesh, held in the cells of one's self-esteem and visions of life possibility. He writes that we must first

> ... grasp that the substance of class in contemporary America concerns differences in people's actual physical, mental, imaginative activity as workers, differences in what people come to learn and master in the course of their general lives, differences in levels of self-respect, and differences in the vision of life possibility [and their children's lives I would add] that attain vivid meaning for people as family members and as participants in larger communities. (1990:53)

And so I decided to do field work in a city in the United States that held one of the widest gaps between rich and poor. I wanted to explore the ways in which individualism (the common-sense discourse of so many Americans) was taken up and used (practically, viscerally, pragmatically) by parents of different social classes while raising their children and preparing them for the futures they imagined they would enter. Wary of directly questioning Americans with bald philosophical questions about their own individualism or lack thereof, I decided to study individualism indirectly, by looking at the ways it is lived, practiced, and conceptualized among parents raising children and teachers teaching preschool. I wanted to talk to individuals about something that prompted a passionate and visceral response, and child rearing always seemed to do just this. Discussions around child rearing (and the metaphors and figurative language within these discussions) also often contain hints at the kinds of trajectories parents and teachers envision for themselves and for their children. For my field work, I set about to understand the commonsensical child-rearing practices that individualism and class co-habited, hoping this would help me understand class conceptions of the necessary relationship between self and world. How do parents both consciously and unconsciously attempt to prepare their children for life within (or beyond) their present social class?

During a theory course in graduate school I began reading the works of the French sociologist Pierre Bourdieu, particularly *Outline of a Theory of Practice* (1977). Bourdieu was the first theorist I had read who really emphasized the ways in which social structures are deeply internalized and embodied by individuals of a certain social class. Bourdieu defines habitus as "systems of durable, transposable dispositions . . . principles of the generation and structuring of practices and representations which can be objectively 'regulated' and 'regular' without in any way being the product of obedience to rules" (1977b:72). Habitus takes root in individuals in large part from early socialization experiences in which external social conditions (e.g., how wealth is distributed) are internalized. In *Outline of a Theory of Practice,* he writes, "Between the child and the world the whole group intervenes . . . with a whole universe of ritual practices and also of discourses, sayings, proverbs, all structured in concordance with the principles of the corresponding habitus" (1977b:167). Habitus consists of deeply internalized subjective aspirations and expectations that seem natural and are taken for granted. ("Of course, you don't talk like that!" "Why would you want to get a Ph.D.?" "Of course, Daddy has to go to work!") Habitus exists in the shared commonsensical realm of what, for example, a working-class mother views as possible or unlikely, reasonable or unreasonable, typical or unthinkable, successful or disastrous for those in her social group. It is "housed" in something quite subtle, quite seemingly natural as everyday knowledge around marrying, child rearing, and the taken-for-granted practices of the body (how one walks down the hall, crosses their legs, how close one gets to you while talking), eating (how one picks up their fork, chews their food), and schooling (how a student responds to a teacher's questions, classroom etiquette). Although habitus is rooted in what is often experienced as private and subjective tastes, aspirations, beliefs, hopes, and dispositions, Bourdieu notes that the habitus "could be considered as a subjective but not individual system of internalized structures, schemes of perception, conception, and action common to all members of the same group or class" (1977b:86). Hence, attributes that might initially seem like individual traits of a child (shy, confident, talkative, or silent) are sometimes rather the subjective inculcation of a class structure.

Reading Bourdieu, I began to explore further the ways in which the deep and "naturalizing" internalization of the objective structures of wealth and poverty contribute to the reproduction of social inequality. Focusing on the naturals of individual agency shifts our attention from the unequal social fabric in which the individual is embedded to their supposed unique talents and natural traits. Who ever thinks of questioning the praised givens of generosity, artistic talent, and hard work? On the upper east side of Manhattan, it is a "given," not a luxury, that the child be allowed to discover herself, what she is good at, through lessons in painting, ballet, tennis, or computer science. In lower-income parts of Queens, it is a "given" that no child should be too spoiled too much, because that's not what the "real" world is like. Everyone needs to look out for herself, that's just part of what it means to live. And yet time and time again, working-class parents often praise the toughness and stubborn spirit of their son, while upper-middle-class parents praise the precociousness of their daughter as if these were individual traits they were born with.

For Bourdieu, there are different types of capital, not just economic in the formal sense. There is also cultural capital (i.e., general cultural background, knowledge, skills, and other cultural acquisitions, passed from one generation to the next) and symbolic capital (i.e., accumulated prestige or honor). For Bourdieu, cultural and symbolic capital refer to "a transformed and thereby disguised form of physical 'economic' capital that conceals the fact that it originates in material forms of capital which are also, in the last analysis, the source of its effects" (1977b:183). Cultural capital, then, includes things like ways of speaking, dress sense, style, a good accent, etc. Children of upper-middle-class parents inherit substantially different cultural capital than children of working-class parents. And yet, cultural capital often includes characteristics that Americans often mistakenly attribute as personal rather than class-learned attributes.

The importance of this cultural capital in allowing for movement between social classes is nowhere better depicted than in Philippe Bourgois's book *In Search of Respect: Selling Crack in El Barrio* (1996). Here, racism and other subtle badges of symbolic power are expressed through wardrobes, accent, conceptions of masculinity, and body language. Crack sellers from El Barrio, in attempting to get better jobs in high-rise, office-corridor culture, are shot down because of their "inappropriate" street cultural capital of wearing "fly clothes," swearing, and talking macho to women. Bourgois notes that one of the crack sellers, Caesar, was hurt when his supervisor accused him of "looking like a hoodlum" on the days when he thought he was actually dressing well (1996:159). Ironically these same "fly clothes" made him "king of the crew" on the street. Or consider Primo, who on starting a job at an upper east side tuxedo shop finds his own street version of masculinity

colliding with the more subservient, "touchy" behavior expected of him. "I
didn't want to be measuring men. It's not for me to be touching men all over
the place like that. That's whack!" (1996:117–118). A far cry from the
psychologized gentle self-expression of Parkside, Bourgois writes,

> Indeed, upward mobility in the underground economy of the street-dealing
> world requires a systematic and effective use of violence against one's col-
> leagues, one's neighbors . . . behavior that appears irrationally "barbaric" and
> ultimately self-destructive to the outsider, can be reinterpreted according to
> the logic of the underground economy as judicious public relations and long
> term investment in one's "human capital development." (1996:24)

For Bourdieu, such deep internalization of "natural tendencies" is acquired
not only through explicit teachings (Keep your mouth shut when you're
eating! Tell me what you're feeling with your words, not your body), rules,
and "structural exercises" but perhaps more so through unconscious,
informal modes of socialization. Bourdieu gives us insight into the more
secretive dispositional, habitus knowledge that is often passed on and
learned without ever coming to surface, crystallizing into discourse or
piercing through to consciousness. Bourdieu, however, would emphasize
that what is so gently and naturally passed from mother to child underneath
the veil of conscious speech, formal lessons, or direct discipline, however, is
just as powerful in its imprint as formal rules insofar as they appear as simply
"natural" actions and everyday ways of behaving. Hence, often "schemes
are able to pass from practice to practice without going through discourse or
consciousness" (1977b:87). Bourdieu speaks of this unspoken knowledge as
the "universe of the undiscussed" (1977b:168) that comprises much of the
very subtle "apprenticeship" between parent and child that starts at a very
young age. A child grows up absorbing the "of course" nature of "the
division of labor between the sexes, household objects, modes of consump-
tion, parent-child relations" (1990:54).

    For example, in my own field work, I was able to watch both the subtle
and blatant forms of this kind of apprenticeship. A wealthy young girl (Liza)
in Manhattan walking on the street with her mother learns a great deal about
hierarchies in America, though perhaps nothing is ever mentioned directly.
As they walk, her mother's face takes on a rather emotionless quality, a slight
look of disinterest in all who pass her by. Her posture is confident and
upright, her pace brisk and full of direction. As they approach a disheveled,
scruffy man who "looks" homeless, she tightens her grip on her daughter
ever so slightly and gives the man a very slight berth, as if stepping around a
squashed piece of pizza, scrunching up her nose slightly, unconsciously
perhaps. She does all this naturally and quickly and seemingly unself-
consciously, while talking of weekend plans. Liza responds to the move-
ments of the mother's body, its subtle waves, crescendos and decrescendos in
voice and posture, the way she is brought closer in or let loose to wander a
few feet at various moments. In this way meaning slides (often, but not
always, unconsciously) from one generation to another.

The next time I walk downtown with both Liza and her younger sister, Willa, I watch her play mommy to her sister, very consciously mimicking her mother's bodily practices and nonverbal cues, proudly pressing these social structures and hierarchies into her smaller body. She models certain behavior for Willa—she becomes more serious and walks with determination, steering her away from potential dangers; for example, men who looked homeless, men who were scruffy in appearance. Unlike the lessons the mother unconsciously passes to Liza, however, Liza socializes her sister with an obvious sense of conscious pride at the new adult role she is playing, so much so that I become annoyed and ask her why she brought her sister closer in to herself around these men. She looks at me somewhat ashamed, somehow aware of the fact that her mother would not want this lesson voiced outright—that in egalitarian America where in preschool it is emphasized that everyone is your friend, this was a lesson practiced but not voiced. Hence, despite the lack of blatant instruction from her mother, she has learned about social hierarchies on the street (the bodies that are to be avoided, the ones that she can open herself to), and yet also seems to learn that this is knowledge that she shouldn't voice outright *to me*.

Hence, reading Bourdieu made me curious as to how children learn and acquire class habitus both formally and informally, consciously and unconsciously (though as Strauss and Quinn note [1997:46], formal knowledge should not be equated with conscious awareness and informal knowledge with unconscious learning).

Perhaps one of the most interesting and subtle forms of socialization I witnessed in my field work was the way in which parents and teachers used distinctly different metaphors when describing the child's self.[1] It is the exposure to certain metaphors such as *flower* (Parkside upper-middle-class community) or *sky* (as in "the sky's the limit" among the Kelley upper-working-class parents) or the fortresslike images of protection that the Queenston parents used in talking about and disciplining their children that begins to establish the child's own *naturalized* conception of her own nature, her "natural" environment, her future place in the world.

And yet for Bourdieu, such internalized knowledge does not turn us into preprogrammed robots locked into fixed routines. Habitus does not simply mimic "outside" culture but structures it as well. Habitus is a set of flexible and agile dispositions that include our personal understanding and knowledge of the world, inhabiting the body more like liquid than solid, at times varying from one individual to the next, one generation to the next, one race, ethnicity, or neighborhood to the next. If we refer back to the mother and Liza walking down the street, we know that every child internalizes the experience of the adult's hand pressure, facial posture, and avoidance of the man in a unique way. Sensing my disapproval, perhaps the young girl I took to get candy will no longer play mommy to her sister regarding scruffy men on the street, whereas another child might continue just to spite me! Because of these varying ways of digesting these structures into our own personal histories, ethnicities, and subcultures, we see that habitus does not simply reflect and reproduce culture but reacts and challenges social structures as well. Building upon Bourdieu's notion that habitus does not simply reflect public culture but actively digests it, I began to wonder, what are the ways that the grand symbol of individualism is digested and inhabited by the wealthy and the poor in America? Surely social classes digest and spit back individualism in different ways! How do different social classes use America's most commonsensical grand symbol, individualism, for its own adaptive purposes?

Perhaps one of my greatest challenges during field work was the cultivation of a nonjudgmental attitude toward the child-rearing methods I saw and heard about. Furthermore, given my own lifelong sense of guilt for all the privileges I have had, coupled with a strong empathy for the poor, I initially had to work very hard not to romanticize the lower-working-class and working-class communities in which I did field work. Given my own resentment toward the wealthy, who so often seemed to be blind to the poor, I had to work very hard not to be judgmental of the psychologized individualism and soft individualism of the upper classes in Manhattan. Given this bias, what I found helpful during my field work was suddenly to insert an interview and preschool visit from a different social class than the one on which I was currently focusing. This brought me back to a more anthropologically distant and "value-free" perspective because I was always amazed by how different the three communities were. Instead of placing value judgments on them, this kind of sudden switching caused me to marvel at the wide spectrum of American individualism and child socialization, in all of its varied forms.

Like many of the parents and teachers I describe in this book, I lean toward one kind of individualism (soft psychologized individualism) but certainly try to practice and value other elements! In some ways I think of myself as an upper-middle-class white woman who will hopefully raise her children with elements from *all* of the class communities I have studied. I greatly admire the resilience, toughness, and fortitude many of the Queens children had, the sheer density of their egos, and would hope to raise a child who is not so delicate that she is blown over by the first strong challenge she is bound to encounter. I also value respect for elders and feel a child should grow up with a true appreciation for those parents, grandparents, and local "elders" who are in many ways wiser and more experienced. Unlike some of the Parkside parents I interviewed, I do not feel a child should be treated exactly like an adult, with the same rights and privileges. I do not want my two-year-old to help decide what kind of car to get next. Ironically, what seems lacking for some Parkside children is the sense of security, protection, respect, and humility that can arise from knowing that one is *not* at the top of the hierarchy, making all the same choices as adults, with the same amount of power in all domains.

What has been fascinating to me in my limited time as a mother, however, is the gravitational pull of my own upper-middle-class habitus, that is to say, the way in which psychologized individualism seems to arise quite naturally in interactions with my own daughter and son. When interacting with them it seems common sense to use the tone of voice I use, to phrase questions, suggestions, and choices in certain ways, all ways strikingly similar to those of the Parkside parents. Hence, despite my exposure to both class and cultural variations in child rearing, I have often been quite surprised by the way soft individualism nudges its way into my own voice and body, as natural as breathing.

Chapter One

Ethnographic Method and Context

I lived in the New York City area from 1993 to 1995, dividing my time between three communities: Parkside, a wealthy, mainly white, upper east side neighborhood in Manhattan; Kelley, a white working-class community in Queens; and Queenston, a mixed, somewhat lower-working-class community also in Queens. All of these names are pseudonyms. When I started my field work, I expected I might find a decrease in individualistic tendencies around child rearing among the lower-working class. Instead, I simply found a different kind of individualism, which leads me to address the issue of the two kinds of individualism I found in my research. I feel strongly that these kinds of individualism be thought of more as tendencies, leanings, or, as Bourdieu might say, "trajectories" rather than homogenous categories or monolithic stereotypes that every parent fulfills. For the most part, I lean toward psychologized individualism, but this in no way prevents me from practicing other kinds of individualism as well. I like to think of these kinds of individualism as akin to the way recent psychological anthropologists have had to rethink the labels individualistic/collectivistic, or egocentric/sociocentric. No one American woman is completely individualistic, just as no one Japanese woman is completely sociocentric. Both elements are contained in every individual, and yet we often find groups and individuals from particular cultures and classes with leanings *toward* one kind more than the other. I like to refer to the parents I study in this book as *individuotropic*, i.e., living and leaning toward one kind of individualism as opposed to being a preprogrammed robot of sorts. Some of the parents I interviewed leaned quite heavily toward one kind of individualism, others seemed more of a mix. In order to elaborate on the various types of individualism in Manhattan and Queens, I have obviously focused more on those parents who lean toward being clear exemplars of hard or soft individualism.

Queens: Queenston and Kelley

Queens is the largest of the New York City boroughs. It has the second largest population next to Manhattan, totaling nearly 2 million people. It is a largely suburban area, and quite ethnically diverse, with Italian, Middle Eastern, Asian, Jewish, Hispanic, and African American neighborhoods. Astoria has the largest number of Greek inhabitants in the United States, and Jackson Heights has a large number of South Americans (Columbians,

Ecuadorians, Argentineans). I conducted interviews and participant observation in two communities of Queens, Kelley and Queenston. Both communities in Queens shared a sense of needing to toughen the child's self but
differed in their reasons why and hence; each Queens community, while
sharing a conception of the importance of a sturdy, tough self, had different
trajectories for their child's self. These trajectories seemed closely linked to
the differences in neighborhood environments between Kelley residents and
Queenston residents surrounding issues of safety, drugs, income, kinship
networks, supportive, or "dangerous" neighbors.

In the southern part of Queens, below the JFK airport runways, is a
peninsula that juts into the Atlantic Ocean. Along the southern tip of this
peninsula are the Rockaways, which form the largest municipal beach in the
country. Off the northern end of this peninsula, is an island in Jamaica Bay.
On the southern end of this island is the community of Kelley, situated near
the tidal wetlands of the Jamaica Bay Wildlife Refuge (part of Gateway
National Recreation Area), between Silver Hole Marsh and Big Egg Marsh.
Almost no people inhabited Kelley before 1880. It started out as a place with
a few shacks, the homes of oyster planters and fisherman in the summers.
With the building of the New York, Woodhaven, and Rockaway Railroad,
however, Kelley became a regular stop, and beach shacks were built for
weekend fishers. A building boom followed this in the late 1800s and early
1900s. According to Vincent Seyfried, historian and author of *Queens: A
Pictorial History* (1982), the beginning of the end for Kelley began when
waste began to be dumped into Jamaica Bay, leading to the enforcement of a
no fishing policy. And yet Kelley was called a potential health hazard
because its septic tanks often spread into Jamaica Bay, making the area ripe
for hepatitis. It took until 1988 to establish a sewer system. Kelley has a
history of banding together in the face of opposition. In the late 1960s the
community successfully opposed a proposal that would extend the JFK
airport runways into its land. In the 1970s, when the city proposed that
Kelley be cleared of all residents and buildings and the island be donated as
part of the Jamaica Bay Wildlife Refuge, again, residents protested and the
city receded.

Aesthetically, Kelley was a rather bleak looking community, with very
little color or extras such as street benches or well-manicured parks. As one
journalist, Sharon Seitz wrote, Kelley is "the black swan in a city where
appearance, wealth and formality are often a preoccupation" (1996:3).
Seyfried says of the community, "I don't think anybody even notices that
there's a community there. It's a curious backwater, an unearthly, unworldly
place" (1990:4). Many Manhattanites considered it culturally deprived. It
had no movies, no theater, little entertainment in general, and no spiffy
sports facilities. People relied heavily on cars and buses and went to the
nearest mall for groceries, a pharmacy, or shopping. It is also an extremely
windy area, with seagulls everywhere, the bay replete with 300 species of
birds. It consists mainly of small shacks or beach houses quite close together
with the larger and wealthier residences along the water. Most houses have

concrete lawns, situated so close together that people can talk from window to window, and often do. The plots for the houses average about 25 feet wide and 100 feet deep. The community is about one and one-eighth miles long (21 blocks), one-quarter mile wide and has approximately 2,500 people. At its widest point it is nine blocks wide. It has its own subway stop and can be accessed by bus. By subway it is 90 minutes from Manhattan. During my field work Kelley had one public school and one Catholic School, a marina, two small deli/grocery stores, a library, a barber shop, two churches (St. Virgilius Roman Catholic Church and the Presbyterian Christ Church by the Sea), a video store, a couple of restaurants and pubs, and a preschool. Many people had boats and spent their leisure time fishing, crabbing, or cruising around the bay.

At the time I engaged in field work, almost 98 percent of the residents of Kelley were white. The remaining 2 percent were black and Hispanic. Most of the residents are natives, whose parents were also born in the United States. In Kelley it isn't uncommon to find three generations living next to each other. Most of the residents are Protestant or Catholic, and a large majority are Irish, German, or Italian. They are employed primarily in the civil services. Most of the adults had completed at least three years of high school. The average number of school years completed by adults 25 years or older was ten. A little over one-third graduated from high school. Three-quarters of the men were employed, compared with one-third of the women. Most of the fathers I talked to were fireman, policeman, or construction workers. Other occupations included mechanics, clerical workers, transport and equipment operatives, or cleaning and food service workers. Many of the mothers were nurses, secretaries, or clerical and kindred workers, or worked in retail or manufacturing companies.

Just outside of Kelley (but still a number of subway stops away) was P.S. 2, a school serving families living on the Queenston part of Rockaway Peninsula. The Rockaway Peninsula is eleven miles long and three-quarters of a mile in width, with a population of approximately 21,000 (86.3 percent white, 5.3 percent Hispanic, 6.4 percent black and 2 percent Asian/Pacific). Rockaway Peninsula is extremely varied in terms of income, often called a microcosm of New York City, with a small number of wealthy residents right on the water and the majority of families with lower incomes living in bungalows on the small side streets off the main boulevard that stretch into Queens proper. Queenston is one of twelve other neighborhoods on this peninsula, including Breezy Point, Rockaway Point, Neponsit, Belle Harbor, Rockaway Park, Seaside, Hammel, Arverne, Edgemere, Wavecrest, Far Rockaway, and Bayswater. During the time I was there, there was a very uneasy mix of a small percentage of middle-class whites in the high rises next to the beach, with lower income whites in houses stemming away from the beach. In the midst of this were housing projects. The area I was in, Queenston, was comprised of a small pocket of working-class whites situated beside a group of housing projects and a school for juvenile delinquents, the latter of which housed mainly black youth. This social mix was made even more diverse on weekends by the number of visitors who streamed through the area hoping to catch some sun at the beach. Teenage birth and unemployment rates for youth ages 17–21 were the second highest in the borough of Queens. High school dropouts were considered to be another big problem in the district. Most people had civil service jobs or were in some aspect of technical, sales, administration, and service-oriented work. Some of the men even commuted to Manhattan for a second job. What struck me the most about Queenston was the relative absence of community and the protective neighborhood gaze I found so prevalent in Kelley.

My field work was done in the immediate vicinity of the school, P.S. 2. Coming from Parkside and Kelley, it seemed the most desolate area, with few or no trees, empty bus stops, garbage, graffiti-covered sign, miles of chipped cement, one dilapidated grocery store, a wasteland of housing projects, and prostitutes at various street corners. I could never wear sandals because of all the broken crack vials littering the street. Queenston reminded me of the poor housing that sits behind the boardwalk in Atlantic City, except there seemed to be less activity, fewer open doors, fewer children out or people walking their dogs. People seemed to keep to themselves. Even the playgrounds were not that busy. Occasionally, I felt I was walking around a ghost town. Unlike the fairly homogenous, tightly knit community of Kelley, this area was quite mixed and quite atomistic. It was a tough and violent area, a place where the white parents I interviewed saw themselves as holding their own in a jungle of violence and corrupt youth. There was very little sense of community pride, or any sense of the patriotic July Fourth–type community found in Kelley. What pride there was existed on the level of the lonely rugged individual. Danger was not in the next neighborhood or subway stop but on the same block or in one's own building. The parents in this neighborhood in general had less money than those in Kelley. Most of the mothers, if married, stayed home with their children, while their husbands often worked two jobs. Many of the mothers were divorced and on welfare. Compared to Kelley, parents seemed to lead very isolated lives, behind locked doors, in front of televisions, suspicious of outsiders, juvenile delinquents, and the "crazy people" right inside their own apartment buildings.

On the subway to Queens (one known for its lack of safety once outside of Manhattan), I tried to undergo a sort of transformation. I took off all of my jewelry, dressed in loose pants and generic t-shirts, sneakers, no makeup, often wore a hat, and looked down the entire time, keeping to myself to avoid attracting attention. I often blocked myself with a Walkman or newspaper, containing myself (in the ways so many Queens mothers sought to fortify and densify their child's self) to avoid getting in trouble or unintentionally "dissing" someone with my curiosity. Rather than interested and intrigued, I appeared bored and disinterested, a facial posture typical of subway etiquette. This same covering and plucking off of key forms of my own cultural capital continued into the homes and stores of the

poorest Queens residents I visited. Conscious even of my upper east side–
looking expensive leather bag, I started carrying a knapsack. At one house in
working-class Queenston I entered the gate to find two women dressed in
black leather jackets pierced in silver studs, with a Pitbull tucked between
them barking at me. Conscious of how "straight" I looked and acted, I
started to speak differently, more casually, less hesitantly, as if I wouldn't be
hurt by their possible rejection. I often walked around the streets acting as if I
knew my way around these parts. On the relatively quiet streets of the tight
working-class community of Kelley, where it seemed every person in each
house knew every person who walked by, I became acutely aware of my
master status as outsider. Walking into the video store, waiting for the bus,
buying something to drink at the store I often felt lonely, exposed and out of
place. It was these experiences of trying so desperately to look "real" that
made me realize how deeply class is embedded in the most subtle postures,
gestures, and mannerisms of the body. Upon returning from these "other
cultures" to Parkside, I became even more acutely aware of the upper-
middle-class postures of the Parkside parents.

Parkside

Parkside is a particular area on the upper east side in Manhattan. The upper
east side has as its boundaries, from east to west, the East River and Central
Park and running north to south, 86th to 98th streets. As many Americans
already know, the upper east side has long been known for its money and
class. The 1990 census shows that the blocks between 59th and 110th streets
from Fifth Avenue to the East River have the highest per capita income of
any urban quarter in the nation.

Before Henry Hudson sailed up the Hudson River in 1609, the
Weckquaesgek Indians who hunted, fished, trapped, and gathered berries,
clams, and oysters for food inhabited the Parkside area. It was called
"Manhatta," meaning hilly island. In 1624 Manhattan was sold to the
Dutch, and after this a steady stream of white settlers came in. The growth of
the Parkside area in particular, however, came about in 1831, when the New
York and Harlem railroad was built and claimed by those who constructed it
to be a better option than the current riverboats. Although much of Parkside
was developed, squatters still lived in shanties and old, shaggy lots.

Over the next 20 years, unemployed Irish immigrants established squat-
ter settlements along the hilly wilderness of Fourth Ave, eking out a meager
existence by milking cows and slaughtering pigs and scavenging coal
dumped by the locomotives (Butler: 1989).

And so before the advent of the New York and Harlem railroad and the
building of Andrew Carnegie's neo-Georgian mansion on 91st Street in
1902, Parkside was still relatively rural, with only a few modest houses,
Christian "charitable institutions" for mentally ill women, and squatters'
shacks. Before the turn of the century, the elite lived south of the park.

Gradually, however, the section from 23rd to 57th streets became more and more commercial, and those wealthy families who wanted to maintain a certain distance from this moved north. Carnegie's mansion and extreme wealth gave the area a distinguished air. In 1896, Caroline Schermerhorn Astor moved to Fifth and 65th, and with her the famous 400. (There were thought to be only 400 families in New York that were "cultured.")

To ensure the residential character of the neighborhood further, Carnegie purchased most of the property on the blocks to the north and south of his lot, selling off only when he was satisfied with the quality of the buyer's plans (*The Encyclopedia of New York City*, 1995). He sold many of his lots to wealthy entrepreneurs such as James Burden, Otto H. Kahn, and John Henry Hammond. Thus began the time of the luxury apartment, which continued until the Great Depression. Since then, the larger townhouses have been converted into apartments, private schools (Parkside and Yorkville probably having the largest concentration of private schools in the city), and social service agencies. The neighborhood now consists of neo-Georgian townhouses, Beaux Art mansions, art galleries, jewelry stores, clothing boutiques, and museums. Even the area east of Lexington Avenue that was traditionally working-class German, Czechoslovakian, and Hungarian, through gentrification, has been spiffed up. And yet to say that the upper east side is comprised of only the upper class actually is not true. According to the *Sourcebook of Zip Code Demographics*, the zip code area in which I lived and did my field work has a fair number of upper-middle-class families as well—families who tended to live in smaller apartments closer to the East River. The 1994 per capita income for my zip code area was $65,000 with approximately 43 percent making less than $50,000 a year. In this area, 87.1 percent were white, while the remaining 12.9 percent were black, Asian/Pacific, and Hispanic in fairly equal numbers.

Arriving in Manhattan, I decided to try my luck living on the upper east side of Manhattan as an au pair, knowing I had the cultural and symbolic capital that was so welcome in upper east side circles. I soon found out that ads for au pairs were placed in a local women's college employment office on the upper east side, and after visiting and interviewing at various homes, I was offered a position by one family who would give me free room and board in exchange for babysitting their nine-year-old daughter after school for a few hours a day.

During my field work, I spent approximately three months of participant observation in each of four preschools (two in Parkside, one in Queenston, and one in Kelley). In the mornings I observed preschool interactions between teacher and child, and teachers among other teachers (as they spoke about the children). In the afternoons I interviewed the parents of the children at these preschools. Why preschools? In large part, preschools were chosen because I wanted to focus on four- and five-year-olds who would be engaging in more advanced dialogue and social interactions than infants. This more complex and more frequent dialogue does not occur with very young children. For example, by observing a three-month-old in day care, I would not have the same access to the cultural and class values embedded in teachers' responses to children's queries, complaints, fights, and jokes.

Preschools were also chosen as an area in which to engage in participant observation insofar as they were bounded sites where the child was socialized into a class and cultural self, and yet I wondered if preschools would reflect the homes of the children whose parents I interviewed. Tobin, Wu, and Davidson in their book, *Preschool in Three Cultures: Japan, China and the United States*, note that in their interviews and observations with American preschool teachers and children, preschools are forces of cultural conservation rather than change. They are:

> not changing the family; they are responding to changes that have already occurred. Preschools, although a relatively new invention, are more a force of cultural continuity than cultural change. . . . work[ing] more to instill than to subvert the values of parents in China, Japan and the United States. (1989:221)

To what extent could I assume that certain schools reflected the same class culture that the parents were practicing in relation to their child? During the time I was shopping around for schools that would allow me to engage in participant observation, I did notice instances in which low-income children in Head Start programs were being taught by upper-middle-class teachers who reflected a type of socialization more typical of upper-middle-class parents I interviewed. I also found this to be true in P.S. 2, the Queenston preschool I observed. Whereas I never found one preschool serving wealthy children that was taught by working-class teachers, I did find instances where more upper-middle-class values were being taught to lower income children. For example, one upper-class preschool in Parkside wrote a description of itself that seemed to match the psychologized individualism of the parents it served.

> Children learn to respect the rights and sensitivities of others while retaining their own sense of individuality. . . . We strive to educate the child so that he has enough strength to remain an individual, to hold on to that precious sense of Self. They need plenty of space in which to Learn about Themselves. . . . For a preschooler an identity crisis is an ongoing process.

This same matching occurred in P.S. 1 in Kelley, and yet in P.S. 2 in Queenston, a certain amount of socialization of upper-middle-class psychologized individualism (handed down by the New York Board of Education) did permeate the classroom. When I finally narrowed down my search, however, with the exception of one preschool (P.S. 2) that was practicing some upper-middle-class forms of teaching and schooling to its children, all the other preschools seemed to match the class cultures their parents were from. Hence, in this study the reader can assume for the most part that the preschools I chose were roughly reflective of parent culture, except for the lower-working-class children who attended P.S. 2 in Queens. Hence, while mainly focusing on the hard individualism socialized in the Kelley preschool (and to some extent in the Queenston preschool), I also point out some of the upper-middle-class socialization of lower income children that occurred in P.S. 2. Unlike the Parkside preschools, I had heard from education professors and administrators at Columbia that I would have difficulty getting into the Queens preschools I had chosen. Administrators at the New York Board of Education said they were schools that valued their privacy and "didn't necessarily like opening their doors to people." Once I received permission to observe in these schools, the principals of both schools warned me of how difficult it would be to approach parents and get them to talk. Both principals said that most parents might be ashamed of where they lived or they might lie about how they really sometimes felt about their children. In both Queens preschools, as in all of the Parkside schools I observed, the majority of the teachers and administrators were women.

Social class was based on the occupation and education of parents and the fee of the schools. I decided to study co-ed preschools with mainly white children to prevent the confounding influences of race and gender. If anything, this book acts as a reminder that Americans tend to confound class and race, on the one hand, equating the lower working class and the poor with people of color, and on the other hand, middle, upper-middle, and upper-class people with whites. My methods are a reminder that we cannot always assume this type of racial diversity in lower- and middle-class neighborhoods. Kelley and Queenston were predominantly white, a reminder that these more homogenous pockets still exist in America, despite simplistic assumptions that all poor neighborhoods are filled with people of color. Why not address the issue of race? For the same reason I don't address the issue of gender. Although gender and race would perhaps influence the types of individualism I describe, these are topics for another book. Early on in my research I decided that looking at class, race, and gender all at once would be too much to tackle.[1]

Like many anthropologists trying to gain access to preschools, I found that certain schools in all of the communities I studied were not open to my "studying them," and hence, as is the case so often in anthropological field work, some of the choices were already narrowed for me. Hence, within these communities, the schools were not randomly selected but targeted with the help of two childcare experts, both of Teachers College, Columbia University. It was because of the personal connections of these childcare experts and their knowledge of areas where I might find predominantly white working and upper-middle-class populations that I was able to gain access to these schools. The participant aspect of my participant observation was minimal, limited to helping the teachers with the children only when they needed it. In general, I sat at the back of the room, observing, and found that students often forgot I was there. In my preliminary research I found that too great a degree of participation (helping teach a class, for example) limited the extent to which I was able to observe.

The focus of my participant observation was on the "practices" of individualism. I take the practices of individualism to be any verbal or nonverbal encouragement of the child's independence, individuality, uniqueness, privacy, personal expressiveness, personal rights, self-assertiveness, self-reliance, and self-confidence. I was also interested in sociocentric practices, which I take to be any verbal or nonverbal encouragement of an identification of the child's self with her social role, the group, group activity, cooperation, empathy, conformity, or knowing one's place in a hierarchy. I was exploring these practices as they are manifested in three main areas: emotions/feelings, creativity/art/play, and morality/discipline/rules. Here I was interested in the ways discourses on discipline and emotions might be veiled discourses, covering up unspoken discourses on what should constitute the normal self, what the child should identify him/herself with, in which direction the child should be developing, and so on. The focus of my observations within these areas was primarily on the interactions between teacher and child. And yet I also paid attention to the ways teachers "retold" (to other teachers and children) activities, emotional scenarios, and fights. The stories told were reformulated stories, embedded with models of the self that the teachers felt (whether consciously or not) the child should learn.

Furthermore, a main part of many preschool activities is creative/art, free play. Some of the questions I considered during these times were: To what extent is creativity praised for its manifestation of the unique qualities of an individual child? To what extent is a piece of artwork, for example, seen as a manifestation of the child's real self, inner core, which is seen in individualistic or psychological terms? To what extent are creative outlets seen primarily as something to occupy the child, keep him/her busy, etc. so that things run smoothly? What is the nature of the discourse surrounding creativity/art?

As Kohn (1963a and b, 1969), Bernstein (1971), and Miller (1989) have noted, there are class differences in strategies for controlling the child, with the working class using position-oriented control and the middle class using person-oriented control. The focus of my participant observation was often on whether a child was punished because of bad intent, negative feelings on his/her part, or because of the negative consequences of the act. Thus, a main focus of my participant observation was on teacher reactions to children's varying forms of disobedience. I was also interested in the extent to which the preschools differed in the reasons given for the rules they establish. To what extent were the reasons given to the child based on notions of hierarchy and obedience to authority ("because I [the teacher] said so"), group harmony ("all of your friends" or "everyone else" wouldn't like you doing that), equality and the rights of each and every individual, how it makes another child feel, or because breaking the rule means being a "bad person?" To what extent were children encouraged to base moral decisions on internal feelings ("be a good boy"), the feelings of others, or conformity to external rules ("because I said so")?

Interviews

My interviews with parents were an effort to unpack the individualistic and sociocentric strains in teacher and parental conceptions of the "normal" self-trajectories they hoped the child would follow. Interviews were not simply a supplement to my participant observation in the schools but formed a significant portion of my field work. I spent over half of my time engaged in interviewing both parents and teachers. I interviewed a total of 60 parents, 30 in Queens and 30 in Parkside. The interviews, including the chitchat of coming and going, lasted anywhere from 45 minutes to two hours.

Among the Queens parents (to a much lesser degree among the Parkside parents as well), I interviewed more women than men. This was sometimes because the mothers felt their husbands "wouldn't want to talk about this stuff" or "wouldn't know as much about these questions," or "wouldn't be good at it." When I insisted that the fathers could definitely answer these very easy questions, sometimes the mothers insisted they wouldn't be good at this, and so I didn't push it any farther. This was the first time I realized that some of these Queens parents felt somewhat nervous about the interview, thinking it was a test of sorts to which they might not have the right answers. When approaching them for an interview, I tried as best I could to get across that it was not an exam or test, that I was not with the New York Board of Education, simply a broke graduate student trying to talk to parents about their kids. The other reason fathers were not interviewed as much among the Kelley parents was that the husbands were literally never home during the day when I visited because of the two or three jobs they held. Some of these fathers worked night and day shifts. In Queenston, sometimes I interviewed mothers because it was clear there was not a father living with them at the moment or they were divorced or separated.

Interestingly enough, the gender division I found prevalent among the Queens parents was also true, although to a much lesser extent, among the Parkside parents. Again, Parkside mothers were more likely to be the ones who picked up their child from school, or were home during the day, or had an office at home, making interviews easier to schedule. Mothers were usually the first person I spoke with on the phone or at school. Parkside fathers were often at work until dinnertime, and sometimes the mother offered to be interviewed, thinking her husband would not want to be bothered after a full day at work. In general, however, Parkside mothers offered up their husbands for interviews much more than the Queens parents, giving me their numbers at work or telling me they would ask their husbands what would be a good time. Hence, sometimes I met Parkside fathers for interviews at work. In general, Parkside mothers seemed to feel their husbands would be "fine" for an interview, that they were just as capable as the women of answering these questions. And yet sometimes, after I pressed them about whether or not they had found a time when their husbands would be free and got no results, I would eventually give in, not wanting to be too pushy.

Selection of parents at these preschools was based on a formal letter sent home describing my research and asking for permission to interview the parents. (See Appendix A.) Not all parents from the preschools selected necessarily consented to engage in these interviews. Occasionally, I tried to interview parents whose children were not at the schools chosen but were recommended by parents as friends of theirs who would not mind being interviewed. Except for the few times when I interviewed whole groups of parents, I interviewed parents separately to prevent a situation in which one parent might overtly or subtly dominate the conversation. Talking with a mother or father alone allowed them to speak as freely as they wanted.

Most of my interviews were relatively informal and semi-structured. They consisted of a list of questions in which the parent or teacher was asked to give his or her opinion. A small tape recorder was used (with permission) during the interviews to aid in later analysis of transcribed responses to my questions. Some of the interview questions were used as springboards, intended to generate an initial discussion and further questions. The lead of the parent was then followed. Not all questions were asked in every interview. I also tried very hard to avoid "funneling," in which the parent or teacher is led toward a specific answer by suggestion on the part of the interviewer. The sets of questions for parents and teachers were somewhat different, but both focused significantly on concepts such as privacy, praise, free choice, creativity, and group activity.[2] I also asked more general questions about what the role of preschools "should" be, what were the characteristics of a good preschool teacher, and what they hoped the child would learn as a result of the preschool experience. (For a list of the interview questions, see Appendix B.) Some of these questions were similar to those used by Shweder and Bourne (1984), Miller (1982), and Tobin, Wu, and Davidson (1989) in their cross-cultural analyses, which I am now applying to social class. When it seemed appropriate, parents and teachers were also asked to describe someone they knew and liked very well. This was asked in an effort to see to what extent a person is described with reference to behavioral acts, what they do, by situating them in place and time and in relationship, or what they are like with reference to decontextualized, abstract, situation-free personality traits. This is based on Shweder and Bourne's (1984) study of person description in India and the United States, which, again, I am now applying to social class.

Interviews: Positionality, Reflexivity, and the Problem of Representation

Context of Parkside Interviews

There is no such thing as context-free knowledge, and interviews are living proof of this. Far from milking out some essential type of pure answer from these Parkside and Queens parents, their answers and my questions were always shaped by the not-so-"peripheral" subtleties of the exchange. The broad range of assumptions, readings, adaptations, and subtexts that were at play during these interviews often struck me. First-time interviews are a fascinating experiment in symbolic interaction and the microsubtleties of public encounters and assumptions. And so, during the time that I interviewed these parents I wondered to what extent my cultural and symbolic capital and presentation of self shaped the kind of discussions and types of "answers" the parents and teachers gave, not simply for the working-class parents but for the Parkside parents as well. My initial assumption that my own symbolic capital as a white Harvard-educated young woman would make it difficult to interview working-class parents was true; however, this is not to say my own cultural and symbolic capital did not also affect the interviews of those upper-middle-class parents who were more "like me."

I will be the first to say that the assumptions and readings I was making of these Parkside and Queens parents and teachers could have been totally incorrect, but nonetheless they were "real" for the interview insofar as I adapted my behavior to them and tried to compensate. My initial assumption in walking into any house or school interview was that the encounter would be somewhat awkward at first. For the most part the parents and I had never met before, except briefly over the phone or at school to schedule an interview. I worked very hard at trying to make the parent or teacher relaxed and comfortable around me. Like most anthropologists, I tried to lean toward my subjects rather than alienate them, imagining what they would find comfortable. In this way anthropologists are ethnotropic, trying as best they can to crawl closer to and inside the heads of those people they study.

The irony of this, however, is that the types of assumptions the ethnographer is making about these people are based on his or her own particular class and cultural background. Hence, the way I lean toward someone is based on my own class-based interpretation of what that person's weaknesses, tastes, desires, beliefs, joys, concerns, and habits are. If I try to appear less Harvard-upper-middle-class-like to a working-class woman, this is based on my assumption that she views my cultural capital in a somewhat negative way. The reader might experience this act of "leaning" as somewhat infantilizing, demeaning, or presumptuous. In other words, how do I know a woman might feel ashamed or proud? To what extent can I represent anyone? Never in an interview did I come out and ask the bald question: How does my presence, how I look, talk, hold myself, etc. make you feel? Such "bald" questions seemed inappropriate insofar as I thought they would hardly evoke honest answers. Who would want to say to me outright, you seem like a nosy, spoiled, rich kid? Who would say, you make me feel good because you remind me of my own days at Ivy League schools? Who is to say this type of self-knowledge on the part of the interviewee is even conscious? My answer to all of these questions is to acknowledge my own bias continually but also to realize that there is no completely bias-free stone to stand on from which to observe these parents.

But this is the kind of symbolic interaction that is best spoken about through particular examples of interactions. Often among the Parkside parents, at times I found that my Harvard dissertation field work and status as an upper-middle-class graduate student reminded them of their own love of education, their ability to speak intellectually and "academically," or the trajectory their own child might take some day. My world was not very far from their own past, or the upper-middle-class schools they hoped their child would someday attend. Hence, my own cultural capital, coupled with my undivided attention and interest in what they were saying, if anything, seemed to cheer them on into memories and discussions of their own times at college or graduate school. Some of the parents began to glow and become quite animated. My presence and my halo of cultural and symbolic capital seemed to be a positive reminder for them of their own status as an educated person. Once various colleges, degrees, courses, and geographic backgrounds were discussed, we also often entered into the game of "do you know so and so," which often proved to us how very close our social worlds were. Parents often seemed comforted by this mutual kinship. Once I mentioned Harvard and my own background, it was as if we had established a common kinship of sorts, and sometimes I had to steer the interview back toward the actual questions, lest the alma mater memories, common connections, common interests, and name dropping go on forever. One father talked about his psychology courses at college with a real sense of joy and nostalgia and seemed to love dipping back into this academic mode as a break from the rest of his day as an investment banker. He also loved musing about what academic area his son would be leaning toward in his early twenties. Hence, I tried to enter into this joyous revelry of the alma mater (not mentioning my flight from Amherst College after spending only one year there). The investment banker father to whom I spoke gave me his card and told me to look him up in the city if I ever needed any help of any sort or just wanted to chat again.

On the other hand, one Parkside woman seemed a little uptight and a bit nervous as we began talking about my own background and reasons for interviewing her. She became somewhat fidgety and looked away from me quite often, talking about her own unfinished education. My presence seemed to remind her that she never did finish college but instead got married and had four children and now was a stay at home mom. There seemed to be a sense of envy in her comments about how lucky I was to be able just to take a year off all on my own and study what I wanted. She seemed lonely in her vast, impeccably neat penthouse, the children away at school. What did it mean, then, for me to compensate? In this case, I spoke more vaguely about my own academic background, dropping the Harvard and Amherst, the countries I had studied in, which seemed to remind her of a path not taken. In this way I covered and highlighted certain aspects of my research and myself all in an attempt to get her to a more comfortable place where she would open up. Hence, I certainly did my own adjusting in responding to my perception of their areas of pride and joy, as well as to their weak, awkward spots.

Context of Kelley Interviews

My Queens interviews also forced me to question my own assumptions about working-class people and, if anything, my tendency to romanticize them as tough survivors who didn't spoil their children. I expected them to be somewhat defensive and not as open to my questions as the Parkside parents, and I expected that my own cultural capital would seem somewhat silly, odd, irrelevant, or offensive to them. Hence, I was determined to shed my symbolic wares. Given my own assumptions then, I was somewhat surprised at the ease, warmth, and nonchalance with which some of the Kelley parents took me into their homes.

However, given that Kelley had a great deal of pride in its solid and upstanding families, I shouldn't have been surprised by the relative ease with which many of these parents welcomed me into their homes. In Kelley, nearly all of the parents preferred to be interviewed at their own houses. There was once again that sense of American community pride, and the usual jokes about the tightness of the Kelley community were made. Some had already heard of me, saying, "Oh, you're that young girl interviewing parents, right? Lisa told me about you." Kelley houses were very small, often one story, and fairly bright. They variously had American flags, pet dogs and cats, big screen TVs, matching furniture sets, refrigerators packed thick with cold cuts and juices for the kids, bikes in the back, and games and sports paraphernalia lying about. They were often rather lively houses, with at least two or three kids. In these houses I never mentioned that I was getting my Ph.D. and that this was field work; I spoke vaguely of my school project and interest in children; and most parents didn't seem to want to press further, some of them thinking I was in college at some New York or Queens school. For some of the parents it didn't seem to matter what school I attended. Many of the mothers my age perhaps wondered why I wasn't married and starting a family of my own; the questions they asked were about where I was from geographically, not educationally, and if I was married and had any kids. The common ground they seemed to seek was through talk of children, not education, degrees, and alma mater. If anything, I felt like an old maid/librarian type around them, with my wire rim glasses, heavy book bag, pale face, and different accent. In these homes filled with life, activity, TV, and children's cross chat, I was sometimes the one who was in need of relaxing, whereas the parents were often very down to earth, welcoming and ready to talk.

And perhaps the parents were so outgoing in Kelley because my key Kelley informant, Lisa (who quite nicely offered to help me track down parents to interview), prescreened some of the parents for me. Lisa loved chatting with me insofar as she was also getting her college degree and could relate to someone doing an educational study. I think she saw us as two of a kind, and she took it upon herself to call her friends and those parents she knew about in P.S. 1 who she thought would be good interviewees for me. From what I could gather, "good" parents were ones who were outgoing and liked to talk, were not too poor or involved with drugs, and had at least one parent working (e.g., as policemen, firemen, nurses, elementary school teachers). Sometimes Lisa would say, "No, you don't want to talk to them; they wouldn't be good." I felt helpless at these times, because despite my saying that I'd still like to talk to them, she didn't follow it up. Sometimes I had the feeling that perhaps she wanted to impress me with her best friends. And so, the same families she didn't track down were also sometimes the ones that didn't call me back. These were poorer families who perhaps didn't want me to come to their homes. Some of these people I tried multiple times but never heard back from and didn't feel I could push any further. Because Lisa's friends had heard about me through her, there was already a level of trust when I walked into their houses. Hence, most of the parents I interviewed were at the higher end of the working-class community of Kelley.

Context of Queenston Interviews

Unlike Kelley, where, thanks to Lisa, I was able to talk easily to a good number of parents, Queenston was more difficult. I never established a connection with anyone who seemed to have the time to help me track down parents, make some precalls, etc. The teachers who had offered to help were enormously busy, and I couldn't add to their workloads! And so I was on my own, often calling people five or six times with no luck. In addition, I had to realize that some houses had no working telephone. Quite often I waited at the school for a parent to show up for an interview and never ended up meeting them. Sometimes this happened two or three times with the same parent, at which point I stopped pestering them. Often I would meet a parent after they had not shown up for an interview and expect them to apologize, but I soon realized that this would have been the reaction had they earmarked it in red pen in their desk calendars, which was hardly the case for these often exhausted, overworked, and overwhelmed women. It was at this point that I realized how irrelevant, passing, and tiny I was in their lives. My interview was not necessarily high on their priority list. In a couple of the houses that did not have a telephone, I visited cold turkey, knocking on doors, feeling completely invasive, more like a stalker, walking in on houses in the midst of dinner or discipline. During these times I felt so bad about invading with my questions that I ultimately decided I would never approach a house cold turkey again. When I expressed to the other teachers, administrators, and counselors at P.S. 2 how difficult it was for me to get anyone to interview, a couple of them mentioned in an almost whisper that it was probably because the parents were self-conscious about where they lived. Perhaps this was the case. I had the feeling that for some of these women I was seen as an authority from the educational system who was trying to see how well they were raising their child. While standing outside of doors that were half closed so that I could not see in, and seeing the hesitancy and suspicion on some of the parents' faces, I felt more like a case worker from the department of child welfare.

In contrast to the Kelley parents, I interviewed about half of the Queenston parents at school. The parents I interviewed at school seemed more comfortable with meeting me there, and although I didn't ask why, I sensed it was perhaps because of convenience (they were picking their child up anyway), or the fact that they liked the chance to get out of the house, or perhaps they didn't want some strange woman researcher nosing about their lives. At these houses, fathers were very rarely home and I can't remember ever interviewing more than a couple of fathers at school. I was also only able to interview three Queenston fathers; this low number was often because the mothers felt the father wouldn't be appropriate, the father was working two jobs, or there was no husband at the moment. Compared to the Kelley houses, some of the Queenston homes were quite dark, with shades drawn and doors locked. At times I felt invasive, as if this was as awkward for some of the mothers as it was for me. These were the same mothers who seemed to view the interview as a test they must do well on or a task they would do because their child's preschool teacher had asked them to. They shifted in their seat as if nervous, as if settling down for a challenging test. They often gave much shorter, succinct "answers" to my questions, and I tried very hard to get them to open up further via lots of obvious interest and encouragement. I then wondered whether I came across as demeaning in my somewhat fawning attempt to get them to open up. These were shrewd women who could also see I was desperate for an interview. Still there was an air of suspicion around these mothers. Sometimes I simply got the feeling they were wondering what I wanted from them, and they were just waiting for the interview to end. These interviews tended to be more structured, with awkward silences rescued by jumping to the next question when the previous one really hadn't been thoroughly discussed. In these interviews I had to work very hard at not telling them verbally or nonverbally what I wanted, despite their obvious desire to pass or please. Often I would make myself just sit with the awkward silence in the hope that the mother would continue without my prompting. These were the hardest interviews I had, and I often left feeling I had not been able to loosen the tightness and defensiveness.

Nowhere was I more struck by the way habitus is embodied than with the mothers of Queenston. These same mothers often seemed pressed for time, harried, overtired, and at the end of their ropes. They had none of the luxuries that most of the Parkside parents had (babysitters, air conditioning, washer and dryer, free time, or jobs arranged according to their own time schedules, just to name a few). They greeted me at the door, in the sweltering heat, one child on a hip, others in the background jumping on the couch, with a barking dog; they did not have enough time to shower, let alone pick up the house for my arrival. I sometimes felt as if my own cultural capital and academic project very subtly reminded them of their position on the class ladder, so I tried to compensate by speaking less academically and couching the interview questions with vernacular buffers and bits of slang. I took on a "no big deal" quality to my approach to the interview. Sometimes I think I must have looked ridiculous. Whom did I think I was fooling? I remember sometimes feeling the chaos of these houses and trying not to appear ruffled by what was to me (and perhaps many Parkside parents) very loud "yelling" at the children: "Get off the couch or I'll smack you, Nathan." "You do that one more time and I'll kick you outta here." Upon hearing these types of direct authoritative commands, I tried to smile as if this were not new to me, as if I had grown up in discipline like this. Every now and then I would comment on the child's behavior with which the mother was struggling, "So she's pretty wild, huh . . . " and smile empathetically, the mother responding with, "Oh yeah, she's a handful all right." This bonded the mother and me together in common loving frustration with "kids"—"Can't live with em, can't live without em." This type of joking criticism or complaining about the child would not have seemed appropriate among Parkside parents, who seemed much more fearful that a louder voice and more direct command would hurt the child's feelings.

Not all Queenston parents were like this, however. Some of the parents seemed totally unself-conscious, relaxed, and quite open about their lives. This immediately put me at ease as well, and in general the conversation flowed much more freely. One father, a prison guard at a local prison, was incredibly proud of his success in life and couldn't have been happier to show me his house and family pictures and talk about his past. Another woman, recovering from drug and alcohol abuse and struggling financially to support her three kids, was also quite open about her struggles in life, her recent divorce, and life on welfare. My own class standing, accent, and academic project didn't seem to threaten her in the least. Another woman, the wife of a local policeman, proudly talked to me about the way she disciplined her child, as if she had already passed the "test," as if her way were the only way any parent would discipline their child.

And yet on the whole, while Kelley seemed bustling with pride, parents in Queenston seemed understandably much more shy, suspicious, defensive, and reticent about having me come to their houses. About half of them met me at the school and we talked while their child was busy with the teachers. I often had to schedule an interview three times before parents would finally show up. Some of them forgot, some were probably too exhausted or had too much to do, and some of them lied in order to get out of doing an interview, perhaps thinking they weren't somehow appropriate, they might not have the right answers, or they didn't want someone they didn't know at all prying into their business. Feeling discouraged one day while riding on the bus into Manhattan on a P.S. 2 field trip, I asked the parent guidance counselor (hired in large part to help increase parental involvement in the school) why she thought I had so many no shows and cancellations, and such a general lack of interest, in my interviews. She told me how difficult it was even for her to get the parents to come in to the school to talk together as a group about their children. Although she encouraged them to come in with activities such as basket making, cosmetic application, and workshops on how to make your own holiday gifts to save money, most often parents said they could not come in because they were too tired, busy, or wanted to watch their soap opera. When I asked one other school teacher why parents were so reluctant to come in, she looked at me sympathetically, speaking of the parents' general lack of interest in the children's preschool, claiming that trying to get them to come in for anything was like pulling teeth. I wondered about the reasons why parents did not want to come into school. Having seen some of the mothers, my first thought was of how exhausted many of them were, trying to run a family on their own and/or hold down a job. Perhaps preschool time was their one time to recover and sleep, or their schedules simply didn't allow any "free time," or, not having the luxury of a babysitter, they needed time away from their kids, not more time with them in a school setting. I also wondered, then, at the ways the school might present itself as irrelevant to the parents, that is, what upper-middle-class activities, suggestions, and lessons were offered that did not seem relevant to their lives.

Chapter Two

American Individualism and Social Class Revisited

My research in New York was primarily an effort to improve upon the rather generic anthropological conceptions of the Western individualistic self in which social class is barely addressed and most often only one kind of individualism is acknowledged. Insofar as my research points to different kinds of individualism in America, I try to complexify and dehomogenize the generic American or Western self used as a foil in so many anthropology texts. The questions I am primarily concerned with are: What meanings does individualism have for parents and teachers from different social classes in Manhattan and Queens? How are these different meanings a reflection of each community's ultimate concerns and daily living conditions? How do various individualisms perhaps reflect different conceptions of the child's self as well as different class visions of their child's life trajectory? How can we understand the reproduction of social inequality better by understanding the reproduction of class differences, particularly the socialization of class-based individualisms? And finally, how are these class differences in individualism passed on to children as natural and self-evident and hence go uncontested and misrecognized? How do different individualistic styles become part of the child's habitus? In this chapter are brief descriptions of the theoretical frameworks that have helped me think about these questions.

The Western Self: Neglecting Social Class

Anthropologists have noted two types of models of the self: the more interdependent, or "sociocentric," way of experiencing the self (e.g., in terms of one's social role, the group, community, land, family or tribe, deities, predecessors, or posterity) and the more individualistic, psychologized, independent ego structure of the "West" (also sometimes referred to as the modern, industrial, or Euro-American self). These theoretical models (individualistic/egocentric vs. collectivist/sociocentric) rightly point to very general differences in conceptions of the self, and yet many have noted the need to move beyond this bipolar dichotomy. Whittaker (1992) writes of the "neo-Romantic North American-European-Christian self" without any mention that this term might hide some of the subtle differences between, for example, the Dutch and the Italians, or differences among those from different social classes in Italy. Throughout his history of the self, the fact that the construction of Eastern conceptions of selves is based on an embarrassingly generic Western straw man is never once questioned. Hence, the bland, generically middle-class, and solely individualistic foil that has acted as a comparative mirror to Eastern selves for decades goes unquestioned.

In recent years, anthropologists have questioned the depiction of the *Eastern* self as solely sociocentric in its orientation, suggesting that conceptions of self are not as bipolar as we think, and that a sociocentric orientation does not exclude an individualistic one.[1] Although recently a few anthropologists have begun to question very thoroughly the oversimplification of the *Western* concept of the self (Ewing, 1990; Stephenson, 1991; Stairs, 1992; Hollan, 1992; Spiro, 1993; Holland and Kipnis, 1994; Lindholm, 1997; Kusserow, 1999a), a reverse Orientalism (an Occidentalism, so to speak) exists in which the Western self is often flattened into a supposedly uniform and rather generic individualism. Often anthropologists who claim to describe the self of the "West" are really describing middle-class America, drawing heavily from literature that focuses on the United States, as if it were representative of the rest of the West (White and Kirkpatrick, 1985; Abu-Lughod, 1986; Lutz, 1988; Danforth, 1989; Erchak, 1992; Becker, 1992). Lutz (1988:55) writes, "Where I do not specify a more precise locus for emotion beliefs (e.g., everyday thought, American academic ideas, etc.), I am hypothesizing a widely shared American ethnotheory of basically Protestant European, middle-class background." Later on in her work, she writes of Ifaluk vs. "the Western perspective on emotion," "Western cultural discourse," "Western theories of human nature and emotion both academic and lay," "the ideological and objective conditions of life in the contemporary West," "Western thinking," and the "Western approach to language." (1988:209–225; see also White and Kirkpatrick, 1985.) These ethnographic references about the Western self are based on studies of middle-class Americans, such as Schachter and Singer's (1962) study of determinants of emotional states among Americans.

Nonetheless, some theorists have begun to bring social class into their analysis of language socialization among working-class Americans (see Miller, 1996; Miller, 1994; Miller and Sperry, 1988; Sperry and Sperry, 1996) and preschools in America (Tobin, 1995). Joseph Tobin argues that the pedagogy of self-expression is insensitive to class differences within the United States. He writes, "Although less often and openly discussed, social class differences in self-expression within American society are as profound and significant as ethnic and cultural differences" (1995:248). He sites Lisa Delpit (1996), who suggests, for example, that by conceptualizing self expression as *natural* behavior, as part of one's true/real self, rather than as something learned and taught, the whole process that middle-class children go through to learn this type of self-expression becomes ungraspable and mysterious to African American children. For example, Tobin (1995) states that many preschool activities such as show and tell emphasize the middle-class ideal of self-expression. For example, Peggy Miller's work on emotion socialization and class also points to these differences (1986; Wiley, Rose,

Burger, and Miller, 1998). Working-class Baltimore adults and children share their feelings and express emotion not by expressing them in a psychologized discourse of emotion words but rather by using action-oriented words such as "I kicked the table" (instead of "I was angry").

The Homogenization of Individualism

A related problem with the notion of a "Western" conception of self is the way in which individualism is treated as if it had the same meanings and uses for all groups. For example, Markus and Kitayama (1991) speak of the independent self of North America and much of Europe. The different aspects of individualism that are given at various times throughout the article include everything from self-reliance, a preference for being alone, boasting, self-advertisement, an inner sense of owning opinions, assertiveness, and, finally, the idea that the self should be consistent across cultures. The question of how and why some groups might espouse different strands and types of individualism is not explored. As we know, individualism has many different strands, meanings, definitions, and forms that are taken up differently by various individuals, local worlds, and subcultures. It is a large enough public symbol to include a multitude of meanings. Its power lies precisely in its ambiguity and plasticity, in the ways different groups can espouse and use its different elements and meanings to fit their local context.

David Potter (1973:143), writing of American individualism in the twentieth century, noted that many theorists falsely assume that all of the different concepts we place under individualism—such as self-reliance and nonconformity—necessarily go together. He notes differences between an individualism of personal self-reliance, hardihood, and stamina vs. one of intellectual independence and personal self-expression and notes the fallacy of using one term, "individualism," to express both these ideas. He writes, "in our historical experience, the believers in self-reliance, in the sense of taking care of oneself, and the believers in nonconformity, in the sense of encouraging dissent, have often been far, far apart. In fact, these two types of individualists seem to be almost natural antagonists . . . " (1973:143). Strauss (2000:108) writes, "teaching children that they have fixed dispositions (Fixed Nature) is different from teaching them that at any time they can remake their lives (Efforts and Choices), even though both of these are individualistic models." Taking up a similar theme, Bellah et al. (1985) state, "[I]ndividualism has come to mean so many things and to contain such contradictions and paradoxes that even to defend it requires that we analyze it critically . . . " (1985:142). It is a word "used in numerous, sometimes contradictory, senses" (Bellah, 1985:334). There are, Bellah says, "different modes [of individualism] even within the vocabularies of each individual" (1985:27). Bellah writes of two main types of individualism: expressive and utilitarian. Expressive individualism is the belief that "each person has a unique core of feeling and intuition that should unfold or be expressed if individuality is to be realized" (1985:334). Bellah et al. relate expressive individualism to the phenomenon of romanticism in eighteenth- and nine-teenth-century European and American culture and to psychotherapy in the twentieth century. Utilitarian individualism sees society as arising from "a contract that individuals enter into only in order to advance their self-interest. . . . [It] has an affinity to a basically economic understanding of human existence" (1985:336).

Since de Tocqueville's (1835) first writing on the importance of individu-alism in America, the question of individualism has been a central theme in writings on American culture and character. Key works in American culture are beginning to chip away at the supposedly monolithic and generic American individualist and to describe its subtle nuances by pointing to sociocentric strains within our midst. Recent scholars who have written on the topic of self and identity in America note sociocentric and conformist strains in our midst,[2] as well as in our past.[3] As Wilkinson (1988) and Hewitt (1989) have noted, for the last 50 years studies on American character have focused on the American attraction to both individualism (see Lifton, 1970; Bellah et al., 1985; Slater, 1970; Sennett, 1976; Lasch, 1979) and a sense of connection to others (Lindholm, 1990, 1988; Varenne, 1977; Goffman, 1959; Riesman, Glazer, and Denney, 1950; Reisman, 1964; WellenKamp and Holland, 1981). Holland and Kipnis (1994) in their analysis of Ameri-can conceptions of embarrassment, provide a rich non-dichotomous analy-sis by pointing to the ways in which, in some contexts, such as embarrassment, the two orientations coexist. They write, "It is only when we acknowledge both the sociocentric and the egocentric that we can understand the dialectic within the American cultural model of embarrassment" (1994:333). Waters (1990) also writes of the ways in which ethnicity is a symbol used by Americans to fulfill two equally important needs of community and individ-ual uniqueness simultaneously, pointing to the presence of both individual-istic and sociocentric strains in one symbol. She writes that ethnicity can accommodate Americans' need to feel unique, as well as their need to belong to something larger than themselves. In his book *Preschool in Three Cultures,* Tobin (1995) points to the ways in which U.S. parents felt preschools should not only socialize independence and self-reliance but teach children how to be members of a *group.* And yet, *none* of these works goes into great detail on the relationship between social class and individualism.

Recreating the Dichotomy Within

One of the challenges in defining individualism within an individualistic society is to avoid the temptation to begin stereotyping again, recreating the East/West bipolar homogeneity, only on a smaller scale, *within* the United States. In comparing a generic United States to the more relational Eastern conception of self, often efforts to dehomogenize American individualism consist of very briefly pointing out sociocentric *groups* in our midst (as opposed to actions, concepts, or discourses that all Americans share and practice at various times). There is usually a perfunctory sentence or two, or perhaps a footnote referring to women (most often Gilligan [1982] is cited) or to the working class as representing more sociocentric, relational, or conformist components of American culture (Lutz, 1988; McHugh, 1988; Derne, 1992; Becker, 1992). These attempts usually constitute little more than a few stereotypical references to a conforming working class or to other-oriented, relational women. The continued glossing of certain groups as "conformist" or "connected" only seems to bring us back to the bipolar reality we were trying to avoid in the first place. The way in which the working class have digested and used individualism in their local worlds is rarely addressed. Hence, one main problem in works on social class is that differences between upper and working classes are often painted in black-and-white terms, in a simplistic dichotomy, with an obedient, conformist working class on the one hand versus an independent, self-directed middle and upper class on the other. To label the lower class as solely conforming/sociocentric (or, as Kohn [1969] does, as obedient) and the upper class as individualistic/self-directed is simplistic and recreates the East/West bipolar homogeneity we are trying to move beyond. The ways in which perhaps a certain individualism exists in the working class and certain sociocentric strains exist in the middle and upper classes needs research. Perhaps it is time to acknowledge that in all groups, both individualistic and sociocentric orientations exist, but in differing styles and ratios, pending on the local worlds they inhabit. In my research, I hoped to move beyond Kohn (1969) and Miller's (D. F. Miller, 1989) too simplistic working class/obedience vs. middle class/self-directed dichotomy by exploring the ways in which individualism is understood, taken up, and used in raising children among working-class parents and teachers.

Clearly what is needed is an unpacking of the homogenous, monolithic term "individualism" itself. While the above works begin to probe the nuances and complexities of American individualism as well by pointing out our need for connection, none of them move beyond noting the multiple kinds of individualism and how these might relate to social class in America. Do different subcultures and social classes "practice" and experience one strain of individualism more than another? How and why has one subculture strategically selected certain components of individualism and not others and what does this reflect about the socioeconomic terrain and local worlds in which they live?[4]

Cultural Models: Individualism

Myths and symbols are part of the public culture; their syntactic looseness and ambiguity facilitates manipulation and choice.

—*Gananath Obeyesekere, 1981*

Very often during my talks with Queens and Parkside parents, seemingly "identical answers" were given. Both groups of parents emphasized the importance of the key values of individualism: independence, autonomy, self-confidence, self-esteem, perseverance, and self-reliance. Although the words "autonomy," "self-confidence," and "independence" could be plucked out of these stories, they remain empty vagaries without the particular fabric from which they were torn. Without reference to how the cultural model (see Holland and Quinn, 1987; Strauss and Quinn, 1997) of individualism is used and embedded in the particular local context of a particular community, social class, or individual, we run the risk of understanding individualism as homogenous and generic, as meaning the same thing to both groups of parents. But culture is not so monolithic. As Obeyesekere writes in speaking of the symbol of the shaven head, "One of the problems involved in the study of symbolism is the failure of both anthropologists and psychoanalysts to relate the symbol to its context. It is useless to lump all ascetic hairstyles together . . . without reference to context" (1981:50). In lumping the cultural model of individualism together as a generic whole, we miss the different ways certain strands of it are taken up and stressed by Queens parents and not by Parkside parents, or the ways in which there are even different types of working-class individualism. We miss the ways in which it has uniquely tailored meanings and uses for Parkside and Queens parents—the various ways in which it becomes a form of explanation or solution to the central issues and meanings in the lives of these parents.

Individualism can exist on many levels simultaneously—among others, on the cultural, class, and personal levels. It works as a cultural model precisely because of its ambiguity, generality, and "syntactic looseness," which allow it to fit into very different local meanings and lives. As its fingers spread out into different regions and contexts, it is taken up in different ways and adopted to fit different molds. Different strata of a society will use and manipulate a cultural model in different ways. Successful cultural models "survive" because they have the ability to act on many levels simultaneously. They are able to meet the needs and concerns of a particular group or individual without changing into something so different that they are not recognized by the culture as a whole. In this way, individualism manifested itself as a cultural model that was simultaneously reflecting and reinforcing the fabric of a community's local context and socioeconomic concerns. It was so effective because it successfully linked levels such as individual lifestyle, local context, and culture while allowing for variation from level to level. For example, a Queenston woman can idolize John F. Kennedy in a way meaningful to herself or her working-class peers, as well as maintain her participation in the spirit of a July fourth parade that displays the shared American culture of individualism. Similarly, Obeyesekere writes,

> The individual manipulates the symbol set in a manner congruent with her needs and the constraints of the culture and her social situation. The individual's use or manipulation of the symbol must be intelligible to the culture, else the hiatus between private image (fantasy) and (cultural) symbol will again appear. (1981:81)

Once a cultural model such as individualism is adopted by a particular group and is embedded in the unique local context, the experience of it is never completely shared by another group, except on a general level. An effective cultural model always exists simultaneously on multiple levels: in the case of my field work, on the levels of cultural, class, and personal, or *idiosyncratic,* levels. Certain theorists (Stromberg, 1991; Keesing, 1982; Kan, 1987; Obeyesekere, 1981; Weber, 1949; McCreery, 1977; Hallowell, 1955) have considered the ways cultural meanings are taken up differently by various subcultures and individuals, and consciously manipulated, as well as the ways individual experience is often not synonymous with cultural belief. Kondo, in her introduction to *Crafting Selves,* writes of how important it is to realize that "conflicts, ambiguities, and multiplicities in interpretation, are not simply associated with different positionings in society—though of course this is a critically important factor—but exist within a single self" (1990:45). Obeyesekere also writes of the variations in the way humans relate to such public symbols,

> . . . collectively held knowledge may vary with individuals and groups within a larger society. The very notion of subculture implies such variation. Also, though individuals may order the world through a set of ideas or meanings, their significance for individual and collective life may show qualitative differences. One does not relate to all segments of culture in the same way. (1981:111)

He considers the ways public symbols simultaneously have individual psychological meaning. "There is no question of private versus public symbol: the symbol acts on both levels at the same time, the one reinforcing the other as in a cybernetic model . . ." (1981:85). Implicit in these statements is the notion of a certain variability in the way each person, subculture, or social class responds to public symbols—my research points to the way the different communities of Queens and Parkside gave different weight to different strands of individualism, elaborating on one component more than another. Where Obeyesekere would say a symbol has both public and private meaning, I would argue a symbol has public, private, and class meaning.

In my research, I am not so much concerned with individual variation in cultural models as I am with how class-based experiences digest and use a cultural model to adapt to the ultimate concerns of their local worlds and to what extent the socialization of these class-based individualisms help keep social inequality intact. I do not focus on the intrapsychic conflicts that are resolved through the symbolic idiom in its totality, as does Obeyesekere (1981), for example, in his study of Hindu-Buddhist religious ecstatics in Sri Lanka. Whereas Obeyesekere focuses on psychological conflict, I focus on the ultimate concerns of a socioeconomic community and how these cause the community to take up individualism in different ways. Thus, my emphasis is more on the ways a particular subculture or social class takes up a public symbol rather than on how any particular individual does.

In this book I look at the ways Queens and Parkside parents take up individualism in different ways such that when speaking about their children, different types of class-based individualism emerge. I will refer to these types generally as *hard* and *soft* individualism. I refer to the individualism of Queens parents as *hard* individualism as compared to the *soft* individualism of the Parkside upper-middle-class parents. The basic difference in these forms of individualism lies in the Queens parents' conception of the child's self as a singular unit "against" the world, as contrasted to the view held by Parkside parents of the child's self as a singular unit "opening up" or out into the world. A toughening, hardening, and thickening of the boundaries of the self is thus part of the process of child development for Queenston parents and is fundamental to their conception of the self of the child. Even within the Queens hard individualism, subtypes emerge, namely projective and protective hard individualism. For Parkside parents, the socialization of soft individualism involves a more fluid conception of the self in which the child is encouraged to loosen the self, express feelings, unfold, and open out into the world.

Thus, I consider the ways we must further explore the variation, ambiguity, and dissonance in the supposedly uniform internalization of cultural meanings such as individualism, such that even within the working class we find variation. I explore the ways local context comes in to place a constraint on the supposedly total and uniform indoctrination of public meanings. I raise the age-old question: How closely paralleled are the cultural model (individualism) and the subcultural experience? How and why does a community take up and emphasize one strand of individualism as opposed to another?

Socialization/Enculturation

Anthropologists and psychologists, especially those interested in linguistic and cognitive development, have made great headway into understanding the ways enculturation occurs simultaneously with linguistic, cognitive, moral, and emotional development. Scholars are now beginning to understand the ways cultural emphases on individualism or sociocentrism are simultaneously learned by a child through linguistic (see Miller, 1982; Schieffelin and Ochs, 1984, 1986; Heath, 1986; Miller, 1989), narrative (see Miller, 1984, 1990; Miller and Moore, 1989), cognitive (see Rogoff, 1990; Stigler and Perry, 1990; Stevenson and Lee, 1990; Peak, 1991), moral (see Lebra, 1976; Shweder, Mahapatra, and Miller, 1990; Shweder and Miller, 1991; Shweder and Much, 1991), and emotional ways. Like Turner's polysemic symbols, multiple "lessons" are embedded in one seemingly thin discourse, such that a Japanese emphasis on the needs, wishes, and feelings of others is learned through the use of directives or an emphasis on individualism and each child's unique differences through mathematics learning (Stigler and Perry, 1990).

Tobin, Wu, and Davidson (1989) in their study of preschools in three cultures point to the ways American preschools differ from those of China and Japan in their emphasis on the development of what Tipton (1982) refers to as "psychologized individualism." In contrast to the "groupism" and more conformist emphasis in Chinese and Japanese preschools, in American preschools there was a large amount of free choice to suit what were felt to be the child's unique needs and tastes. That these unique tastes and needs be satisfied was considered a natural right of the individual. Efforts were made to teach the right of free speech, individuality, independence, and self-reliance. A strong emphasis was placed on verbal articulation of emotions and inner feelings. This was seen as helpful in the promotion of autonomy, individuality, and self-expression, as opposed to an expression of group solidarity. Play was seen as an avenue for self-actualization of the child. And yet, as illuminating as this comparative study is, the American preschool used for comparison is typically based on a middle-class preschool. Other studies that have explored individualism embedded in the moral socialization of the American self (Shweder, Mahapatra, and Miller, 1990; Shweder and Miller, 1991; Shweder and Much, 1991), socialization in the home (Richman, Miller, and Solomon, 1988), or American conceptions of the person (Shweder and Bourne, 1984) are also based on middle-class populations.

Other studies on how the child learns to be a member of a group in preschools in Japan (Lebra, 1976; Hendry, 1986; White, 1987; Peak, 1989, 1991; Lewis, 1989) point to the ways individualistically oriented American preschools differ from those in Japan. In Japan it is felt that it is the school's responsibility to socialize children in group behavior and to foster an enjoyment of group experience. Peak (1989:107) notes that in the Japanese preschools she studied, the minimum standard for appropriate behavior that the teacher set was comparatively low compared to American preschools. "Problems" such as screaming or a high level of noise were not necessarily corrected; rather, the class was "indirectly encouraged to set its own limits." Fights between children are not followed by apologies on both sides because there is not a strong feeling for the "rights of the victim." A booklet distributed by the Tokyo Board of Education for parents reads, "When children fight, watch them fight and allow it to happen. . . . Through fighting, children come to understand others' viewpoints, learn tolerance and self-restraint . . . and self-assertiveness" (Peak, 1989:107–108). Both Peak (1989:122) and Lewis (1989:143) note that when children are encouraged to control their egoistic tendencies, the reasons given are not because the teacher says so or because "those are the school rules," but because "all of your friends," "everyone else," or a "group life" must place limits. Authority to place limits on behavior lies in the group itself. Lewis (1989) also notes that, in contrast to American preschools, strategies for social control in Japanese preschools include minimizing the impression of teacher control, encouraging self-management by children so they learn how to behave and be in a group, use of small groups (as opposed to individual) as units of activities.

Socialization as Adaptation

To speak of child rearing in adaptive terms is to understand the ways in which early childhood practices prepare children for the specific settings into which they are heading. Parents often envision trajectories that they hope the child will head down, but the nature of these trajectories (with their obstacles and requirements along the way) obviously can differ tremendously from culture to culture, class to class, subculture to subculture, parent to parent. LeVine's theory of human parental care as adaptive behavior includes the notion of varying "parental investment strategies," which best prepare the child in foraging, agrarian, or urban-industrial societies for the future economic self-maintenance necessary for their society. LeVine (1983, 1990; Levine, Miller, and West, 1988) writes of the ways in which parental behavior in a specific setting can be interpreted in at least two ways: "as a utilitarian pursuit of adaptive goals, given certain environmental contingencies, and as symbolic action, given certain meanings embedded in prevailing cultural models of the mother-infant relationship." (1990: 458–459) He suggests that in agricultural, labor-intensive countries where subsistence resources are scarce and infant mortality is high, families have a large number of births and invest a great deal in the safety and health of the child for the first vulnerable 18 months. Independent, assertive, competitive, and demanding children are not valued, and, hence, the degree of visual and verbal stimulation that leads to these traits is not practiced. What is needed in these labor-intensive, high-fertility societies are children who are not emotionally demanding but obedient and can do without a great deal of attention when the next child is born (1983).

For example, on a most general level, the Gusii of Kenya share the goal of achieving a child's survival, maintaining economic security, and learning cultural values (including the subtleties of cultural capital, I would add). The Gusii are an agricultural people living in southwestern Kenya. They have one of the highest birth rates in the world; the average woman bears almost nine children. LeVine notes that although the Gusii maternal and child health situation has improved greatly and is relatively good by African standards, the infant mortality rate still runs about eight or ten times that of middle-class America, and it is not hard to imagine that Gusii mothers are primarily concerned with minimizing survival risks to their infants (1990, 459). Thus, utilitarian considerations such as maternal work load, infant mortality and fertility all act as environmental pressures to which Gusii mothers respond (1990, 460).

The Gusii believe infancy to be a time of high degree of risk and thus, with a cultural goal of protection, soothe the child, respond to any stress immediately, and provide almost constant physical closeness, as do the

Japanese. Given the need for children to enter hard labor and to support their parents economically, the mother's high workload, and the likelihood that another child will be on the way, one of the goals of the Gusii is to raise a child who is compliant and obedient, who will not be too demanding, and who knows his/her place in the age hierarchy. No effort is made to talk or to excite the child, as this would create an expectancy for attention. As the child gets somewhat older, the mother, having work and more children, keeps the child's expectations for constant attention low, letting other children care for the child. The child learns to do what the mother says, rather than initiate an activity on its own. It is placed on the knee of the mother facing outward toward the group, as if to deny the importance of a special, single bond and promote a healthy reliance on others. The child must also learn *omoigweeri* (obedience) and *omosikani* (respect). These are taught in part through language socialization: Children are not to interrupt or talk too much since they are not yet wise enough. *Omoigweeri* (which could often mean "silence") is seen as the child being intelligent enough to know her lower rank. Thus, intelligence for the Gusii is not necessarily divided from social skills.

Thus, the Gusii, who until recently were agropastoralists, "define economic competence in part in terms of their children's manifest obedience and responsibility, which they see as essential to their future economic careers as well as their present tasks" (Levine et al., 1994:13). Parents avoid giving the child high degrees of visual and verbal stimulation, as this would lead to the development of an emotionally demanding child. Individuality and egotism are much more useful traits for a child headed into a highly competitive, urban-industrial society.

Social Class and Adaptation

LeVine's notion of childcare as culturally adaptive can be taken to the level of social class. As Miller states of day care centers,

> the manner in which each of the settings is defined may be seen as an interpretation by caregivers of the world as they see it. . . . There seems to be some powerful urge in human beings to replicate for children the social reality they perceive from their own experience in the larger society. (1989:93)

Sociologists and others[5] have considered social class in relation to parental values concerning children and the socialization of children into socioeconomic strata. Many of the studies suggest that parents with blue-collar jobs stress conformity to externally imposed rules rather than the self-direction, initiative, and independence stressed by parents in professional and managerial positions. Kohn (1969) was among the first to write of differences between working- and middle-class parental values. He wrote, "the higher their class position, the more highly they value self-direction and the less highly they value conformity to externally imposed standards" (1969:71). Kohn (1963a:163) suggests that parents value these traits because these are what constitute success in blue-collar and professional jobs and that "parents come to value self-direction or conformity as values in their own right, not simply as means to occupational goals." Kohn and Schooler (1983), in their study on work and personality and the impact of social structure on personality, claim that the higher men's social-stratification positions, the more likely the men are to value self-direction for themselves and their children, and that this is substantially attributable to degree of occupational self-direction, which is higher in middle-class jobs. However, this study was based only on men, and, needless to say, job conditions are not the only experiential links between position in the larger social structure and personality. And yet, despite Kohn's conclusion, each social class has too often been saddled into bipolar procrustean beds of conformity vs. self-direction, which hardly illuminate the varying individualistic and conformist styles present in all groups.[6]

Hochschild (1979) also notes that each class tends to prepare its children with the skills necessary to its type of work environment and to pass on class-appropriate ways. She notes that "feeling" rules vary by social class. Middle-class jobs call for a more emotional investment in work and management than do working-class jobs, which call for external skills and the products of them. She writes, "The class difference in socialization amounts to different degrees of training for the commodicization of feeling. This is yet another way the class structure reproduces itself."(1979:571) Thus, citing Kohn (1963b, 1969) and Bernstein (1971), she notes social class differences in childcare that act to prepare children for different jobs. Kohn (1969) notes that among the middle class, parental punishment is often based on the intent of an act, and the child's motives, feelings, and "internal dynamics" become the focus, whereas among the working class, parental punishment is often based on the consequences of an act rather than the intent.

Other studies have focused on the differing linguistic socialization used in different social classes. (See for example, Heath, 1986; P. Miller, 1982.) Heath describes differences between rural white working-class conventions of language use, which employ strict literalism, with those of the middle class, which are increasingly flexible with meaning. Wiley, Rose, Burger, and Miller (1998:833) in their article on constructing autonomous selves through narrative practices, note how two European American communities in Chicago differed in the types of autonomy they promoted among their children: Expressing one's view is a natural right for middle-class children, but something to be earned and defended for working-class children. Bernstein (1971) in his study of class differences in linguistic codes among parents with their children, notes that working-class children tend to be socialized via restricted linguistic codes and that middle-class children are socialized through elaborated linguistic codes (where the speaker does not assume the existence of shared knowledge and context), systems of meanings, and role relationships. Bernstein wrote of position-oriented versus person-oriented strategies for control. In social relations where the group is emphasized over the individual, authoritative positional reasons are often the basis of rules ("You shouldn't do that because the teacher said so"), whereas in groups where the individual is stressed, personal reasons are given for rules ("You shouldn't do that because it will hurt you"). The former tend to be found among the working class and the latter among the middle class. Cook-Gumperz (1979) also studied social class differences in parental presentation of rules to children.

One of the works I use as a stepping point for my research is D. F. Miller's *First Steps toward Cultural Difference: Socialization in Infant/Toddler Day Care*. Basing her work on that of Bernstein before her, Miller (1989) studied the linguistic codes used in day care centers from different social classes. In her study of two-year-olds in four day care centers, Miller's focus was on the differing linguistic codes and strategies for social control used by the teachers. She found that the working-class day care center was characterized by a restricted linguistic code (context-dependent meanings, few linguistic markers, nonliteral speech) and positional social control (imperative commands, hierarchical structure, adult-centered curriculum, and gender differentiation). The middle-class day care center was characterized by restricted linguistic code and personal social control (egalitarian structure, child-centered curriculum, mixed imperatives, appeals), and the upper-class day care center was characterized by an elaborated linguistic code (literal speech, linguistic markers, context-independent meanings) and personal social control.

Through different studies, Miller, Bernstein, and Kohn suggest that obedience, conformity to set routines, and knowing one's place in a hierarchy are intrinsic parts of a working-class world. If so, then how do the ethnoconceptual categories of the self among different social classes vary? Do the upper-middle and working classes espouse the same "kinds" of individualism or does each group possibly have different meanings and uses?

Socialization, Education, and Class Reproduction

For some time now, social theorists have addressed the question of why working-class children so often end up with working-class jobs, and why upper-middle-class children so often end up with upper-middle-class jobs. As Jay MacLeod (1987, 1995) writes in his book *Ain't No Makin' It: Aspirations and Attainment in a Low-Income Neighborhood,*

> In the most general terms, social reproduction theory explains how societal institutions perpetuate (or reproduce) the social relationships and attitudes needed to sustain the existing relations of production in a capitalist society. . . . On one end of the spectrum are theorists who advocate deterministic models of reproduction; on the other end are those who put forth models that allow for the relative autonomy of individuals in their own cultural milieu. (1987:9)

Perhaps the theorist who has had the largest influence on my thoughts about social class and the perpetuation of social inequality in education is Pierre Bourdieu, insofar as he strikes a better balance between the two poles of structure and agency and moves beyond the economic determinists (Bowles and Gintis, 1972, 1976) through his concept of habitus. In *Reproduction in Education, Society and Culture,* Bourdieu and Passeron (1977: 177–219) argue that education's most central role is the "function of conserving, inculcating and consecrating" a class culture, including the cultural and symbolic capital that determine who has power in a society. Even though for Bourdieu one of the institutions most responsible for the perpetuation of social inequalities is the educational system, where seemingly "natural" conceptions of the world, self, life possibilities, and "realities" are taught, through his concept of habitus he resists a vision of humans as passively accepting their class status and simply mimicking the class structures that exist. He writes,

> I do not see how relations of domination, whether material or symbolic, could possibly operate without implying, activating resistance. *The dominated, in any social universe, can always exert a certain force,* inasmuch as belonging to a field means by definition that one is capable of producing effects in it. (Bourdieu and Wacquant, 1992:80)

In "Cultural Reproduction and Social Reproduction," Bourdieu (1977a) also writes of the ways in which the pedagogic culture that schools transmit is closer to the dominant culture. Pedagogies of the upper-middle class are privileged in schools such that those who have no previous socialization in these forms of cultural capital are at a serious disadvantage. Why? In large part because the transmission of school knowledge and culture "depends on the previous possession of the instruments of appropriation. . . . [It] requires initial familiarity with the dominant culture" (1977a:493–494). Hence, a child of Puerto Rican immigrants who is told at home not to talk back to adults, to be quiet, to speak only when spoken to, in a New York upper-middle-class preschool is written up in an evaluation (which his Spanish speaking mother cannot read) as anything ranging from "naturally" shy to sullen, rebellious, recalcitrant, stubborn, lacking in communication skills, or dull. This is a classic case of a division of power parading as a "natural" difference in intelligence and social "skills." Social hierarchies and the reproduction of these hierarchies are seen as natural hierarchies of intelligence, gifts, skills, personalities, or merits (1977a:496). Bourdieu writes of this catch 22:

> An educational system which puts into practice an implicit pedagogic action, requiring initial familiarity with the dominant culture, and which proceeds by imperceptible familiarization, offers information and training which can be received and acquired only by subjects endowed with the system of predispositions that is the condition for the success of the transmission and of the inculcation of the culture. By doing away with giving explicitly to everyone

what it implicitly demands of everyone, the educational system demands of everyone alike that they have what it does not give. (1977a:494)

Hence, for Bourdieu, particular cultural capital is inherited by children from each social class. This upper-middle-class cultural capital is valued and respected in schools, while lower-class capital is devalued. Academic achievement, then, is often retranslated back into economic capital; e.g., the job market rewards those who excel academically. And finally, the school naturalizes and legitimates this whole process by making cultural capital look like natural talents, traits, gifts, skills, or merits, "by making social hierarchies and the reproduction of those hierarchies appear to be based upon the hierarchy of gifts, merits, or skills established and ratified by its sanctions, or in a word, by converting social hierarchies into academic hierarchies" (1977a:496).

A number of other theorists have written on schools as sites for the learning and reproduction of class cultures. (See Bourdieu and Passeron, 1977; Willis, 1977; Apple, 1982; Giroux, 1983; Collins, 1971; Foley, 1990; MacLeod, 1987.) Willis, in his well-known work *Learning to Labor* (based on his field work among white working-class males in a British secondary school), resists what he feels are the overly simplistic and reductionist notions of some social reproduction theorists where passive agents simply mimic larger socioeconomic determinants. Willis believes it is important not to deny the autonomy of the boys' own local worlds and cultural practices and, hence, their ability to talk back to and contest their class position. He states,

> We must go to the cultural milieu . . . and accept a certain autonomy of the processes at this level which defeats any simple notion of mechanistic causation and gives the social agents involved some meaningful scope for viewing, inhabiting, and constructing their own world in a way which is recognizably human and not theoretically reductive. (1977:172)

Hence, Willis focuses his narrative on the "lads'" own experiences of social reproduction and describes the ways in which they resist school rules, school authority, and poke fun at those ("ear'oles") who obey them. The "lads" feel that trying to achieve is somewhat futile since they're going to get crappy jobs anyway, with or without an education; they feel they might as well have fun. MacLeod (1987), in his ethnography of working-class males in the northeast city of Clarendon Heights, also talks back to overly simplistic social reproduction theorists (namely Bowles and Gintis, 1976, in *Schooling in Capitalist America*) who emphasize the role of educational tracking in the process of class reproduction by describing the ways in which two groups of boys (the black "Brothers" and the white "Hallway Hangers") from the same social class, living in the same housing project, and attending the same school "nevertheless experience the process of social reproduction in fundamentally different ways" (MacLeod, 1987:137). The Brothers ironically have *higher* aspirations than the Hallway Hangers. He writes,

What the Hallway Hangers and the Brothers demonstrate quite clearly, however, is that the way in which individuals and groups respond to structures of domination is open-ended. Although there is no way to avoid class-based restraints, the outcomes are not predefined. (1987:139)

In my own research, I was also struck by the ways in which most of the preschools I studied were (as Tobin et al. 1989:219 state of their own work in preschools) "agents of cultural conservation rather than change . . . working more to instill than to subvert" the class-based individualisms teachers socialized. I would argue, especially in preschools, along with learning the ABCs, the child learns the class culture of hard (protective or projective) or soft individualism, a particular conception of self and its relation to the world. In my field work in two working-class preschools, one did not socialize the dominant upper-middle-class culture of psychologized, expressive individualism, while the other tried it, with half the teachers embracing this and half laughing at it. In the one preschool where working-class children were taught upper-middle-class psychologized individualism, this was largely because the New York Board of Education insisted teachers socialize the child's self in this *softer* way, not because the parents or certain working-class teachers felt it was the correct way to treat a child.

Chapter Three

Queenston and Kelley Ethnoconceptions of the Child's Self: The Soft-Hard Continuum and Establishment of Firm Boundaries to the Self

Although Queenston and Kelley parents differed markedly in the type of hard individualism they espoused (defensive vs. offensive), they did share certain themes in a general ethnoconception of the child's self. Queenston and Kelley parents' discussions about their children often centered on descriptions of the importance of moving from soft selves to hard and tough selves. If the boundaries of the self were too porous or soft, the negative influences of the street (prostitution, violence, drugs, alcohol, peer pressure, gangs) could penetrate and take over. Unless you were careful, there were plenty of people that would "walk right over you." The boundaries of the self could be trespassed through conversion, lack of resistance, softness. As one quite protective Queenston mother said of her child, "If you don't have your own self-awareness, then anyone can get inside of you and change you. People can, if you don't believe in something strong enough, can be converted. If you don't believe in yourself, then yourself can be converted." A Kelley mother described her son Edward as "very happy-go-lucky, sweet personality, easy to get along with, sometimes a little too easy. I fear that somebody will smile at him and he'll say, 'OK, I'll go with you.' I try and teach him that not everybody is his friend." One mother who was planning on moving from Queenston because of the violence in the community spoke of the self-confidence needed in order to resist the world's corruption.

> Self-confidence, God you really need that to face the world today. If you're strong about your confidence, you struggle by a lot of things, but it gives you an outlook, you know, about the whole issues. The most important one, perseverance, is also something that to be strong and to be tough, make sure that you go through all the things. [Sighs.] Ach! There are so many things, I don't know what to say—everything, there's prejudice, racism, murders, people being selfish being greedy.

What were some of the ways Queenston parents attempted to toughen the self? In my interviews, through watching how parents interacted with their children, I discovered that much of the thickening and toughening of the boundaries of the self occurred through using techniques such as humor and teasing, by instilling a "get over it," "move on" philosophy, by using a relatively loud, strict voice in discipline (which also often included spanking and hitting), and by not necessarily saving face in front of the child when they were angry or frustrated. Nor did the parents always respond immediately and seriously to crying, yells, or questions from the child. Socialization of toughness also occurred through open encouragement and praise of independent acts done without help from anyone. Furthermore, unlike the Parkside parents, Queenston and Kelley parents tended to feel there should be limits on praise so the child didn't become too dependent on it or become too "full of himself" or "puffed up."

Queenston and Kelley parents often used the word "tough" as a positive quality in their child insofar as it showed the child's ability to resist outside influences that might be harmful. It was the ultimate survival skill. "Tough" was often part of a constellation of other words and phrases stating the child "isn't a pushover," "speaks her own mind," or is "her own person," which portrayed a solidity to the self that the parent was quite proud of. The words "spoiled," "fresh," "whiny," "weak-minded," "prissy," "soft," "mushy," and "pushover" were used in reference to qualities the parents hated and would not tolerate in their children. One young Queenston mother of two children, who had recently had a family member killed because of neighborhood violence, felt her daughter was too dependent on her, too overly sensitive and emotional. She described how her daughter didn't want to have her birthday because she was already worried about dying at the age of five. When I asked her what were some of the characteristics she'd least want her kids to develop, she replied,

> I'd hate it if they were like my motha, like she always thinks she's sick, there's always something wrong with her, there's always something to complain about . . . considering all the stuff she'd been through also, is pretty strong considering, but like she's always [imitates someone in pain] uh, uh, ow, owh, you know, this hurts, that hurts. She always has somethin' to complain about. Even if the world is that bad, I don't want my daughter goin' around and complaining all the time. There's a lot of things to complain about, but there's always somebody worse off than you. I don't want her growin' up thinkin' that's normal.

One Queenston father talked with pride about how he wasn't a "softy" the way his wife was with the kids. "Yeah, but I never give in to the whining, crying thing. If you're whining, you're not getting it, even when the guy comes around with the truck that they're guaranteed an ice cream every night when mom's home, but not me."

I also interviewed one Kelley mother, Sara, who talked about how silly and "soft" her sister's discipline of her children was. She also spoke disparagingly of the "mushiness" of her oldest son. Of her sister, she says, "She's into all that time out stuff. She says to her kid, 'You're not bad, what you've done is bad.' I mean, give me a break. Of course, the kid is bad sometimes."

Sara did not feel that telling the child she was bad would significantly hurt the child's ego, self-esteem, or development. The notion that a child could not be told he was bad seemed ridiculous to her. She talked about how when she grew up her mother used to sit in the corner with her coffee, and if Sara did something wrong, she'd get a spoon thrown across at her. She was also afraid her husband was getting "too soft" with the kids. Despite her shy personality, during our interview she would switch suddenly into loud, harsh yells and she would scream at the kids to leave her alone while she was talking. Neither the child nor the parent flinched from these outbursts. Both resumed normal play or conversation, as if it were part of the natural ebb and flow of life in the house. She then went on to talk about her eldest, who was the "mushiest" because he got the most attention. When I asked her if too much attention leads to that, she talked about how "you shouldn't pay too much attention to any emotion and you shouldn't baby them too much, give them too much praise. You don't want them to be too soft."

Of course, this is not to say that Queenston parents never spoke of a child's softness as positive. Sometimes when I asked parents what qualities they liked about their child, being "a softy" or tender was mentioned, just as was respecting other people's feelings. One Kelley father said in speaking about his son, "As much as I like Matt for being the soft guy that he is, I tell him all the time, 'Don't be a pushover.'"

Another woman spoke of her son's ability to show his emotions as positive: "He'll cry at the drop of a hat, you know, and that's one thing. When I watch a movie, I'll cry, and I've instilled that in them. They will sit here and cry in a movie, which I think is good, even for a little boy. They should have emotions, show their emotions."

Others spoke of their child as being caring or understanding, sweet or kind. "He'd do anything for you, give you the skin off his back." Hence, talk about toughness did not exclude talk about the positive aspects of being soft. But softness, if left completely unchecked, could cause people to walk all over you. Traits associated with softness or an opening up of the boundaries of the self (kindness, gentleness, sharing, empathy, selflessness, helpfulness, cooperation) minus self-respect or self-confidence was dangerous. When I asked Queens parents what they wanted their children to learn in preschool, aside from independence, they answered that getting along with other kids, sharing, and sensitivity to other's feelings were *extremely important* for children to learn, but not to the point where the child's self is walked all over or taken advantage of. This attitude was also clearly demonstrated in Tobin, Wu, and Davidson's (1989) study of an American preschool in Hawaii. When I asked one mother about what qualities she wanted her child to develop, she said, "concern for others and the environment, and perseverance, not to give up too easily." As one mother said while emphasizing the importance of self-confidence, "You have to believe in yourself, in order to have anyone believe in you."

Much socialization of toughness occurred during my interviews with the parents, and, thus, I learned a great deal by observing how they treated and interacted with the children who were around during my time at their apartments. Discipline was an excellent area in which to discover what could be done without causing psychological damage to the child. Interestingly enough, even among the few Queenston working-class parents who had adopted some of the more lenient, "softer," less-hierarchical approaches to disciplining their children, there was still a way of talking to their children in terms of voice level (loudness, yelling) that would have been judged quite harsh by the Parkside parents and some of the Kelley parents. Unlike those Parkside parents who adopted an image of the child as more delicate, vulnerable, and easily damaged by a parent/child power differential when the parent was yelling, not saving face, or when hitting or spanking was performed, Queenston parents often slipped quite easily into a (relatively speaking) very loud, harsh voice without any apparent sense of guilt, concern, or regret. Yelling, shouting, and issuing direct commands without a "please" or "thank you" were part of the natural training of the child and were not necessarily distressing to the child's psyche. A couple of the parents laughed and rolled their eyes as they took up conversation with me again, as if to punctuate the child's unruly behavior, rather than their way of dealing with it. Queenston and Kelley parents thus slipped in and out of high volume direct commands very easily without distress in themselves or in their children.

Phrases from war and fighting such as "defend yourself," "fight it out," "ok, big guy, just try and knock me down," "get tough," and "stick up for yourself" were used at times. In talking about interactions with their children, some of the parents used phrases like "smacked her in the mouth," "beat that out of him," "knock that out of him," "whack him," "go after him with a belt," "give you a shot," "whip them," "I wanted to sock her," "Shut up. Mind your own business," "If I could leap across the table, I'd strangle her," and "I'm like, I'm going to kill you. Get away from me." These phrases were often used in the presence of the child without the parent feeling this would severely hurt the child's feelings.

Furthermore, among these parents there was often less of an effort to "save face" or voice in the presence of the child. In contrast to many of the Parkside parents, who made an effort to appear interested, gentle, and enthusiastic toward the child even when it was clear the parent did not feel this, many Queens parents simply acted annoyed, bored, or disinterested in the child without fear that this too would be detrimental or damaging to the development of the child's self. One mother said in front of her four-year-old daughter, "Jessica is very sweet also. She's also a wimp. Whiny and a wimp too." Often these parents also did not respond immediately to loud noises or signals of distress by the child. At these times the child would often be rough housing with a sibling or playing with friends and be screaming at the top of his lungs without the parent immediately responding. It was very common for me not to be able to hear the parent's voice due to the child's loud screams in the background. This was viewed as part of rough play, and the child was not seen as being in any real or significant danger. I remember one mother kept talking without a response of sympathy toward the child, even when I stopped the interview and looked over at the child, signaling to the parent that I didn't mind if she needed to interrupt the interview in order to attend to the child. Nor did the parents always respond to their children's questions. Even when I stopped the interview so that the parent could answer the child's question, the parent did not always answer. With one parent there was simply silence as she waited for me to continue with my questions. It was assumed the child could manage with whatever slight mishap or problem he had gotten himself into, or, if not, he could at least wait until the parent was ready to respond.

Not always responding immediately to a child's questions or crying, and using a loud voice and direct commands were not seen as damaging to the development of the child's healthy ego. Such behavior on the part of the parent encouraged stamina and self-reliance on the part of the child, whether in dealing with his siblings, friends, or a glass of milk that had just spilled in the kitchen. It also encouraged the child to "move on" and not dwell on a worry, fight, or emotional upset since he learned that it would not necessarily lead to an attentive response on the part of the parent. One mother said,

> I hate when they bicker. I hate it when they don't stand up for themselves. That bothers me. I have one child who whines. She'll keep coming to me. As opposed to defending herself. I don't want them to fist fight and dwell it out, but anytime he hits her or . . . I don't want her come running. I'm like "defend yourself and fight it out, get over it. It happens, this is going to happen and you don't need to turn to me every single time something bad happens." That I can't stand, when they can't speak up for themselves.

When parents spoke of hitting or spanking their child, such acts were not believed to significantly damage the child in any way. It was sometimes described as a final measure and, at other times, the first method of discipline used. "Sometimes I just give 'em a quick slap on the backside of the head—that works. Like when they say something wrong, I smack them and say, 'what'd you say? what do you mean?'"

One Kelley father, a fireman with five children, told one story about disciplining his sons:

> Recently he was bouncing the basketball in the house and broke a cup, and I've told him a million times, "Don't bounce the ball in the house," and I'm at the stove cooking, and I hear the glass break, and I look inside. The basketball's down, and he's already on the couch and he's crying because he thinks he's about to get it. I won't even touch him. I say "Get up and pick up that glass," and he knows. That's happened, but this guy Kevin is exactly the opposite. I've already whacked him, and he's a two-year-old. I'll whack him, and he laughs, and I know that I've hit him hard enough because when I pull his pants down, my fingers are there. I think "Wow, I hit him hard enough" and Kevin laughs. That makes you want to hit him harder, but you've got to stop. So what are you going to do? He's done that. He did it to me last night. He and Matt sleep

together in the same bed. They have bunk beds but I let them sleep in the top bunk together. Kenny's kicking away and hitting away and I'm trying to get Kenny out of this hitting routine. So I tell him, "If you hit anybody, I'm going to come up and give you a shot." It doesn't work. It's not working so far. I'll have to change up on it. I said, "I told you." Wham, and he's laughing. "You think that's funny?" I give him another shot, and he's laughing. So what are you going to do? I stop. I just put the cover over him, and I said, "Now stop." He fell asleep shortly after that, so I don't know.

One Kelley mother said that the parent should not be "soft" either but should have the stamina and strength to stick with certain spanking or hitting practices.

> You know when I say somethin' and they have to get hit for it or whatever, I'm not gonna baby them for it for very long. That's one thing I don't believe in that. If you're gonna have the strength or whatever just to go in and spank your kid in the first place, then you should have the strength just to turn around and just keep it at that. Don't say, " Oh well, mommy's sorry for hittin' you, but you were wrong."

In these ways, not only did the Queens parents differ in how much tougher they wanted the child to become, but they also had a different notion than the Parkside parents of the "base" they were starting with. In other words, the child's confidence and normal development were not put in jeopardy each time they engaged in one of these acts of socialization. Toughening the child in these ways was not a risky endeavor insofar as the basic stuff of the child's self was viewed as tougher and more resilient *to begin with* than that conceptualized by Parkside parents. Hence, the starting points in Parkside and Queens parents' ethnoconceptions of the basic *substance* of the self were perceived as quite different.

For many of the Kelley and Queenston parents, other images of hardness or solidity were mentioned when speaking of the importance of sturdy moral blocks and pillars within the self's domain such as principles, family, structure, consistency, discipline, "strong" values, and the lesson of hard work. These seemed to give the self a backbone, a foundation, a solid skeleton that would last over time. When challenges arise, these would hopefully remain rooted, acting as a foundation in times of upheaval, questioning, or danger. A child should be given what I refer to as the *architecture* of the self, the wood that builds them up and gives them a solidity much needed in an environment where it is quite easy to be knocked down, corrupted, and diluted. A life was based on this idea of one parent: "I would like him to have his own. His own mind and his own ideals based on the morals that we try to live our lives by here."

One father mentioned how important work was, how it made you harder, more resilient. Upon hearing I was interested in studying various cultures, he said Americans were "too soft":

> I've heard that the Japanese kids go to school incredibly long hours—like they don't have Saturday or Sunday off, very few holidays. The harder you work as

a younger person, the harder you'll work as an older person, and good habits are hard to break. If a kid only knows hard work, he'll always be a hard worker. I think Americans are a little soft. Our kids, you look around. . . . I go to public high schools sometimes, and the kids are just. . . . There's just no drive there.

After Mrs. Timson talked about a murder on her street and a child molester in her building, I asked her what things she did to protect her children. She talked about principles in terms of blueprints and lines that guided the child and that the child could always fall back on in tough times.

You have to give them a very strong background, give them principles, give them meaning, values, values. You give them strong values about everything, you give them principles that you have to rely on, and you just say to them, you draw the line for them. If they have that, they know where they're going, where they're coming from.

Like a backbone?

Yes, they rely on, and you know, that's the way I was brought up and I'm trying to do the same thing. I contested it a lot, but today I'm very thankful the way my father brought me up.

When I then asked her if she could pick a public figure whom she would like her children to be like, she talked about Jackie Onassis. I asked her what she liked about Jackie. "She had a head on her shoulders and a lot of principles and you could see that she was a very mature, very structured woman, I love structured women . . . not because she's famous or a star, she brought up a family, and that, she's principled, a structured life."

When she went on to tell me about her father whom she greatly respected and admired, she said,

He went in the army, got his education, came out, met my mother, finished college at University Canada, and he was financial. He worked very hard all his life, with three kids and the way, his whole life. Today he's retired—a good life. He deserves it because he worked his ass off, and I look at the way I'm doing and I think I'm following in his footsteps and I'm trying, and I admire my father the way he is, because I think he brought up three great children and a lot of time I ask him, "What do you think of this?" and he gives me his opinion, and I make a decision after that, and my mother was more like the backbone, the woman that stayed home and like I'm doing.

You admire your dad mostly for his work?

Not his work because he had a good job and all that. His work for giving us shelter, food, education, principles, values of life, you know, everything.

Another Queenston woman talked about morals and values as important blocks of stability:

I would rather my children have the same qualities as, you know, the same way that I grew up. Yeah, I would really love them to have the same qualities as my parents, the same morals, the same values that I grew up with, a little too strict, but I mean there's also a way of doing that too and not being as strict. I would rather that they have the same morals and the same values that I had when I grew up that my parents instilled in me that their parents instilled in them, you know, cause we've had the same morals and values passed on from generation to generation. I would like them to have, to have the same respect, for whatever decisions they make in life, morals and values.

When I asked one woman what qualities it would take for her child to get a good job today, she talked about how the child must have a certain amount of structure and routine.

> I guess to try to be at home. To be consistent. Wake up, go to school. You know what I mean. I think consistency is a big help. To make the child, so then he can follow. That's how . . . you know what time you go to bed, what time you do your homework, you know, have a little bit of structure to get the best.

Another woman, the librarian at the local Kelley library, spoke with pride about her community, referring to its good old-fashioned values that were strong enough to endure over time. She mentioned that this was one of the few places left where you saw mothers "out with their children, taking them for walks in carriages." She spoke of how a community also needed a certain moral architecture to withstand the struggles and corruption of the New York City environment. Many other parents in Kelley spoke with pride about the sturdy moral architecture of their community and what it "stood for." This was a good place for their child to grow up insofar as it validated and built into place the hard values and moral structure that they felt needed to be key components of the architecture of the child's self.

In contrast to this, among the Parkside parents, such *firmware* instilled in the child would often be conceptualized as too limiting, too harsh. Of course, the Parkside parents taught their children values, but the difference between their values and those of the Queens parents was similar to the difference between cartilage and the hard bone of the spine. Cartilage does not act as the main architecture of the self. It does not support the body in a way that the spine does. Furthermore, it is bendable. The child can move his ear or nose if he wants. He cannot do this with bone. Parkside parents' conceptions of the child's self did not allow for values that were as rigid, hard, or permanent as bone. Rather, they emphasized the importance of room, space, lightness, softness, and flexibility in which the child's unique qualities could emerge and grow outward. Their greatest fear was that the child would be locked into some rigid procrustean grid imposed by certain basic, hard values.

Privacy

Privacy was one of the concepts that also revealed a less psychologized conception of the child's self by the Kelley and Queenston parents than by the Parkside parents. I discovered that much can be learned about conceptions of the self by asking parents whether and why they feel their children need privacy. During these interviews I tried very hard not to give a sense of what I meant by "privacy." As an upper-middle-class woman I often associate privacy with psychological privacy, as opposed to physical privacy for the body. I did not want this bias revealed, so I avoided any type of prompting in which I would further explain what I meant by "privacy." For example, I never elaborated, "privacy such as when your daughter feels hurt or sad and just wants to be by herself." Interestingly enough, the Kelley and Queenston parents were quite a mix in terms of whether they felt their children needed privacy at all. Many of them did feel the child needed privacy, but not necessarily a psychological privacy aimed at protecting or nourishing the unique emotional terrain and feelings of the child. In this way, the child's psychologized self was not seen as needing shelter or space to the extent that the Parkside parents felt it needed them. Whereas Parkside parents almost universally spoke of the privacy needed for the psychological aspects of the child's self, at least half of the Queens parents used "privacy" in relation to the general sexual aspects of the child or said that the child did not need privacy at such a young age.

Some of these parents felt that the child did not need privacy until puberty, at which point it was this sexual aspect of development that deserved space and shelter and not necessarily the emotions, moods, feelings, or personality of the child. In this way, often what was meant by "privacy" for the Queens parents was a privacy and shelter for the budding sexuality of the body. Privacy from the opposite sex was especially noted; most often girls were said to need privacy from their fathers. One young Kelley mother, Ellen, in response to my question as to whether children needed privacy at the preschool age, spoke of her four-year-old daughter:

I don't know. Yeah, I think so. Dawn is very private. The other kids would run around with no clothes on, but not her. She can't even change her shirt in front of her grandfather. . . . So yeah, I think they have to learn that. . . . I have three girls, and we're all the same sex. They have to learn what's theirs is theirs. No one's allowed to touch.

Another mother, Dawn, spoke of the need for privacy in terms of the daughter's need to respect her own body: "Privacy shows them to respect . . . themselves and to respect everybody else—don't want them growin up fourteen, fifteen years old usin' the bathroom with your mom, walkin' in the room like it's no big deal."

Another mother, Nancy, said that her daughter needed privacy and tied it to her daughter's shyness about her body. "At home she's very shy. She doesn't want anybody to see her without her shirt on, and she won't. In the bathtub if my husband walks in, it's like, 'ahh!'" Another father, Tim, mentioned his seven-year-old daughter's shyness about her body. "My older daughter needs her privacy. She doesn't like me to see her naked when she's walking around the bathtub and all that stuff."

When speaking of privacy from siblings, parents also referred to the rights of ownership of various objects that belonged to the child. One mother went on to talk about her daughter's possessions:

> You don't go into Dawn's room and start playing wit her little games. That's hers. What I also did with each of [my daughters], since they share a room, and they have bunk beds. So I build shelves in each of their beds for their own private things. If they go to a birthday party, and they bring home like those little things in goodie bags, they put it on their shelf. No one else can touch what's on their shelf.

When I finally pointedly asked one mother about privacy that might not be related to the body (i.e., a more psychologized privacy), she said she wouldn't push it, because then they're going to expect it and it's hard to get that in a big family. Privacy was seen more as a luxury they could do without than as a basic need.

I also discovered that at times, the parent would be talking about privacy only in relation to older children, because the presumption was that the preschool-age child did not need privacy. Sometimes these parents would automatically switch to talking about their oldest child, assuming that's whom I meant the privacy question was for.

One father, James, said,

> At four, no. I mean privacy when he goes to the bathroom, I'm sure. In his own room, I don't, no, not important right now, doesn't need it 'cause he wouldn't want it anyway. He's just three. I mean, if you say, "Here's your private time. Go in your room and think." I mean [laughs], what privacy do they need? I mean these questions are for a little bit older children.

At the end of the conversation, I decided to ask one father about a more psychologized privacy to see how he would respond. I asked, "What about needing to be alone and think?" He responded, "She doesn't do that. If she wants to go to her room and read a book, she'll ask me to come and read a book to her, things like that, so she's not caught up in that."

However, when the parents *did* refer to a more psychological privacy, it was usually spoken of as a positive thing, tied to the nurturing of independence and self-reliance. Privacy was when the child got to practice doing what she wanted. It was part of learning how to contain certain objects and information (e.g., secrets) within the bounds of herself, as well as an exercise in self-reliance. One mother Tanya, said,

> Oh they definitely need space. See, my daughter is now in Pennsylvania with my girlfriend. She went by herself to Pennsylvania; that's giving her space ... so I have no problem with my daughter going into her room and playing by herself. I say, "Christian, stay away from her."

What do you think would happen if they didn't get any privacy?

They would never know; they would never have any of their own little secrets. You know how every person has their own secrets—they have secrets. If they never had any privacy, they always talked about everything, then they would never have their own little secrets.

When I asked another father exactly what about privacy was good for his sons, he replied, "showin' that they can do what they want by themselves; they can relax and just do what they want."

One mother, Michelle, a nurse and mother of three who said she was trying to "get her son to be less of a follower and more independent," answered my question as to what would happen if they never got any privacy not in terms of how detrimental it might be to the growth of their personality and expression of feelings, but rather in adaptive terms as a kind of emotional resilience of learning how to cope when you don't get what you want, which is an "inevitable part of life."

They wouldn't know how to be alone, and there are gonna be times when you're gonna be left alone, in your job, in your social life, love life or whatever. They would not handle it. I wouldn't want them breaking down if their wife or husband said, "Leave me alone for ten minutes . . . " I don't want them to not be able to handle any privacy. You have to do something alone, college studies or whatever. You're not gonna have your friends there to help you. My daughter, like, homework's her privacy. She'll bitch and scream and say, "Well, why can't you help me?" And I say, "If you can't get it by the time you're done, then when you make mistakes, I'll come over and help you, but I will not help you and go a and b and c, you know?" They need it for their independence and their privacy.

Another Queenston mother who adopted some of the more upper-middle-class methods of child rearing, similar to those used in Parkside, emphasized the same thing:

My son has his own room. The oldest one Matthew, has bunk beds. Both of them and Mathew has the upper. When it's time out, you go upstairs, you play by yourself, you relax.

What's good about privacy?

To see themselves, you know, to, a question of independence. They won't need another person to play. They can play by themselves and relax and Matthew reads his books and stuff.

For these parents privacy was tied to learning self-reliance. As one of the strands of individualism felt to be important among these parents, it bound itself to an experience where the child learned that he would not always get what he wants. And so Kelley and Queenston parents responded to questions about privacy in a variety of ways, ranging from feeling that privacy was not really needed much at all among children so young; to feeling that privacy was needed for the sexual aspects of the body, personal objects, and information; to feeling that privacy was a way of learning how to be alone or to be self-reliant in a world where there won't always be people around to help you.

Resistance to the Psychologization of the Child's Self

Portfolios were a perfect example of the Board of Education's attempt to integrate more upper-middle-class psychologized teaching methods in preschools in Queenston in which most of the teachers were working class and had not been trained in these methods. When I was doing my field work in Queenston, portfolios had just been introduced into one of the classrooms that I observed. Portfolios were books of samples of the child's "work," put together by the teachers for each child. Each portfolio was supposed to express the child's unique self through selected pieces of artwork, the activities he or she chose in class, and things said by the child. All of these together were said to represent the uniqueness of the child's self more fully than a mere grade sheet or generic teacher report. While I was at this preschool, one of the educational administrators from the New York City Board of Education, Miss Thompson, came in for a weekly meeting with the preschool teachers to make sure the portfolio process was being "correctly implemented." To about half of the preschool teachers, those who had been teaching in the school for some time and were not presently pursuing a degree in education, Miss Thompson was quite a nuisance. The teachers felt they did very well on their own, without what they described as a rather nosy, controlling, and uptight woman telling them what they should do with their class. Most often her words were taken with a grain of salt. The teachers nodded as if in agreement and then secretly rolled their eyes when she turned away. Miss Thompson represented the new, upper-middle-class, more "sensitive" and child-centered teaching methods and techniques that the Board of Education was hoping would filter down into every New York classroom. These methods often focused on not damaging the child's self-esteem and showing appropriate appreciation for his or her uniqueness and individuality.

Around the preschool classroom were a sprinkling of small poster-size pieces of paper with different ways a teacher or parent could phrase something so as not to hurt the child's self-esteem. For example, one phrase might be: "It's not that you're bad, Megan, it's that what you've done is bad." These sheets also included advice on how to ask children what *they'd* like to do, instead of commanding them to do something, as well as various clever ways to praise a child, thereby raising her confidence and belief in herself. These stayed on the walls but did not seem to receive a great deal of attention. While in the Parkside preschools these exhortations were practiced on a daily level without any reminders hanging on the walls, most of the Queenston teachers (with the exception of the youngest, who had a higher degree in teaching than the others and seemed to mimic the posters word for word), did not seem to feel their teaching needed more sensitivity, attentiveness, praise, or warmth.

What was most interesting were some of the parents' responses to these portfolios. For example, I asked Mr. James, a prison guard and construction worker living in Queenston, whether his child needed privacy. He said without hesitation, "no," and went on to talk disparagingly and bitterly about the children's "portfolios" at preschool. In this conversation, we see Mr. James resisting the psychologization of a four-year-old. He felt kids shouldn't be treated and thought about so seriously all the time.

> I went over there—they have a class, a school meeting, and Miss Tarlin is telling me, "Well, we drew these pictures with finger paints. What do you see in them?" I said, "I see a mess. What do you see?" I mean, don't try to read into a four-year-old finger painting. It's not too—I mean, can you pick out a psychological murderer at four years old? I don't think, I mean, don't try to read into it. I mean, don't even give me all this hogwash. I really don't want to hear it. This is a four-year-old kid. Don't tell, I mean, they have stacks of paper on a four-year-old kid!

I then asked him if he could tell me about his child's portfolio:

> Portfolio. It's how they get along. They put their pictures and try to analyze them. What do you see after this child paints a picture? What is it? How do you see your father here, or where do you see the flower in this? And then they'll try and explain it to you.

"Psychoanalysis?" I said jokingly, sensing his frustration.

> Psychoanalysis, yeah. I mean, you're psychoanalyzing a four-year-old kid that is standing there with their hand in paint. If you ask them draw a picture of a flower and they drew a weed, maybe you could figure something out there, but I don't think you're gonna figure out hand paintin', so I told her it was just a little too much, and I said you're gettin' a little too serious with four-year-olds. She said, "Well, this is the Board of Education's rules, now, so we have to do it, we have to explain it." And I said, "Well, I don't want to hear it. This is bullshit." You know what I mean. I'm not—there are people I know in Manhattan . . . who have a two-year-old and the two-year-old says instead of da da, says ta ta, and they fuckin' analyze it, and I mean, shit! It's unbelievable. You're better lettin' em go into a pile of mud and put it on the wall. It's the same shit.

There was a Parent Room in Queenston, which also had many of these small posters hanging on its walls. The Parent Room was intended to be a meeting place for parents to come and talk about their children and take mini-courses on crafts, cooking, and holiday gift ideas. Very rarely did I ever see parents in this room. Mothers and especially fathers had to be pushed and prodded to come in. I interviewed a group of about four Queenston parents whom the Parent Room coordinator, Ms. Costado, had urged to come in one day so I could talk with them. I would ask the group a question and most often the parents would reply one way and Ms. Costado would tell them the way they should have responded. The whole dynamic of the group interview was one in which I asked "serious" questions and the parents made jokes in response. I remember not knowing whether I should just give up on the interview and hang out and laugh with them or continue with my role of prudish anthropologist asking serious questions. At no other time did the child-centered psychologized philosophy seem more foreign than at that moment. The whole time I was asking questions, Ms. Costado tried to get the parents to answer in the "right" way by emphasizing the more child-centered philosophy espoused by the New York Board of Education. She brought up ways they could be more sensitive to the child's needs: be more empathetic, to try to understand how the child is feeling, build the child's confidence, sometimes let the child tell you what he wants to do instead of dictating to the child, praise the child more, and remember to tell the child that her *behavior* is bad, but that she is not a bad person. Most of the parents did not seem to take her advice that seriously, and, in fact, the "interview" turned out to be more of a laughing session where the parents joked around about their children, gossiped with each other, and snickered at the craziness of some of Ms. Costado's suggestions. Ms. Costado seemed embarrassed by how the parents were responding to my questions and would often say things like, "Oh come on, you know better than that. How should you really do it?" Ms. Costado had grown up in the area and was very well liked by the parents. Unlike Miss Thompson, she was very down to earth and unpretentious, more like "one of them" despite her attempts to change the way they raised their children. Ms. Costado was able to get close to the parents because of her similar background, sense of humor, and understanding of where the parents were coming from. As much as she could, amid the mutual teasing and laughter, she tried to introduce suggestions on how to treat children with respect, but most of the parents did not pay much attention. When I asked a question, they would often reply with a joke.

For example, I asked, "When are you most proud of your child?" One mother, a very large, gruff woman whose husband was a police officer and whose son was the class rabble-rouser, replied, "When he shuts his mouth!" and she laughed. The whole group laughed with her. Ms. Costado looked disappointed, trying to get the parents to stop joking around and answer things "seriously." She tried to get the interview back on track, saying, "Be serious, now. Come on. You know that's not what you mean. Go ahead, Adrie. Now listen to her; listen up."

Occasionally the parents were having such a good time laughing and joking that I couldn't be heard. The interview itself was not something they felt needed to be taken seriously. Nor did child rearing or the child's feelings need to be taken so seriously. I meekly asked, feeling totally out of place, "What are some qualities you are most proud of in yourself that you hope the child will have?" One young father, John, part Mexican and full of machismo, said, "I'm a great sex lover; that's what I hope he's like." The whole group laughed again. I laughed along with them, trying not to be too serious but also trying to get them to engage with me. I asked "How do you discipline your kids?" The large woman, Mary, answered, "Smack em upside the head." To this John, said, "No, spank em on the butt; that's better." Most of the interview continued like this, with Ms. Costado piping in afterward with, "You know you're not supposed to hit them first. Come on, John, be serious. Help this lady out. She's trying to do her school thesis." In response to this John tried to contain his laughter, finding it hard to resist the chance to entertain the group, but this only made them laugh even harder. Most of the time the laughter seemed to be over the difference between the actual way they did discipline their children or sometimes felt about their children and the ways Ms. Costado was suggesting they should act and feel. Spanking and hitting and being sick or frustrated by the child were offered up as answers, and laughter soon followed over how incorrect their answers were.

Humor as Resilience and the Importance of Moving On

For some of the Queenston and Kelley parents with whom I spoke, humor was an extremely important part of the socialization process. They wanted to teach their child that you couldn't be too serious in life, too hypersensitive, too worried. Seriousness would result in snapping and breaking, as opposed to resiliency. In order to get through this life, you have to ride with the punches, make do with what you've got, and not get too bent out of shape. For Mr. James, a correction officer at a nearby prison and father of seven children, this was a key part of his philosophy of life. Humor was one way of coping with some of the struggles of life. In talking about some of the characteristics he wanted his children to have he said,

> Don't take life so serious. Life is to be enjoyed . . . confidence is one of the main things that's gonna get you through life, confidence and a good sense of humor, to be able to laugh at yourself, because you have to laugh at your mistakes. You know what I mean. Every mistake, as they say, is a stepping stone to success, so I mean I try to give these little quotes to my kids all the time.

Later, when he talked about John F. Kennedy as the public figure he would most like his children to be like, he said,

> Like John Kennedy, perfect. I mean, all his political life he made jokes. When he messed up, when he screwed up, he admitted it with a joke. "Oh, I messed that up." I don't know what speech it was when they asked him about was he doin' enough for women's rights. He politically, in front of a million people said, "Probably not," so he has the sense of humor to know, "I'm not doin'

enough, but I'm gonna let you know, I'm tryin, with a joke. I'm gonna laugh at myself," and everybody laughed at him. He said, "I'm the guy who came with Jackie," so he has enough sense of humor to know, "I'm in a spot, come out of it" and also know who you are. He says he gives his wife the credit . . . I mean, now you can pick a comedian—I mean, I'm, I keep sayin' like laughing at things, but if you laugh through your life, you're not gonna have so many problems. You have to pay your bills, but you can laugh and say screw this guy this month, you know.

Later he commented on how if you've got to do certain things in life you might as well take a fun, lighthearted attitude toward them.

> I mean, if you have a family, you have to work, whether you like it or not. You have to keep goin', so I mean, what the quality, perseverance, you have to have a little fun on the job. You have to. It all boils down to, can you laugh at things, when you come home, leave your job there and have a good time. You know you gotta go back tomorrow, but you make the best of it. You can only make the best of a bad situation, not that work is a bad situation, but without work, there's no play.

I spoke with another father, Nathan, a construction worker and fireman with whom I talked while he drove into Manhattan for his sixteen-hour shift as a standby supervisor at a fire station on the upper west side. In talking about the types of people he likes and what's important in life, he said, "Most of the people that I call my friends will have a good sense of humor, be generous, and will help me, give favors as well as return favors. Good sense of humor is very important." When I asked him why, he replied in an incredulous tone, "Why? 'Cause they're gonna be a lot of things in life you gotta laugh off."

Humor was part of teaching the child not to be too sensitive, teaching him to move on. These parents felt that if you treat every struggle as a tragedy, you'll never get anywhere in life. The child needs to "weather himself" against the nature of the world, one in which as one Queenston father said, "shit happens." One woman, a mother of five, said about her daughter, "I just tell her all the time, get over it and move on." Another woman said, "I think kids should be taught to fall on their face a couple of times. Plenty of people have done it and survived. Try and get everything you can out of life, and not be overwhelmed by it."

One mother spoke of how she dealt with her children when they cried or got hurt. She talked about the importance of getting over a hurt quickly and not making it into a tragedy.

> I think that if you pay too much attention to any emotions that they have. Like when they cry, I give them a little pat, "o.k. you're all right." If they fall or something, "o.k., o.k." We don't dwell on anything. If you dwell on things, I really think that that's what makes them the whinier. You fall down, you get hurt, o.k. it's done, unless they're really hurt, which is very few and far between. I don't react to falls. My mother always says that I'm so calm. But the

more that you react, the more they react. You know like, "Be careful." That type of thing when they fall, unless it looks like they really skinned their knee, but then we clean it, and they go right back out and play. Let's not lay on the couch with our leg up in the air and say, "Oh my God." Get over it.

One father, Mr. James, told me some of his favorite characteristics about one of his children:

Megan is seven, very confident child, not afraid to tell anybody off, if she doesn't know you she's not afraid of, does well in school, but also doesn't care, she's doing well but if she didn't do well she'd be the same way, like who cares, it doesn't, ha, I go every day what more can I do for you, that's basically her theory, but she happens to be doin' very well.

So, you think that'll be good for her to have that attitude?

Oh yeah. Later on, sure, oh yeah, definitely, most definitely.

Why?

Because every failure is not gonna be a crisis . . . so Megan is the type, you know, she will, if the roof fell in, she'd just move to the next room. It's no big deal, you know.

Thus, much of the toughness taught to the children is about not being overly sensitive. The goal is to have the child "move on," not get stuck in an emotional tailspin where they feel sorry for themselves. Because these parents were closer to struggles than Parkside parents, it became even more important that their child learn to get over troubles quickly.

Hierarchy/Power Differential between Parent and Child: The Child Is Not a Small Adult

In contrast to many of the Parkside parents, many of the Queens parents I spoke with did not feel it was harming or inhibiting the child's development if they asserted their power as an adult over the child. Hierarchy was part of life, the way things were, and something the child would have to accept. As one Queenston mother, in speaking about life in general, said, "We're all slaves to a master in some way or another." When talking about the inevitability of hierarchy, another father said, "In life someone's always goin' to tell you what to do, you're always gonna have a boss so as long as you can follow the orders with a smile." One mother told her youngest son, in a buck-up tone, "I tell this guy all the time, 'Listen, you're number five. There's not a lot of time here. Don't expect it all.'"

Examples of the child's lower status were manifested in the child not having access to all parts of the house or pieces of furniture (for example, the parent's bedroom, the dining room for guests, a father's chair), the child having to use a respectful tone of voice in talking with parents, and certain parents not feeling they had to knock on the child's door before entering. One woman adamantly asserted her superior position in the house by stating adamantly, "I'm the mother, I don't knock on their door." In another scenario one three-year-old child, Tommy, sat in what he knew to be his father's chair. The mother immediately said, "Tommy, get outta there! When you're grown up you can have your own chair, but until then your daddy gets first dibs cause he's older than you are; that's just the way it is."

The issue of hierarchy in the home was an area that most Queenston and Kelley parents seemed very adamant about. I could not help noticing the strength of their convictions, especially in contrast to the more insecure voices I heard at the Parkside Parent Guidance Workshop, where parents struggled with the question of how much power they really had over their child. Interestingly enough, the few interviews I had with Queenston and Kelley parents in which the child was treated more like a small adult had been with those parents exposed to upper-middle-class teaching styles through their own involvement with the educational system. Either they were teachers themselves, or their child was enrolled in a preschool that was trying to implement a more child-centered philosophy to discipline and education.

However, for most of the Queens parents I talked with, often direct references were made to the fact that "I'm the mother; she's the child." Unlike many of the Parkside parents, who made an effort at least to *ease* the hierarchy so as not to make the child feel more powerless, many of the Queens parents did not feel there was anything wrong with the child feeling less powerful than the adults. It was not seen as impeding the child's expression or development of self. Nor was it seen as constraining the child's development of tough individualism. If anything, it blunted and fortified the boundaries of the self, making the child "get used to it." Many of these parents disagreed with viewing and treating the child like a "small adult." On the contrary, respect for adults was emphasized as important for the child to learn. In many of my conversations with Kelley and Queenston parents, parents vacillated between hierarchical commands and demands for respect, and statements about their pride in the child's self-reliance, independence, self-confidence, and perseverance. Never once was an emphasis on respect for the parent's authority seen as blunting the development of the child. Rather, the blunting action that occurred against the child's self in statements such as "Get outta that chair now, it's your father's" was seen as part of the necessary and important lesson of respect. It held the child's self within the structure set by the hierarchy of the household. This in no way drained the child of the independent fight for life he would need in the world at large. Nor did it turn the child into a softy. Unlike the Parkside parents, individualistic and authoritative discourses existed side by side, without tension or seeming contradiction.

Whereas Parkside parents often disciplined indirectly in the form of a question, using a high, soft, tentative voice ("Do you think you should be doing that?"), most of the Queenston and Kelley parents simply stated,

"Don't do that." Many Parkside parents felt they had no right to address the child with direct commands except in extreme situations of danger. If the child were about to run across the road, they might say, "Stop that right now!" a type of direct, authoritative command that many Queenston and Kelley parents felt comfortable using most of the time (even after praising the child's individualistic/independent behavior).

In a conversation we were having about whether kids should have the same status as adults, one Queenston father said,

> I seen that with a couple of kids right down here, and I find those kids to be so fresh. The mother will say something like, "You've had enough." The kid says back "Don't tell me I've had enough. I know when I've had enough." I heard that before. That guy needs one right on the mouth. I've heard that, and that is their philosophy on rearing a child.

Another Kelley father, a fireman and father of five sons, spoke of how he hated fresh kids. "One of the ways I was brought up, you never talk back to someone older than you." Another man, in talking about what kind of rights he thought his children should have, said

> Not that children should be seen and not heard, but there's times when they should be quiet, and you know when I'm talkin' to somebody else I don't like to be interrupted, you know, "daddy, daddy, daddy" cause I'm talkin', but then when you're done, you have to go talk to them. You can't forget.

When I asked, "Do you think there should be more of a difference between the rights kids have and the rights the parents have?" he answered,

> Well, I don't mind that my kid doesn't use "Mr. and Mrs." terms with the parents, I'm not that strict about it, but kids are kids and they should do what they're told when they're told. I see a lot of parents that give their kids an awful lot of free rein and they get told what to do by their kids and they have to make special menus for their kids. I think you're lettin' the kid run your life then. I don't think that's why we have children. No, I don't think parents should cater to their children.

He then told me a story about the type of behavior he would never put up with.

> I had a guy over to my house the other night and him and his wife came over and their son and the son wouldn't eat chicken and whatever else we had, but he had to go out to the store and get groceries for the kid. Right before dinner he went out and bought it, and I said, "Listen, Steven will eat it when he gets very hungry. You know, my kids are gonna sit here through dinner and then when they get hungry later, they'll eat it." That's how spoiled kids are made, and that's kind of ridiculous.

The concept of being *fresh* represented the child not respecting this power differential. Being *fresh* meant talking back to adults, acting as if the child had the same rights as an adult. This was not tolerated. One mother spoke about her daughter Laura's temper. "She has a temper, she's very—what do you call it—she's the motha [she imitates Laura in an adamant, authoritative voice], 'I told you I want something to drink and I want it now.'" I asked, "What do you say to that?" To which she replied, "I tell her, 'You're not the motha. I'm the motha, and when I get it, you'll get it.' And I tell her this too, that she'll wait until I get it." She paused and thought for a moment:

> She's not really, I don't know if it's really say, forward, but like how you see some children, they're like quick to say something to an adult, and they're not afraid to do anything, or say anything.
>
> *How do you feel about that?*
>
> I think that's wrong. The parents should show there are certain times that, I also learned, certain times children should be seen and not heard, and she'll come and tell you something that wouldn't be comin' from an adult, and that's wrong, so I try and teach them that, there are times when children aren't to be hearin' anything.

She then spoke of the sharp division between the rights of adults and the rights of kids.

> I may say to my kids, you know, I'll give my kids their rights, but not to where it comes to adult things. You know, like they'll come in and you'll see some of these kids where they'll just be talkin' to an adult and asking you off-the-wall questions or tellin' you something and you think to yourself, "What kind of mother does he have?" When it's certain things that are goin' on my daughter may come out and may take something out here and she'll really understand it. It's not the time now, you know. You shouldn't be seen. Children should be seen and not heard . . . then as they grow up they'd say, like well, "I'm an adult and I'm gonna be," not that they're responsible, but they got their morals all mixed up, really. What comes out of their mouths would, if I see that happen to any of my kids, I would whip their, they wouldn't see daylight until they were thirty.
>
> *You mean swearing and stuff like that?*
>
> Just like cursing and things that you would normally hear out of an adult's mouth. Like there's this family I know, the kids are always swearin'. If you couldn't control them all, you shouldn't have 'em, you know.

Another mother talked about how she hated it when her children whined. When I asked her why, she said, "Because I really feel that the child is now controlling the parent. The parent has no control. Some parents have more patience than others as far as putting up with a whiny child. I don't."

Unlike the Parkside parents, which, as we will see, found it quite a challenge to socialize soft individualism while teaching the child what I refer to as the more sociocentric values of kindness, group identity, manners, group conformity, respect for authority, and politeness, Kelley and Queenston parents did not find the insertion of sociocentric values into their hard individualism to be conflictual or problematic. (This was most evident in the behavior of teachers in preschools, which I will explore in another chapter.) The two modes of discipline were not seen as mutually exclusive. For the Parkside parents, the sociocentric values were often viewed as a constraint upon the soft individualism they espoused for their children, and socialization of the sociocentric was often done with the nagging doubt that perhaps they were stifling the individuality of the child. This was the main theme of the Parent Guidance Workshops I attended in Parkside.

Among the Kelley and Queenston parents, what struck me most was the ease with which parents "switched" from practices of hard individualism (think for yourself, praise for independent acts), to loud, direct, and authoritative commands that reminded the child of his place in the family hierarchy or implied that he had better conform to school, group, or family rules. One woman shouted, "Because I'm your mother and you do what I tell you to do" right after proudly talking about how her child needs to "be her own person." Statements about how the child needed to learn to follow the rules at school and get along with other children were mixed with tough talk of sticking up for yourself and not letting anybody shove you around. These two ideas were not viewed as problematic, contradictory, or in anyway stifling the development of the child's self. Children simply needed to learn both. My surprise at noting that these differing types of socialization didn't seem to be perceived as contradictory by the parents only reveals my own upper-middle-class bias, in which my own desperate concern for the child's independence and individuality leads me to wonder whether such a hierarchy will blunt or hinder the process of individualization or self-confidence.

During one interview, a four-year-old Queenston child spilled grape juice on the table where his mother and I were talking. The mother yelled at her, "That's just great, Laura, just great. Clean it up before I smack you one." The mother then raised her hand as if to hit Laura when she didn't immediately begin cleaning it up. Narrowing her eyes and pursing her lips, she gave Laura a look of, "Don't even try to challenge my authority." Laura quickly went to the pantry, where she got some paper towels. After that, the mother continued to answer my questions about what was important to learn in preschool. She spoke of the equal importance of learning how to be an individual and sticking up for yourself and learning how to get along with the group. Alongside learning to be tough and how to stick up for themselves, Kelley and Queenston children also learned that they don't give lip to their elders. They learned respect. Discourses of respect, hierarchy, and obedience were woven together with an unthinking ease and nonchalance by these parents. Yelling quite hard at the child or giving no reason why they must stop a certain behavior except that an adult told them to was not seen as incongruent with the lessons of hard individualism. In some of the interviews, children would come into the kitchen when I was talking to a parent. If the child did not greet me right away but rather went and got a cookie or drink from the refrigerator, or played with his toys, he was reprimanded. During one interview with Mike, a Kelley father, his seven-year-old son Tim walked in the room while we were talking. He went over to the cookie jar and started fumbling around for some cookies without addressing me. Mike yelled loudly, "Hey! Tim, what do you say to an adult in the room?" Tim didn't say anything but shyly shrugged his shoulders. "You say 'hello, nice to meet you.' You don't just walk in here and not say, 'hi,' and just do what you want. Where are your manners?" The father then looked at him with disgust and exasperation. And yet, never did the parent then look back to me almost to apologize or check my response to this harsher discipline. There seemed to be no sense of guilt or conflict in the father. He turned back to me and smiled. Rolling his eyes, he said sarcastically, "Kids, you gotta love 'em!" as if to imply what a pain they could be to raise. This is in stark contrast to a few Parkside parents who looked at me after they told their child not to do something with a somewhat tormented look, as if they were unsure about issuing direct commands for obedience based solely on their authority as an adult and were looking for my reaction, perhaps even my approval. Among the Kelley and Queenston parents, it never occurred to them to look my way after a harsher, authoritative form of discipline in which group rules were being stressed. There was nothing for them to feel guilty about, no sign of hesitance or embarrassment on their part, so why should they look to me to see how I reacted? The harsher demands they issued to their children were naturally woven in and out of the socialization of hard individualism as it was needed.

Chapter Four

Queenston Hard Protective Individualism vs. Kelley Hard Projective Individualism

During my field work in the New York City area, I observed the ways in which children were socialized into *hard* styles of individualism, within which various substyles of individualism, each with its projective and protective stances, also emerged. Hard individualism emphasized a tough, resilient self that was hardy enough either to *protect* itself from violence, poverty, and misfortune (as in Queenston) or *project* itself into a higher social class (as in Kelley). Hard protective individualism involved protecting the child's self against the violence and hardships of the local world that surrounded them. It involved a more defensive stance of putting up shields of armor through pride, self-sufficiency, privacy, independence, toughness, and self-resilience. Projective individualism involved a more outgoing, upward-moving trajectory in which the sky was the limit and one's socioeconomic terrain could be bettered with each successive generation. An "offensive" rather than a defensive trajectory was woven into strands of individualism such as self-assertiveness, self-confidence, self-reliance, doggedness, and persistence. In this chapter, I try to highlight the differences between these projective and protective trajectories, and the ways in which they are woven into specific strands of individualism.

Queenston Lower-Working-Class Hard Individualism: Surviving in a Tough World

When individualistic values were referred to among Queenston parents, not only were they often situated side by side with more sociocentric values (conformity, hierarchy), but they were also surrounded by an entirely different set of meanings, a different semantic web than those used by Parkside parents. Individualistic values were part of stories of struggle that could not have been told by Parkside parents. Independence and self-reliance were spoken about with a great deal of pride and bitterness, fueled by anger and resentment against "the system," the violent environment, or a difficult past or person the parent had been disappointed by.

In most of my conversations with Queenston parents, individualistic values could not be extricated from a difficult past (e.g., child abuse, alcoholism, drug addiction, divorce, or what they felt was an overly strict upbringing), the environment (e.g., gangs, drugs, an unsafe neighborhood, or a society rampant with racism, prejudice, and violence), or the government "system" or vision of the future in which there would be a lot of struggle, work, and hardship. Individualistic values were woven into discourses about how they had made it through various difficult events. It was a philosophy of the lone individual standing tough against a world that threatened to knock him down. Even though the degree of struggle varied among different individuals (with the exception of certain parents in Kelley, who bordered on middle-class status), individualism's raison d'être was usually an attempt to deal with something "tough," perhaps the most common word used by these parents. Though the stories varied, individualism was inextricably tied to and arose out of a sense of difficult struggle.

Individualism, in the form of "not relying on anyone else" and "not trusting anyone but yourself," was often seen as the way out of a bad system, a system that could not be trusted. Standing up for oneself arose out of experiences of being pushed around "too much." Some mothers said they'd had enough, they'd been pushed around enough, and they were standing tough against the world. These were strong women, without husbands, raising and supporting kids on welfare, exhibiting a toughness that was palpable in their voice and body. Some of the poorest of these parents were very lonely figures, keeping to themselves, angry at the "system," mistrustful of people not within their immediate circle of family and close friends. Many of them were extremely suspicious of what I was up to, and it took three or four tries to get them to speak with me.

For these parents, independence represented an intentional separation, distance, and isolation from past or future disappointments—it represented a barricading of the self, a closing and hardening of the boundaries of the self. Unlike the Parkside parents, because of what they'd been through, Queenston parents often wanted their kids to be even more independent than they were, to "not to need anyone." They felt a sense of independence, a strong self-determination, self-reliance, and self-confidence in their children's beliefs was what was going to make their children's lives better than their own. Independence, self-reliance, and self-confidence were what would keep their children from getting mixed up in the wrong group, gangs, or street life.

Individualism and the "Tough" Neighborhood

It was not at all uncommon for parents to tell me they were planning on moving because of the violence in Queenston. Parents complained of gangs, drugs, prostitution, the projects, gunfire, child molesters, or "low-class people" as dangers they were trying to avoid. Most of the women I spoke with who spoke about the violence surrounding them seemed extremely exhausted, some of them to the point of acting numb, dazed, and jaded. If they were married, their husbands were at work, and often held another night job on top of the work they did during the day. One day in the public park, I spoke with Mrs. Tackett, a mother of three children. She was a large woman with disheveled hair and a bit of a slur in her voice. She seemed completely exhausted and a little distracted. When I asked her why she was moving she replied,

> There's a lot of low-class people around here. That's the reason why I'm moving. Yes, I don't like it. No, it's not safe. This school over here is juvenile delinquents. St. John is all—they all have felonies. They all known by their cuff and things. Two weeks ago they tried to put the boardwalk on fire, so you know, I'm moving for safety, for a better school. It's a better area.

When I asked her where she lived before, she mentioned Bensonhurst, from which she had to move because of violence as well.

> [T]here was a problem over there. They killed a black guy. He was visiting his girlfriend and they told him that he didn't belong in this neighborhood and they killed him. [It was an] all Italian [neighborhood]. I was pregnant with Matthew . . . it was during the summer. It was a block away from where I was living. It was very scary when you have a newborn baby. And you know, and I have black friends, I have Chinese friends, I made a party for my husband and I had every possible nationality.

She and her family had considered moving from New York, but because her husband had invested so many years in his job with the telephone company, they found it hard to give it all up.

Often the resentment that arose from telling one story led to the telling of another. She then told me,

> Yeah, and in my building there's a child molester. Somebody, one of the landlords in the next building who I know very well, whose child is mentally retarded got molested two nights ago. So you look at it and you say, "I'm staying here?" It should be a little bit better where I am but. . . .

When I asked her what she wants her child to learn in preschool she says:

> Perseverance and self-confidence are most important. . . . God, you really need that to face the world today. It's something that if you have, if you're strong about your confidence, you struggle by a lot of things but it gives you a, an outlook, you know, about the whole issues. The most important one, perseverance, is also something that, to be strong and to be, tough, make sure that you go through all the things.

I then asked her, "When you say face the world today, what kinds of things are people facing?"

[She sighs] Achh! There are so many things, I don't know what to say. Everything. There's prejudice, racism, murders, people being selfish, being greedy, you don't want your child to be doing, things you have to consider and if they have self-confidence in themselves and they see that in their parents they have a better outlook of the world.

When I asked her to pick three characteristics she'd like her kids to have, she said self-confidence, independence, and self-reliance. I then asked her why these are so important, and she talked about how you just have to be independent, you just can't depend on anyone else. She felt that by the ages of 20 or 25 you should be largely responsible for yourself. Otherwise, "You're not gonna have the common sense about what goes around in life." She was trying to get her son Matthew, in preschool, to get out into the world more. "I don't want him to be—he likes to be under my skirt all the time. I don't like a mommy's boy."

One of the women whose individualism was inextricably woven into her particular tough past and violent environment was Tracy Volk. She represents the Queenston women who espoused a certain degree of individualism both because of the struggles they'd been through and the violent area in which they lived. Tracy was about 21, had her first child at age 14, and now had three children. Her husband was a civil engineer. She was a very strong, hardened woman, and it was obvious she had endured a lot and had developed a "thick skin." She had a great sense of humor and often laughed at past and present hardships as if to make the best of them. When hearing how much time I spent on the New York subway she told me how her sister had been killed on the subway a couple of years before "so she never rode the subway anymore."

When I asked Tracy about this area as a place to live, she laughed at how unsafe it was.

By the time she's gone into third grade, we're not gonna be livin' here anymore, 'cause there's nothing here; it's a bad neighborhood. You can walk down a block, there's crack vials all over the place, there's little kids her age. Some guy was drivin' around all last summer trying to abduct them. I'm afraid. I don't even let her, we live in a building, she wanted to go downstairs and play with my niece which is only three flights down. She could take the elevator. I won't let her. She won't—I don't let her do anything by herself, which is bad because she's never gonna learn how to do it herself, but I'm too scared.

I asked her what the kids were like around the neighborhood.

I can't even take her to the park across the street from my house. The kids come in—they come in from other cities. They come over to fight here, and they're rude. They call her names, 'cause she's not exactly skinny. They call her names, they tease her. We were up there and some man was urinatin' on the playground. He had some little girl with him about ten years old watching him. I was like, that's it, grabbed my kids and left.

So the drugs are a problem too?

Oh yeah. You can't drive down a block without five to ten girls tryin' to flag you down, hookers . . . by where I live, between here and my house . . . these girls are girls that I've known since I was younger . . . half of them look like they have AIDS cause they're so, you know, but that could be from the drugs also. I don't know.

Is it pretty divided black and white here or no?

In some parts, in some parts, in my building there's everything. Across the street there's the projects, that you can't walk past at night because you'll get attacked [laughs] every weekend. Like from where I live you can listen and hear the gunshot, so it's like it's not safe [laughs].

What are your fears for your kids?

I'm always worried about her, always, even with some of the mothers whose kids go to school with mine. "Oh, could she come over to play?" And I'm like, "No." [laughs] I just can't. I mean, I'll take their kid to play to my house, but I'm like, "No. She can't play at your house." I'm too overprotective with her, but then I'm not.

Theresa Feldman also worried about the wrong crowd that was prevalent in her neighborhood.

You know, it's very easy to get influenced by the wrong crowd, you know, so I would rather that they choose people that aren't the ones that are hanging out and going out and . . . otherwise, you'll get involved with the drugs and alcohol at a young age and unfortunately, you hear about so much of that down here because it's all Irish and there's nothing for the kids to do down here. There's sports, but sports only go from this time to this time, and after that, what do you do? They end up drinking on the boardwalk, going into, half the, most of the bars down here are all underage drinkers. They don't proof. It's a disaster down here.

Another mother, Diane, a very small but feisty woman with a gravely voice, spoke bitterly of the drinking in her neighborhood and the wild kids. "This weekend, they have this Irish fest over there, another excuse for Queenston to drink. I'm not, I mean I take the kids cause they sell little jewelry, but then at night time it gets crazy with all the drunks." In mentioning the people down the street, kids especially, she said, "I mean I see a lot of kids in the street that will tell their mom 'shut up,' or 'do this or do that' . . . just a person walking by on the street. I don't want, God forbid, they'd push, you know, I mean, 'cause these kids are wild. They push older people down and everything." When I asked her what happens when children don't learn to be independent, she refers to a world where "people will take advantage of you."

Another parent, Debbie, spoke of how she never took the subway and was "sincerely afraid of the city, the influence of the city. . . . My sister-in-law moved away from there [a nearby neighborhood]; that's not a good neighborhood, used to be, but not anymore. It wasn't safe." She told me about the high school she went to and described why she would never send her kids to the same school, why she's moving:

> It's not safe, it's ranked third worst in our district, most unsafe, in terms of violence and drugs, weapons coming into the school, they have security. . . . I plan on moving before my kids go to school, move out of New York City to New York State, probably Rockland County, Manuette, not far, within an hour. My husband can still work in the city, but I don't want my kids educated here, I don't like the experience of the train and the buses. You can't really send your kids on the train and expect them to come home at three o'clock when school is over because three o'clock is a very unsafe time to travel on the train, so what a lot of people do, my in-laws, friends, and relatives do, is have them either join clubs or teams or sit in the library and do their homework and then come home at rush hour at five o'clock. The kids get out of school and they rampage the trains. Gangs are very bad on the trains.

Deborah spoke of the importance of independence. Because in New York it was so easy to be "led around by the nose," you needed to have a strong sense of self. When she talked about the self she emphasized the importance of strength, hardness, durability. The self needed to stick *to itself,* bind itself tightly and not naively venture into unknown territory. In talking about "following the group" she said,

> I don't want them to be not part of a group, but I don't want them to be, 'cause gangs are very prevalent here and that's the extreme, but it's very common. It's an extreme but a very common extreme, and I definitely don't want my kids to be part of one, even part of a group that has a specific ideal.

When I asked what would happen if her children grow up to be dependent she replied,

> I think it's acceptable and I think that they can thrive but I don't think it's as well if you were more of an individual. I think you definitely need to be an individual, especially in New York. In this country you need to have individual ideals and outlooks on things and I think you'll have a very positive life. I think if you need to have a group and you need to be group oriented and you need to be, there's a follower and a leader. I don't ever want my children to be a follower [with emphasis]. I want them to be not necessarily a leader and a dictator, but I want them to be able to make their decisions on their own, not because of what the group is doing. I don't want the leader to be able to tell them what to do, I want them to be able to argue with the leader and say this is what I think you should do, definitely not being just the group being led by anybody. They should have their own individual ideas, and outlook and opinion. . . . I think it's very important in New York because it's so easy to be led around by the nose . . . then you find out later that you're screwed, so I think you definitely need an individual outlook on things.

I also spoke with one father, Mr. Dunleavy, a very shy man who had lived his whole life in Queenston. He was married to a very bossy, tough, and outspoken wife whose self-confidence he seemed to envy. He seemed as if he did not like the quiet qualities of himself and thought that his kids would need to be tougher than he was in order to resist the gravitational pull of the streets and gangs, drugs and alcohol. When asked what characteristics he would most want his children to develop and have as adults, he replied: "Mind of their own, confidence . . . independence yeah, not followin' everybody else." "Why?" I asked. "'Cause sometimes other people aren't doin' the right thing. Do what *they* think is right, not follow everybody else." When asked what his fears for his children were, he mentioned, "gettin' mixed up with the wrong crowd, fallin' in the wrong way, get into trouble, like smokin', drinkin' things like that, mischievous things."

A young mother, Lisa, also spoke of the *pull* of the wrong crowd, how individualism and strong self-esteem helped the child resist that and get above it all. She spoke about the survival tactics she had to teach her child: "We do try to give them warnings and advice on what to do in the worst cases. Julianna even, I've even talked to her about like if she's in the play yard at school and you hear gunfire, you get down on the ground. Can you believe that I had to tell this to my child?" She talked about the South Bronx, where "I don't think there's a hope no matter what you do. Kids gotta worry about getting shot when they walk out the door."

When I ask her what makes one child a more likely candidate for not getting in the "wrong crowd," she tells me they have to be "individuals." She spoke of how the environment could pull a child into the wrong crowd, of the importance of the strength, resolve, and hard qualities of the self, the importance of a self that is bounded, that knew the difference between its own and foreign terrain. The boundaries of the self could not afford to be sloppy or porous, since "the group" was perceived as contagious and boundary less. She said:

> Well, if they're not individuals, if they're not comfortable being . . . to get away from that, they're going to fall into the crowd. There's more of a chance that they're going to . . . if they're in a bad environment, that's how you get into bad crowds. You do what everybody else does. So if you've got some kind of strong self-esteem that you can get above it all. I think that can help a child.

Another mother, Penny, spoke proudly about her "little one being outspoken. I like that because I don't like her to be pushed around. I like her to be able to stand on her own two feet. She's her own person. She really speaks her mind and what she wants."

When I asked her what makes a child "go bad" or get into trouble today, she said, "If they're a follower. That's why I emphasized the fact, I like my kids to be independent and stand with their own ideas. You try to instill in them, if you think it's wrong, then it's wrong. In your head if you think it's wrong, no matter if ten other people tell you, like come on do this or whatever. Like I say, I think if they're a follower, then they'll do anything that anybody else is doing."

In this way being a follower was associated with going bad, or getting into trouble, or having walls of the self that were more open, fluid, susceptible. She spoke of the contagious quality of the group: "Like I try to tell my son . . . even if you're not doing it and you're there, you always going to be considered a part of it. I said you have to watch yourself that way too. You could be an innocent bystander by just being there, but still you're with the group. You know, the so-called 'group,' I always say. You know, hang out with your group."

Individualism and a Tough Past

For those who had struggled with the system, marriage, or drugs in the past and come away defeated, individualism served as a legitimate philosophy that espoused a certain degree of isolation and time to be left alone. A time when parents licked their wounds in solitude, often peering out into the world they had removed themselves from with a great deal of bitterness and mistrust. These were parents who had often been in positions of dependency on or trust in a person, community, or system, been disappointed, and thus built a philosophy of "You can't rely on anyone or anything except yourself. Therefore, stick to yourself, rely and believe in yourself, only." Another element of their tough pasts was what they viewed as overly strict upbringings. This harsh treatment ranged from parents beating them when they (the parents) were drunk or high, to repeated verbal abuse, to no communication between parent and child.

The accepted tenets of individualism allowed these parents to be respected as individuals and left just to "live their own [lives] the way they wanted." Individualism served a protective, healing role. It was one way of rationalizing why they needed to remain in a distrustful, relatively defensive position toward the world. It legitimated their isolation, couching it in an idiom of strength, and even arrogance, rather than cowardice. These parents often spoke of independence as something they adopted later in life, after being stupid enough to think that they could be dependent on the system or a person. They spoke proudly of the process of "wising up." Understandably, they seemed distrustful, suspicious, and yet prideful of what they still retained and how they had made it through.

I got to know Lisa Shickey, a small thin woman with long dark hair and a strong Queens accent, through the parents' group at P.S. 2. She'd come in with a few of the other parents to learn how to make baskets or dolls for the kids and to take makeup lessons from one of the Queens Mary Kay cosmetic consultants. She was quite hesitant about being interviewed, seemed very suspicious of me, and made a point to let me know that she could barely, if at all, fit me into her busy schedule. She wanted me to know that she had things to do, and that she wasn't someone who was desperate or needy. She seemed intensely insecure, lonely, and yet prideful and not about to give up. She was one of the parents who came in to school everyday, hoping that the leader of the parents' group would have arranged an activity. When I mentioned that it might be too noisy in the cafeteria to interview her, she said, "Well, that's my life, it doesn't get quieter than this, so you'll have to deal." Over time I found out she was divorced, raising her three kids on her own, and on welfare. She grew up in a family where she was beaten when her mother was antsy from trying to stay off drugs. Lisa was typical of the parent whose initial foray into the world had been rough but who felt that "at least it wised them up" enough to know that one could only trust oneself. She said:

I'd be born to somebody else, uyum. Yeah, my parents just always did their own thing and they were never involved in what was important with us, you know. They never did homework with us, they never came to church with us, they were hypocrites, you know. They got high and stuff like that, so then when you get high, they start beatin' you up cause you're bein' bad, but they tell you when you're eighteen you're allowed to, which is total nonsense. You should never, ever plain and simple—it is never normal, right, and that's why I won't do it and I won't have it in my home, because you know, they would say bad words, you know. I say to my mother until I never say that word, or if I never say that word in front of my child I'm not gonna start smacking him. . . . I didn't live with my fatha but, wit my motha, you know, she wouldn't tell you, you know, she would be doin' the same thing, and tellin' me but you gotta wait till you're eighteen to do them. Then you can do them all you want. She treated me good when she was high, but when she wasn't high, she was all miserable because she wasn't high, but when you're high, you're feelin' good and then you can be loose.

When I asked her to pick three characteristics she'd like her child to have as an adult, she said "independence, definitely," and gets along well with others, self-confidence, and self-reliance. I asked her if independence was really so important: "Absolutely, definitely, 'cause other people are gonna let you down, and it's a burden to other people if you can't do it yourself, and people will start main' you feel like you owe them things, or are obligated to them if you're always relying on them. You really need to be able to rely on yourself or else you're in big trouble in the real world."

Later she talked about today's world, where it's hard to trust people "especially today, man, people, like 'whichever way it works that's the way I'll go whether it's right or wrong, or steppin' on somebody or not.'"

I asked her if there were any ways independence has helped her in her life. "Definitely, because then, you know, you're in control, you make the decisions of your own life. I wasn't independent, really I wasn't, but now I have to be because I'm raising three kids by myself. . . . Aha [she talks as if she'd wised up], so it taught me to be independent [laughs]." When I asked her, "What if you don't learn to be independent? What do you think happens?" she replied, "I think people take advantage of them, I do. I think people can pick up, like when people are not confident. People can sense that. It's not good." I asked her what she does to teach her kids how to be independent. She told me a story: "I told them, you know, if somebody tries to say, 'Oh, you're a faggot; you're a wimp; you won't do it; you're a chicken,' you just tell them, I tell the kid, I tell them to tell the kid that I ain't no faggot, no chump [she says this all with conviction, as if she is defending her own pride]. I do what I want to do, not what somebody else wants me to do. That's bein' a faggot or a chump is lettin' other people push you around, you know, and not to feel that way, you know, things like of that nature. I give them answers to say to these kids when they're pressured, so they'll know what to say. They won't be like dumbfounded and embarrassed. I just tell them . . . 'you don't have to listen to them, just walk away. Say that to them and walk away.'"

Tracy Volk said "it was crazy how [she] grew up." She was left alone from the time she was six. Her parents were divorced and her mother had to work two jobs. Her father had moved out; he'd come visit on weekends and then her parents would fight. When she was fourteen she got pregnant, and she moved out when her daughter was four months old, since her parents didn't support her or do anything for her. I asked her if she was glad she had kids.

> Yeah, what I figure if that with Amanda, when I had her, if I didn't have her when I did, I probably would be dead somewhere, because the guy that I was with when I was with her is into drugs, lived in one room, depended on his mother. Without her I probably would be following him and I probably would have been dead by now. [She said this in a very matter of fact, almost chipper tone.]

She went on to tell me about her mother.

> We pretty much did everything for ourselves . . . that's why I figure, all this stuff that they did to me when I was little, I just reverse it. With my mother she used to pile medication, like fifteen to twenty pills in a pile, and she'd just take 'em, at one time . . . she was just like the biggest hypochondriac in the world. . . . She used to flip out all the time. . . . There was fifteen of us. I was the youngest out of fifteen kids. My mother had seven and my father had seven and they got together and had me and all my father's kids lived with us when I was one, and all my mother's kids lived with us, so there was fifteen of us in one house.

I met Theresa Stedman at her apartment, an extremely run down "bungalow" in one of the small side streets off the boardwalk. She was at home with her three-year-old son and one-year-old daughter. Her other child was seven. She was separating from her husband, trying to raise three kids on welfare on her own. She was very proud of how she was now clean from alcoholism and had also gotten over cocaine and marijuana addictions. She went to Alcoholics Anonymous and Narcotics Anonymous. She described growing up as a "nightmare." She grew up with strict parents who hit her a lot and were alcoholics. They were divorced when she was three. She seemed very tired and rundown (her father had just died), but still had a good sense of humor. As soon as we sat down to talk she told me, "I had never been real close to my mother or my father, but my grandmother died and then it's like then I got close to my father and he just died. Well, I'm handling it, I mean it wasn't easy."

She talked with pride (emphasizing resilience and stoicism) about her mother, who was still working and hanging in there after the death of her husband. "It made her go on. Yeah, that's the one thing. My mother still works. She'll be 59, she still works, she's carrying two houses, two cars."

When I asked her what she wanted her children to learn in preschool, she said self-reliance, self-confidence, and perseverance: "If they don't learn how to be self-confident about themselves, they'll never go on." I asked her if you need that before you can get anything else.

Oh definitely. I had to learn that the hard way, you know. A child cannot resist any of the rest of them, unless they have perseverance, number one. When things don't go the way they would have liked them to, at least they will be able to have the self-reliance and confidence to say, "Ok, I made a mistake. That's all right. I have to go on instead of sitting on it."

She talked about how important independence is:

I want them to have their independence too. I want them to be independent. . . . I was very dependent, I was very dependent. I was the youngest and everything like that, and it took me having to go through partially a divorce to finally gain some independence. I had always relied on my husband to pay the bills, to work, and granted, right now I still can't work 'cause I can't afford to go back to work full time, with three young children, you know, but um, if you're dependent, you don't know how to take care of yourself.

When I asked her how independent she'd like her kids to be, on a scale from zero to ten (with zero being independent and ten being more of a group-type person), she said,

Oh, I'd like them to eventually be a zero, independent, because I mean you can't, I mean it's ok to be dependent like you know, dependent on electricity, water, and stuff like that, but it's not normal for a child to be dependent at the age of whatever age, like you know . . . oh yeah, I would like them to be independent, very much so. I knew so many people that are almost 40 years old and they still live at home with their parents. That's crazy. My recent ex-husband is 30 years old and he went back to live with his parents.

Debra Smith was a blonde-haired, blue-eyed, very young mother with a haggard expression and an angry, fed-up edge. She also lived in one of the beat-up bungalows off the boardwalk. She sat smoking in her kitchen, her body slumped and exhausted, while her three kids and their friends ran amok through the house. Every couple of minutes she screamed at them, threatening to "smack 'em." Debra was very private and seemed suspicious of me, seemed bitter about life in general. She kept to herself and let few people in—a few friends and her husband, who was out working his second job. She told me she got mixed up in the wrong crowd when she was young and got pregnant at a young age. Her parents were divorced when she was ten. She spoke regretfully about how she dropped out of school in junior high. Her brother was 13 years older than she, so she didn't have much in common with him.

When she talked about how she wanted her daughter Laura to be independent, it was usually mixed with talk about experiences in her past in which she stupidly "followed the group." Like other parents, talk of independence was inextricably tied to talk of the "bad" groups in school or on the street, peer pressure, dropping out of high school, drugs, and alcohol. Independence was what would save one from giving in to the group as she had in the past:

> I think independency would be more important, because then as they get older they learn to make their own decisions and not to have that group say, "Well, your decision is wrong. You have to follow what we say." To have to make their own choices and to know what decisions to make is right. Then they're not going to grow up to be independent and certain situations show—always depends on the situations—don't do it just because you're friends are doin' it. That's more independent, and don't just drop out of school 'cause you see you're friends doin it, you know, which, you know, those are the things as I was growin' up I'd want. . . . So depends situationwise, if she's out wid her friends and you know, whatever, there's one thing to be group oriented but then also to be able to make your own decision and know that if somein's goin' on, whatever, you know you can walk away from it without havin' to get grief from your friends and stuff, or put down.

The individualistic socialization of her child grew out of the memory of her "too-dependent" past where she had been let down.

The self should be resilient enough to get the child through the hurdles and mistakes that are an inevitable part of life (hard work, low wages, little vacation, separation, loss, loneliness). Independence, self-reliance, self-confidence, and resilience were spoken of as the tough fiber that would help the child buck up, move on and keep going through some challenging situation that would arise, when, as one parent said, "things don't go right for them."

When I asked Tracy Volk what were some of her favorite characteristics of her children, she replied:

> [She talks with pride about her sons.] Like my boys, they do for themselves. They're smaller than [their sister] is, but they do for themselves. They don't let anybody mess with them. They're smart, they're tough.

Street smart?

> Oh yeah!, [she says, smiling with pride]. He's two and the other one's three . . . my three-year-old has been in school in like a special education school 'cause he's hyper since he was about a year and a half, and he's very, not that this

makes a difference, but he's the only white kid in his class. Like whatever the other kids say, my son'll say, "Can you top this?" and he'll beat them to it. He doesn't let anybody get away with anything. His favorite thing is, like if I'm driving and he says he wants something and I tell him "no," he's callin' the cops on me. He says, "I'm callin' the cops on you, bad girl." Like he'll be like, "I'm thirsty, get me a drink or I'm callin' the cops on you." So and he's the same way. He gets it and he gets whatever he wants done. . . . They're both very tough little kids.

I talked to her about her daughter, Sheila, five years old. When I asked her what characteristics she'd like her daughter to have as an adult, the first two she mentioned were independence and self-confidence. I asked her why she picked those and she answered: "'Cause I don't want her to have to depend on anybody, you know, when she gets older, and I want her to think the most of herself, 'cause now she's very shy and she can't do it, so I want her to think that she can." I then asked her, "How will independence help her in the world?" She replied, "She won't have to rely on anybody. She won't have to ask for anything, unless she desperately needs it." I asked her about personality characteristics, if there was anything that she would want them to be more like or different from herself.

I want my daughter to be pretty much just the way I am, but different, pretty much everything, attitude the same, 'cause if I want something I go and I get it [she says this in a very determined voice], so I want her to have the just, the same mentality for that. If she wants something, she can go for it and get whatever she wants, 'cause right now I give her whatever she wants, and I don't want her to think somebody's gonna give it to her all her life. I want her to be able to go out and get it for herself.

I then asked her, "Beyond food, shelter, and love, what are some of the things you think children need to be happy?"

Well, in this neighborhood they need karate lessons. . . . [She nods.] There was this instance, ah, this kid Katie in her class, her older brother was out in the schoolyard and they beat him; they stuck pencils in his ears. I was like I don't want anything like that happening to my kid, nothing like that. This was the preschooler's older brother, about eight, that's one thing, like even with each other, like if he hits you and you didn't do anything to cause it, then you hit him right back so he knows how it feels. That's what I taught all of . . . so I taught all of them that if you get hit, you hit them back, and I mean you don't just walk up to strangers and boom, but if somebody hits them or causes them or hurts them, then do it right back, unless the kid's smaller.

I also asked her what other things she tells them about how to respond to strangers.

Oh yeah, my daughter, I forget where I was, but we were at the park and it turns out that a little boy that's in her class now, with his mother, came up to her and said something to her and she screamed, "Shut up. Get away from me." Ahh! Like this [Tracy smiles proudly], and I get up and came over to her and said to her, "What's the matter?" And she said, "This strange lady's trying to talk to me." And I was just like, "I meant like strangers," but I guess that's how she took it 'cause this lady was telling her what to do and she screamed bloody murder, told [the lady] to shut up, told her that if you came near me, I'm gonna kick you and run [laughs], so my daughter pretty much knows if somebody she doesn't know comes up to her, unless they're introduced by someone she does know.

I asked her if she shows them actual physical things to do.

Oh yeah. I tell them if there's a man that comes up to her, I told her right where to kick him. I mean, she hasn't done it to anybody yet [laughs], thank god, but she knows exactly where to kick a person, and I told her if there's anything on the floor that she can throw at them, bend down, pick it up, and throw it at them, like rocks or glass or something like that. She knows.

I asked her what some of the qualities or characteristics are that make a child go bad today or get into drugs. She said, "If their parents ignore them and well if they're dependin' on other people, if they're followers, doin' what their friends are doing, and they'll say, 'He, he's doing it,' and they can't be themselves, so they'll follow whatever the other guy's doin'."
She said she wished her children would be more independent than she is. When I asked her to describe someone she knew and liked a lot, she replied that she really "didn't like that many people [laughs]. To be honest, I don't." When I asked her why, she replied,

I don't know, 'cause like, the way I grew up I had two people that I trusted. One was my brother, one was my grandfatha, 'cause if I asked them I needed something, they'd be there to get it for me. I'd break my arm for somebody if they needed it that bad. Like I've taken in my friends who didn't have apartments. I've taken them in just for them to turn around and stab me in the back, so I really don't like anybody anymore [nervous laugh].

But, in general, you stay pretty much to yourself?

Pretty much I stay to myself. My husband has a lot of friends. I just stay away from people pretty much [laughs]. See, I got my kids to keep me company. That's pretty much enough for me [nervous laugh]. That keeps me busy.

Kelley Hard Projective Individualism: Getting to and Staying on the Top and the Importance of Success

Although they represented only about a fourth of the parents I interviewed, these Kelley parents were in a slightly higher income bracket. Individualism did not bind itself as much to violence and poverty because they were not as prevalent; hence, in speaking about the goals for their children, they had a less tight and hardened defensive stance.

Compared to Queenston, Kelley was a fairly safe and neat community on an island in Jamaica Bay, with a great deal of pride. Although parents were quite suspicious of strangers in their community, toward the world in general they exhibited a greater sense of trust and hope. Many of these parents were proud of how far they had come. Kelley parents did not always have the beaten-down, shameful, haggard quality that Queenston parents so often had. They spoke at great length about their houses and boats, their pension plans, the way they were successfully taking care of their families through hard work. They saw themselves as wealthier than their parents and hoped their children might be wealthier than they. Individualism for them allowed the child the means to reach out to the world successfully, to "make it." In this way, individualism had more of a pioneering sense about it. Rather than the more protective individualism of the Queenston parents, there was a definite outward momentum to the hard individualism they socialized, based on the perception that their children could forge into new domains and head down trajectories usually inhabited by the middle and upper-middle class.

Kelley's sociocentrism was reflected in their shared child watching and the frequent instances of multiple generations living in the same house or nearby each other. Most parents and teachers talked about how tight the community was, how residents watch out for who does what and where. Parent after parent jokingly remarked about how you couldn't do anything in Kelley without somebody knowing about it. Some of the residents jokingly referred to gossip, and it became obvious that gossip was accepted as an established form of social control, one of the prices you pay for living in such a tight community. Father Martin of St. Virgilius Church has lived on the island for 23 years and jokes that he is still not a local. One resident implied he felt most of the people in Kelley were related. It is also fairly common for people to marry within their community. Many of the parents I talked with told me of their nearby parents, how they liked to stay near them, how important family was to them. In Kelley it isn't uncommon to find three generations living next to each other. On one of my first walks down the main street, a woman on a bike, named Donna, came up to me and asked me who I was. She had never seen me before and she knew everybody in town. She turned out to be a modern day *Muchona the Hornet*, informing me of town gossip and filling me in on who was who. She told me after we talked on the street that now everybody would be asking her who that woman she was talking to was, because they'd all notice I wasn't from around there. This was my first introduction to the watchful and suspicious eyes that pervaded the town. Strangers were not warmly welcomed but watched very carefully and without reservation.

During the time I did my field work, most of the residents were white (only 2 percent black or Hispanic) and either Protestant or Catholic, with a large majority being Irish, German, or Italian. What struck me most about Kelley was that it had a great deal of pride. Parents emphasized that their community had good values and good, solid, upright, decent people. In Kelley I noticed some of the houses had American flags in front. "It's a very patriotic community," said the head librarian. "You see mothers out with baby carriages, people with good values." One of the things parents were most proud of was Kelley's upstanding residents and the way people took care of each other. They were also very proud of how they took care of their elderly, instead of locking them up in homes. Even the recluses were well taken care of. Fundraisers were occasionally held for someone in need of surgery or a family whose house had burned down. Some Kelley parents also prided themselves on the fact that their kids could play outside without worrying whether they'd be mugged, shot, or hurt. Since families lived so closely together (you could look across the street or next door and see into your neighbor's kitchen) and all of them knew each other, a child could play on the street and no matter where she went, she was sure to be looked after. In this way there was a very convenient joint babysitting that occurred on the street, with many of the young mothers sitting out on their porches, watching three or four children from nearby houses. Often you'd hear mothers yelling to each other from house to house, saying, "Hey Mary, Tommy's comin' over. Is that ok?" and then sending their children over.

Still well aware of the "hard reality" the children were up against, one Kelley father, in speaking about his own upbringing, said, "If you have to get a couple of hard knocks, you grit your teeth and work through it." Later he said, "I want them to learn that ahead of time; it's not all rosy." Many Kelley residents viewed the New York world immediately outside of their community with much caution and even disdain. They spoke about how Kelley was safe in comparison to adjacent communities, like Queenston, which was only one subway stop away. When I mentioned I was going to walk back to the subway stop after the interview, many parents warned me against taking it. Most Kelley parents I spoke with have not taken the subway for quite some time and in no way let their children go on it alone. The subway stop in Kelley seemed to be a symbol of the danger and corruption that was hovering around Kelley and of the many sordid types that existed outside of their neighborhood. The stop brought together a wide variety of people that the Kelley residents obviously didn't trust. It was a rough stop, a place you would not want to be alone at for too long at any time of the day or night. It always had a desolate feel, and it became quite clear that if you were a respectable Kelley family, you rarely took it. At around 3 P.M., parents said it was particularly dangerous. Groups of mainly black school children on their way to East Manhattan mixed on the platform, playing loud music, shouting, swearing, joking, and pushing each other around. When I took the long subway ride out to Queens, I learned that during the times when school was let out, you dressed down and kept your eyes to yourself. What I called "streaming" was very common around three o'clock, when wild boys would stream through the cars looking for fights, trouble, fun, money. They would often perform rap moves to the music they were playing in their tape box, smoke, and tear apart the advertisements lining the upper part of the subway wall. They had an air of untouchability about them—they seemed ruthless, invincible, powerful, and tough and only needed the slightest of provocations (eye contact, invasion of space by sitting too close to them or staring at them) to ignite their anger. Kelley residents got on and sat quietly, eyes down, keeping to themselves. It was only at home or safely ensconced in their own neighborhood that they got angry with these "streamers." Otherwise, they seemed to play it safe.

However, Kelley parents did not only see individualism as a way of strengthening the self against the pressures and bad influences surrounding the child. Individualism was not solely needed as part of a survivalist mentality but helped one to gain success and achievement in life, to arrive and stay *on top* of a recently reached status or level of success, to be a leader rather than a follower. Many of the Kelley parents were cautiously optimistic, full of hope that their child would make it but simultaneously well aware of all that was "out there" to influence them in a negative way. They were, on the whole, much more chipper, confident, outgoing, and hopeful than Queenston parents. They seemed to have more energy in the interviews and, on the whole, were more receptive when I approached them about talking with me.

In general, these parents spoke much more positively about their children and their achievements in sports and with high grades. They saw the values of individualism as what the child must have to be a leader, to gain success and achievement. There was a certain feistiness to these parents in regard to their children—the feistiness of parents who, having climbed a certain distance up the economic ladder, had gained momentum and wanted to keep going. The individualistic socialization of their children constituted a large part of that momentum. Here we find the beginnings of a philosophy of the child opening out into the world, but in a less soft and delicate manner than that described by Parkside parents. Children needed to stand firm in order to get anywhere, not simply to avoid violence or drugs. Kelley children were described more like supermen or a Nike ad than as emerging delicate flowers, a phrase that Parkside parents often used as a metaphor. As some Kelley parents said, the child's individualism was a chance to "try things out," "stand out," "get a lot more out of this world," "break away," and "go for your dreams." They emphasized being self-determined, persevering, and pushy. It would not be as delicate a process as among Parkside parents, nor would the parents constantly be there to help the child emerge. They spoke less about assisting the child through this process through emotional encouragement and empathy than about getting their child into good schools, with good teachers, good coaches, and good teams.

Hence, the strands of individualism these parents tended to focus on were more the self-assertive, self-confident aspects than the protective, defensive, self-reliant qualities Queenston parents emphasized. And yet, there was a hardness and toughness to their talk about the child's entrance to the world, as if the child had to build momentum and develop a tough skin to break into new socioeconomic domains. One father emphasized the importance of a high school degree, computer skills, and that the child not expect to get a great job automatically. He says, it's not easy "To get a good job [laughs] cause they're not many out there."

Mrs. Ramacca spoke to me at length about her children. She had two daughters, both in a local gifted program. She seemed quite intent on making sure they got whatever they needed in terms of academic encouragement: support, transportation, a packed lunch. She felt her environment was pretty safe compared to the South Bronx and therefore, didn't feel she needed to move.

> We have a saying in our house, "when your mind says stop, your heart says go." I get it mixed up a lot, but you know. You want to give up, maybe in your heart, you can give that little bit of extra.

> *How does this help them later on in life?*

> Well, you'll go out and go after your goals. If you know that you're not afraid to try and that you can achieve just about anything you try, then I guess there's no limit to what you can do. You can have any dream at all and go for it. You have to break away and make yourself independent to be able to accomplish things. If somebody's always doing it for you, you're not going to be able to do it on your own.

When I asked her what would happen if her daughters weren't independent, she talked not about danger but about achievement and dreams, binding individualism to this more projective outward trajectory. Instead of talking about how individualism helps her daughter defend herself against the world, she talked about how it helps people get more *out of* the world:

> I don't think they're going to achieve their goals then. Everybody's got a different dream. If you're not comfortable being individual, I don't think you're going to be successful. You gotta know what you want in your heart. Everybody is different. . . . it's what you do in the beginning that either gives them the courage or the perseverance they need to be that individual or they might just be too afraid to try anything and too comfortable relying on family or friends that they'll just fall in with the crowd and not look to stand out.

For her, independence and self-determination were tied to success and achievement. She taught her children to keep trying and never to give up. She didn't want her daughter to be concerned about others to the extent that she didn't do what she wanted to do. When I asked her, on a scale from zero (independent) to ten (group oriented) what number she would like her children to be, she replied,

> 3, 1, or 2 because I'm not happy about . . . I am concerned with what others think to a degree. I wish that wasn't so. I'm afraid of hurting someone's feelings to get what I need or what I know is mine or something like that. I'm very careful with people's feelings. I think I could get a lot more out of this world if I

just stuck up for myself a little bit more. . . . I'd like to see my children a little more independent than I am.

Aggressive individualism is important in a competitive society. One woman spoke of her aggressive and outgoing child and praised her for speaking her mind. She valued this trait in terms of ideas as opposed to avoiding gangs and drugs. She felt kids needed a certain aggressive individualism in today's world. "That way other people don't step all over them. They'll get their ideas across." Another woman emphasized the importance of perseverance: "It goes back to being independent, being not really outgoing, but being able to express themselves. I guess like not really giving up, like if you have a set thing and it doesn't go right the first time. I'm one that always believes to try, try again."

Sharon Tarmas linked being dependent with not getting very far. She felt being independent forces you to put your best foot forward. "They'll be dependent on other people and they won't get far. I don't think they'll get far if they have to depend on other people, cause they can't take care of their own. It's not good to depend on your family, friends or anything." When I asked her why, she replied,

> I don't think that's good. I don't depend on my family. I mean, if I need something, if I run short or through bad times or something, you know, I can always get something. But I was raised to take care of yourself. If you make your bed hard, lay in it. Long as it's not the point where you're laying there to die. If you have to reach out for a little bit, get a couple of knockers. You don't get anywhere because you don't put your best foot out. You don't give it all you have. You don't try hard enough. You don't give it all you have, because you know that if you don't make it, someone is there to pick you up. If you knew that you don't have that person there, then you try and you'll do it; you'll make it. You know you'll make it as easy or at least you'll make it easy enough so that you live with it.

Climbing the Socioeconomic Ladder

Certain Kelley parents seemed very conscious of their rise in social standing. Some of them spoke of how they were wealthier than their parents, some of whom had been extremely poor. For these parents, individualism was situated in an attitude in which some viewed themselves as having "gotten out," or "made it" and were determined to stay up at the level they had reached. Individualistic values such as leadership, stepping out, self-confidence, perseverance, and self-determination were the lifeboats that had both got them there and were going to help the next generation stay afloat or go for the next level. These parents spoke with pride about the socioeconomic level they had reached.

One mother talked of the importance of self-confidence and how her children should believe the sky's the limit:

I think that when I was growing up, we weren't really taught to thrive for the ultimate goal. We were taught to get as far as we can, but that's not really being taught to get to your ultimate goal. I think children today are being taught that you can achieve anything, where I was told you can achieve something, but we're really not sure what that is. But today it's you can achieve anything if you put your mind to it. Being from a lower class or middle-class blue-collar family you could turn yourself into an upper-class white-collar family with no problem, where I wasn't taught that. I was taught blue collar, middle-class ideals don't go too far 'cause you're really not sure where you're gonna go. Kids now are being taught to really strive for the ultimate, whereas we were taught don't get too confident in yourself because you don't want to fall on your face. . . . They shouldn't be taught enough is enough. I want my kids to definitely strive for everything they can possibly get—not take it, but work for it. I don't think you should take anything. You should definitely work for everything you've got, but I think that kids should definitely be taught that you can get everything if you really work for it.

Ellen Higgers was a young mother who was very proud of Kelley and felt it was a great place for her children to grow up. She told me about how in Kelley, everybody knew everybody. Her best friends lived a couple houses over. She loved the fact that her children were watched by the neighbors and were very safe on the street. She had an extremely neat house, one of the larger ones in Kelley, on the water. When I asked her to describe some qualities she'd like her child to develop she replied,

I want them to have confidence. I want them to be leaders, not followers. I want them to have minds of their own . . . be loving and sensitive and kind and strong at the same time, not so much opinionated, but strong as if they feel something that they can back that up, and that there's right and there's wrong also, and be able to walk away. You have to raise them to understand that you can walk away, and that's ok. I want them to go to college. My husband and I both went to college. I want them to be somebody. I want them to do something important with their lives. You don't just want them to grow up and [then she stops, as if conscious of her possibly too-pushy attitude] . . . but I think also, at the same time, whatever they do as long as they're happy. I want all of them to be happy in their own way.

Ellen described herself as not necessarily from a "lower-class" background and wished to keep her kids in schools where they wouldn't be around the lower-class type as much. She decided to send them to a Catholic school not because it was better academically than the public school, but because the Catholic school had "a better class of people in it." "For some reason I do feel that in the Catholic school there's more mothers who, I don't know, better families. That sounds terrible, but they do care more. They have a different class . . . and it's not just totally against the public schools, it's more that type of community."

Later, she said in a confiding tone:

I think kids and the families that go to the Catholic schools down here are more along the lines and the ways of how I'm raising my children. That's the best way to put it. Not the whole public school, but a good portion of them are really just low class. You can walk through this town and see some of the houses and some of the ways the kids look and the way, the parents, no teeth. . . . I never said this to anybody else—that's even more so why the kids are going over there, because it's more along the lines of the kind of people I want them to be as they grow up. Not even that the Catholic education is such a great thing.

After this I asked her if she could pick a number on a scale from zero to ten (if zero meant independent and ten meant more group-oriented) that she'd like her children to be, and she replied, "I would say zero. I want them to be individuals. Different. And as far as you would say . . . community goes, I would say people that really care, that are on top of the school, on top of the work, and on top of the children in general. Just good families. The same kinds of people that we are is who I want them associated with."

She went on to talk about the importance of sports in their family and how she wants her girls to be sturdy, hardy. "Whining. I can't stand whiny kids. Spoiled, prissy . . . we go skiing in the winter. In the summertime we're working, or we're out on the boat, or we're swimming, or we're upstate hiking, and we go camping. We do a lot as far as sports. I don't want to hear any whining. I love camping. Weak-minded girls, I hate that."

Another father from a very large family, with six children of his own, spoke to me at his fairly large house near the water. When he described his mother he spoke with pride about how she raised kids who were successful and accomplished. Instead of talking about the importance of independence in warding off the violence or the gangs, he spoke of the importance of each generation climbing higher financially.

My mother . . . really never had much, ten kids. My father and she worked for the city, never had a lot for herself, not as much as probably I have today. . . . They were of meager means, they were actually poor. When you look back now, ten people livin' in four rooms, but we were happy. Everybody was happy, one bathroom. She's strong, confident, not afraid. She had ten kids. That in itself is a feat, and everybody is well adjusted. Financially, everybody is secure, everybody owns their own, nobody is on drugs, that's an accomplishment. . . . I would say my life is better than hers, and I hope my kids will be better than mine. Every generation should go up a little bit. You don't have to hit the stars, but some people do. She was a token clerk and it was important and something, just to be happy. To have what you have is great. I'm happy with what I have but I want more. Because I'm the next generation, I want more than. I don't want just one house. I want two or three. I want a rental so when I retire I can make some money. They didn't think like that back then, you know.

When I ask him about where he falls on the spectrum from zero (individualistic/independent) to ten (more group oriented) and where he'd like his kids to be, he felt he couldn't say which way his kids' personalities would take them, but he hoped for leadership. I quote him at length:

On the scale I see myself about a five, because I know you have to be with certain groups to follow the system—how it works. But also in order to change things, you can't be all the way, always following everybody. Otherwise, you become a follower and never a leader. So you want to be closer down to the zero—be the leader and enjoy the other line and go the other way and make your own scale, have people following you. I'd rather see my kids go toward the zero, to be not all the way to the zero but in the middle, to be a group player, but if you're gonna have that leadership quality, you've gotta stay closer to the zero . . . the farther down toward zero you go, you're gonna be a leader, start something different. Every system can be changed. It takes a lot of work, a lot of time, but if you're the one who started it, you'll get the credit for it.

I don't want them to just be a follower all their life. There's a time when you have to be a leader. Everyone will be a leader even if it's just on a small construction project like this. Someone has to run it, start it, make the decisions, so those guys are the ten and I'm the zero 'cause I'm leading. So to be a leader you have to be more toward zero, you have to be a little of both, seize the opportunity, grasp the moment. If there's a time to lead, step out. There is a time where everybody will get their chance to step out and take charge, and if you take it—otherwise, you step back and go back into the group. Sometimes bein' with the group isn't all it's made up to be. It's secure, it's this and that, but you all got to step out, feel the waters yourself. Everyone has to do it, whether you go back into the system—like yourself, I'm in the system—we all have to be in some system, but there is maybe one of my kids will step out of, will be one of those who steps out of the system, and leads a new way, the road less traveled, but you know they're too young to tell. They could get a nice easy teaching job, follow the system or open up a wholesale retail and make a million dollars in three years. You don't know. Would I like to see them do that? Of course, for their own sake. Maybe they'll throw me somethin', a bone when I get a little old.

Mark Timmerman was a father who had four kids. He was a fireman, very proud of his community, proud of his accomplishments, proud of his family. He spoke of how he had gone farther than some people he knew: "You see some people don't get to where I am, owning a home, a family. Some people don't want to go that far. They're happy with an apartment or living in mom's basement. I could never be like that. I have like three jobs now, and I manage to keep a smile on my face."

He then talked with pride about his family.

I had brothers and one sister. We all function fine in society. We all have jobs. Half of them went to college. Half of them are professionals. Some of us are civil servants, but we all have been successful, married, have children, own homes. So I give my mom and dad a lot of credit. We lived right in the city. I know a lot of guys I grew up with. They didn't make it. They're in prison. I went to Catholic school too, and I know a lot of guys who didn't make it. But to get to my level in life, for four years I cleaned toilets. Then I took the civil service exam.

He talked very proudly about his daughter Katie, who he thought would be a rebel rouser. He said she'll be " . . . a handful as a teenager. I can see her.

She'll be a handful. She likes stirring the pot, but that's the way it goes. She just loves her own personality."

I asked him if he thought that this was a good personality trait to have.

> She's independent. She's across the street right now with one of her friends. I go, "Are you ready to go home?" "No, I'm not ready. I'll call you." And she loves to call on the phone. "I'm ready. Come get me." I think Katie is a very strong personality and very independent. I think she would be able to make her own decisions, where my other daughter Jessie might be a little frightened to follow the leader. Probably Katie's personality is a little better, to be more independent. She's strong. I, myself, was always like the leader of my friends when I went out. I kind of made the decisions of what we were going to do. "What do you want to do tonight?" I'd say, "Let's go to a movie," and we went to a movie. I was always the leader. I went into the military. I did fifteen years there. I still do that.

Hence, in comparison to the fortress-like "stand your ground" images of the child's self the Queenston parents described, during my interviews Kelley parents mentioned the following action and sports-oriented phrases:

Go after your goals
Go out/go for it
Have any dream
No limit
Achieve just about anything you try
You can work your way to anywhere you want to go
On top of the school
Lead a new way
On top of work
Hit the stars
The sky's the limit
Every generation should go up a little bit
Step out
Take charge
Stand out
Reach out
Put your best foot out
Give it all you have
Get to your ultimate goal
Strive for the ultimate/everything you can get

Chapter Five

Individualism and Ethnoconceptions of the Child's Self in Parkside

Individualism and Capitalism: Success and Achievement in a Competitive Environment

Individualism binds itself to the dominant themes and core concerns of a local context. In Parkside (where most were not worn down by the daily confrontation with physical safety and financial struggle), most often the values of individualism were linked with success, achievement, and leadership in a competitive society. Parkside *soft* individualism was thus less of a toughening against a harsh environment; rather, it was tied to ensuring that the child opened out into the world, into a successful career.

It was quite evident that by age three Parkside children were already considered little competitors—small but complete "little people" with their own tastes, desires, needs, and wants. All of the Parkside parents I interviewed had their children enrolled in private preschools. Among the Parkside parents, competition to get into private preschools was fierce. There was quite a complex and long application process, consisting of multiple interviews with the parents and the child, the parents alone, and finally the child alone. Intelligence tests and recommendations were also required. Many parents experienced a great deal of angst over whether their child would perform well during the interview process in the preschool they had chosen. The parents knew the child was amazing, but the challenge was to get him to show this to the interviewer. One mother, an artist and textile designer, said jokingly, "With my luck she'll bite the director. Forget it then. After that, she doesn't have a chance." The world the child enters is challenging and competitive. As one mother said in an uncharacteristically "hard" fashion, "I want my children to be strong enough to be who they are and put up with the flack."

Interestingly enough, it was among the fathers of the Parkside parents that the language of individualism and competition was often linked. When I asked one father, an investment banker whom I interviewed in his office, if his three-year-old child needed privacy, he answered, "It's important. I don't see any reason why not. That is a right, because you have to think that for them they're out there competing, developing, and learning and so they need this down time where they aren't under a microscope, they aren't being pushed."

Another father, a lawyer named David whom I also interviewed in his office, said of his extremely bright and precocious child, Chaz, "There's a great deal of metaphor possibility between the venture capital business and the upbringing of a child. . . . This has to do with what children are like. Entrepreneurs, successful entrepreneurs are absolutely driven and single minded and megalomaniacal and in many respects they are children." He went on to say, "If there's anything I would credit competitors or even myself I suppose to some modicum of success in life, is not necessarily what I knew or didn't know, but that I had the persistence and determination to go find out."

Another father, Jordan, spoke proudly of the dogged, entrepreneurial qualities of his daughter: "She's a risk taker, self-determined. She'll test and she'll try and to go not only with the behavior but with other things. I think it's a personality trait that in the end will serve her well, somebody who's willing to try new things, to be successful . . . be smart, stick to it, be very aggressive and perseverant."

Of all the strands of individualism, appreciating and developing one's psychological uniqueness and individuality was perhaps most strongly emphasized and linked to success and happiness. One parent stated very simply, "I think you have to be individually oriented to achieve."

Another mother said,

> I want my children to be the best that they can be. We are fairly competitive . . . I believe in individual excellence. I do not believe in the lowest common denominator. I think America is really clinging toward the most common denominator in all aspects of our society. I don't believe in that at all. I really fight it, and that's why I don't believe that if everybody does what you do, that's a judge of what you do, ever. I do believe in the golden rule, but I think the only interesting thing in life is being different . . . better than everybody else.

One mother, Celia, spoke candidly, with a certain confidence and fierceness I wasn't used to from Parkside parents. She was very frank and quite blunt. She said there was nothing that would stop her children from being the best, and though developing the child through various lessons and classes cost quite a lot, it was what must be done. When I asked her what characteristics she would least like her children to develop, she replied, "To be afraid to not be the best. As people, I think the idea of competitiveness is good and I want them to be successful."

Celia was very open about how much she paid in order for her child to be extraordinary.

> I'm not interested in the normal, I'm interested in the best. I don't approach anything from the normal, so if there are certain things that will give them an advantage, whether or not they can use that or how they can use that is up to the individual. My daughter is extraordinary at chess and ice skating, for which I pay through the nose for her to be able to be extraordinary at.

One father, John, an entrepreneur, emphasized the way uniqueness helped the child stand out. He said of his three-year-old, "I think it helps they are forcing themselves to do their own thing, come up with their own conclusions, not just be swept along because that gives them more ability to be a leader, a self starter, a stand-out."

A young teacher, Sara, spoke of uniqueness and the *true* self of the child. She also linked this with being successful in the world. I asked, "You mentioned it's kind of nice when you see their true self, so is it good for them to be authentic to that?" She replied, "I think so. I think they should be true to themselves. They shouldn't have to change for school. It makes them what they are—unique people and if they can be comfortable with themselves, then when they go out into the world and they're older, they'll be so comfortable."

Being true to the self's genuine idiosyncrasies was thus tied to taking risks, being unique, standing out, and having creativity.

One father, Robert, said, "It all comes back down to this creativity thing. The more individual she is, the more creative she's going to be. . . . We want them to free wheel and do what they want to do."

Self-confidence and feeling good about the self were also linked with success and happiness. The following are some quotes taken from various Parkside interviews in response to my question about what characteristics might make a child *successful* (whatever that might mean to them):

> You need it [self-confidence] to succeed in life.
> If she can feel good about herself, that she can accomplish something, then she can go after a job.
> You can take two children with equal intelligence and the one who really believes in himself and what he can do is just going to do much better than the one that doesn't, and this is obviously a competitive society and the people who believe in themselves do much better.
> Self-esteem—my older one doesn't have nearly as much as my younger one. They can achieve anything with it; they can do anything when they feel confident in themselves, they can just do anything! . . . If you feel good about yourself and determination, you can do anything. You can do anything!
> When they feel very confident and capable—if you don't feel good about yourself, you can't learn. When you emotionally feel good, you can really take the world.

Parents stressed the child's cultivation of her emotions and the development of a good sense of self as crucial foundations for being happy and successful. The child must fully acknowledge and honor her emotions, tastes, and desires so that she can find the right societal outlet for them. The energy of true desire, authentic preference, feelings, and tastes will naturally motivate her to be good at what she loves. If she does not know and have confidence in her unique feelings and preferences, she will have little momentum to carry her forward in a quite competitive society. Parkside parents thus had two discourses: one of the importance of success, achievement, and "going for it" and another more psychologized discourse in which emotions, likes, preferences, and feelings were seen as the emotional fuel that gave the child energy and drive needed to be happy and get ahead. Parents implied that being in denial, or shut off from the unique parts of you that are the "most you" would only hurt the child. Many parents tied this psychologized individualism with success when I asked them what the child needed to achieve:

> [A] good sense of themselves.
> If he knows what he wants to do and takes responsibility for it and doesn't try to get somebody else to make him happy by telling him he's doing a good job or whatever, I would think that's what's the most important—know what you want, and take responsibility for it.
> If the child can begin to understand who he is and where he's weak and strong, his development will be very, very outstanding in terms of himself.
> Having a clear focus, knowing what she wants to do . . . a certain amount of self-confidence and awareness of abilities and capacities which comes through in terms of communicating your abilities.

In Parkside, individualism thus made a large part of its territory the emotional health of the child. Individualism became what Tipton (1982) refers to as a *psychologized individualism*. It was a philosophy used to protect and legitimate the unfolding of the child's psychologized self. Talk of autonomy, uniqueness, individuality, and self-determination was intertwined with talk of the importance and rights of the psychological self to emerge and be the best it can be.

One preschool teacher, Sara, spoke of the importance of teaching the child to explore and release the emotions and how this was tied to leadership and a sense of liberation.

> To give them skills about expressing and redirecting emotions, exploring their emotions, recognizing and respecting their emotions and then finding ways to deal with them because this is where the emotions can go from unbridled to so held in that the kid just can't function because they're so afraid that they'll mess up in school. You really have to look for the times when you release and explore those emotions and let them feel confident that they can lead, whether it's leading a line or getting up, and it's that whole sense that you are an equal among your peers, everything is within the realm of possibility.

Another mother, Linda, spoke of wanting her child to really know the vast terrain of her feelings: "Develop an ability to know what she's feeling . . . self expression, to know yourself, you feel safe to express it, and that includes negative stuff. Our job is to help them express the negative in an acceptable way."

One father, John, described to me what "mirroring" a feeling was, a technique he had learned in a Parent Guidance Workshop. He said,

> No, I absolutely believe in all the nurturing stuff. I never got mirrored when I was a child, and I learned mirroring when I was in the Parent Guidance Workshop, and it was foreign to me to mirror my child's feelings 'cause in my

house you never felt anything. But then to say to your child, "oh, you must be really sad about that," and "would it help if we talked about why David took your doll away from you?"—it's amazing how that works. It is such a helpful thing. She left the group, came to me, and told me what was happening. I mirrored her feeling rather than discounted it and held her and talked about it, and she was right back in the group again. It was validation, which is important.

One mother Jane, talked at length about raising children. She was a very emotional woman, and at one point, she started to cry in the interview when speaking about her mother. Raising children seemed to be a very intense and serious experience for her. Every move she made had consequences. She tried, more than any parent I met, to accommodate the child's needs and feelings. She very much emphasized empathizing with the child and not crushing that vital, spunky part of them that she felt they needed in the world (that gave them the momentum they needed to get through the world), but was also sometimes exhausting to put up with. Even when it felt like a roller coaster ride and was quite emotionally exhausting, she felt there was a certain joy in seeing the child's unique will assert itself. This assured her that the child would not be stepped on in the world at large. She said, "It's all so exhausting. Here I am encouraging expression of emotions and it's so melodramatic—up here one minute, down the next, and then they're fine, at least in my case, 'cause Chauncey is very, very erratic."

Independence, individuality, and self-confidence were also seen as bringing mental health and happiness. An individualistic and independent child was felt to be a happy child insofar as independence was proof that her feelings were not being stifled or blocked. Happiness came about when uniqueness (which was seen as residing mainly in the child's feelings, impulses, and desires) was able to flow freely. Once this process occurred (an opening up and freeing of the child's unique character), a natural strength arose in the child, the strength to be "who they are," to be unique and stick up for those very qualities that made them different from others.

When I asked one parent why self-confidence was so important for her child, she answered: "You need it to feel good about yourself. You need it to succeed in life and to feel happy. . . . A good strong ego and self-image are basic for an appropriate personality and just being able to function in the world."

Another parent said, "If she learned nothing but came out feeling [a] strong character inside, it would be a success."

The goal for most Parkside parents was a child who asserted her own thoughts and feelings as valid in their own right while still accommodating certain basic societal constraints (manners, politeness, kindness, and group activity when necessary). Continually operating with a "false" self (too often doing what others want you to do when this is not what you believe in) was akin to operating at half mast, in a victim stance that made the child less spontaneous, assertive, creative, and perseverant because she was not doing what she wanted to do. The genesis of unhappiness thus lay in the repression and invalidation of the child's unique internal cues and needs, which vary from individual to individual. In an effort to ensure a certain health and happiness, aside from wanting their child to learn the manners and rules of society, parents often worried that their child was trying to please others too much. While still admitting the need for group cooperation and support, health consisted of overcoming certain inhibitions and acting from the wellspring of the child's true thoughts and feelings.

Psychologizing Self: Parkside Ethnoconceptions of the Child's Self

Although Parkside parents lived in New York City, crime, drugs, gangs, and violence were not a major part of their daily lives. Because they had the material means to protect and insulate their children from the violence of the city, these worries were not of primary concern. Furthermore, most of their experience of "the city" consisted of other equally affluent parts of Manhattan. Places like the Bronx or Harlem were not areas thought of as part of "the city," nor did the parents ever think to frequent them. Some of these families also had country clubs or homes in Connecticut or upstate New York that they went to on the weekends.

All of the parents I interviewed lived in an area that was quite safe. I never thought twice about my safety when going to Parkside homes or preschools. Most often the buildings had doormen and high security systems. The children were taken to and from places by a babysitter, and were thus guarded by an adult at all times, and cabs were often taken instead of the subway. Parkside as a community was quite concerned with keeping its particular blocks safe and clean. Lexington Avenue, a busier, more colorful and chaotic street with a range of social classes represents the "line" where a class mix begins. It is the line they most often do not allow their children to cross unaccompanied until high school. On Park Avenue, where I lived, most parents let their child out of the building and onto the block if the doorman could still see them. Some young children were allowed to walk their dog on the block of their street. It was considered safe and clean enough for them to go unaccompanied by a babysitter. Strolling down Park Avenue, it was not uncommon to see only doormen and babysitters with young children out for a walk. Many of parents I interviewed had either a live-in babysitter/au pair or one that came every day for any number of hours depending on whether both parents worked or one parent needed a certain number of hours off to do some errands or see a friend. Live-in babysitters were usually older immigrant black women or young women trying to get through college. They received room and board and a small stipend in return for their services.

Park Avenue was a very wide and quiet street, immaculately clean, with gardens running down the middle and beautifully pruned Christmas trees or tulips, depending on the season. It was very rare to see the homeless on Park Avenue. Anyone who tried to make a home under one of the awnings of the apartment buildings was quickly shuttled off the street. Doormen were constantly on the lookout for this, but it was never much of a problem, since nearly all of the homeless knew enough not to even try and instead continued across Park Avenue, toward Central Park. The homeless tended to cluster either closer to the park or on Lexington Avenue and farther east. On each block there were neighborhood watch signs, alerting people on the street that this was a monitored area.

Most of the residents in Parkside were white-collar professionals. They lived in buildings with high security systems and sent their children to private schools, mainly on the upper west or east sides of Manhattan. Most parents I interviewed were investment bankers, accountants, lawyers, and successful entrepreneurs. Others I interviewed included a photographer, filmmaker, journalist, teacher, and dancer. All of the parents had college degrees and some of them had advanced degrees (M.B.A., J.D., M.A., Ph.D.).

Each day at around three o'clock, when school was let out, the streets in Parkside were flooded with children in uniforms. At this time, different private schools in the area assigned two parents to patrol a group of blocks for a few hours to monitor the safety of the area. They wore bright orange rain capes so that they could be easily identified in case a child needed help. They also had walkie talkies that were connected to safety patrols in the schools. These were often two mothers who walked around casually chatting as they perused the streets. During the day there was a certain relaxed, family-like atmosphere to the area in which I lived. People were not as frantic and driven as you would find in the midtown business area or amid the hectic, loud commercialism and chaos of Lexington, First, Second, and Third Avenues.

Not surprisingly, all of the parents I interviewed seemed less exhausted than the Queenston parents. Most of them, while perhaps sometimes nervous about the interview, were relatively encouraging. In general, there was an eagerness and freshness in their reception. They were, on the whole, less suspicious and defensive than the Queenston parents. Their apartments were quite calm, clean, and spacious in comparison to the homes in Queenston. Fresh flowers often sat in a crystal vase on a piano, a housecleaner often dusting quietly in the background. Only once or twice was a TV turned on, and this was only so the child would not disturb us during the interview.

During my field work in Parkside, I lived with a family for two years. I took care of their nine-year-old daughter (helping with babysitting, homework, transportation to school, and dinner) during the week in exchange for room and board. The father was an investment banker and the mother owned her own production company. Their daughter went to a private school in the East End. Living with them enabled me to sink into the community in a way that I could not have done if living alone or commuting from some other part of New York. Were it not for their gracious eagerness to welcome me into their family and help me get to know the ropes, I would have remained very much an outsider in Parkside. Meeting their friends, talking with them at dinner, working for them at their parties, and having them as general resources for information on preschools proved remarkably helpful.

Deborah Gordon and Margaret Locke (1988), in considering biomedicine in terms of the two major Western traditions of naturalism and individualism, point to certain assumptions found in the modern self. Spontaneous emotions and feelings are viewed as more natural and less cultural than thoughts and thus take on many naturalist assumptions. A feeling, like nature, is conceptualized as being not only separate from but prior to culture. Furthermore, very rarely is a feeling associated with the larger group, society, or public. Rather, private and public are divided and natural feelings placed on the side of the private. In my conversations with Parkside parents, there was a strong emphasis on the child finding or discovering her true self. Lutz and Abu-Lughod (1990) claim that in the modern West, feelings have been established as the core of one's self, the most real part, the seat of individuality, in a way that thoughts are not. They write, "The heart (the emotions) are commonly seen as the true, real seat of the individual self, and things of the head (thoughts) as relatively superficial, socially influenced aspects of the self" (1990:68). Feelings are seen as the most real part of the self. In writing about the nineteenth-century Romantic movement, Susan Sontag states, "Emotions are Me in a way that thoughts are not." Sontag (1978) also notes that in the nineteenth-century Romantic movement, sadness was seen as making someone interesting. Thus, emotions are seen as constituting "the perspective of the individual on events. . . . [T]he subjectivity of emotions in this sense gives them a fundamental—even sacred—role in individuating the person" (1977:35).

Feelings were then protected insofar as they constituted a large degree of what made the child unique. Tautologically, individuality and uniqueness then became the explanation for why feelings should emerge: "because they are hers." Lutz and Abu-Lughod (1990) point out that emotions often stand for inviolatability and privacy. One of the greatest injustices one can make is to tell someone else how they feel.

Among many Parkside parents I found that vertical metaphors were often used to describe the true self's location on an axis that ranged from superficial (top) to natural/real/true (bottom). As the "deepest," most private, subjective part of the child's self, beneath the outer layers of the public self, the feelings were the most natural part of the true self. The naturalist assumption sometimes taken up by these parents was that the social/cultural (false) self is epiphenomenal, analogous to surface layers, which can be wiped off to discover the natural bedrock beneath.

In talking about the real self, a bipolar public/private dichotomy was also often invoked. Although spending time with "the group" was described as equally important as time alone, if overused, the public domain could be enervating, depleting the self's energy. During my interviews with Parkside parents and teachers, I was often struck by the wide array of negative connotations that accompanied the word "group." Some parents described their children as collapsing after their time at preschool, as needing private time to recuperate and recover. Time out was often suggested when a child was socially overstimulated. Sometimes the mother would interrupt during her child's play group and suggest the child needed to cool down and spend some time alone. Thus, sometimes culture/society/the group was described and understood, as Gordon and Locke write, "largely as external constraints that *limit* rather than enable or empower. . . . To be socially determined is to be weak, trapped, limited" (1988:27). Social relationships, as Gordon notes, were often seen as "a potential threat to freedom. Involved relationships with others are less often understood as being a potential source of freedom, power, and resources" (1988:37).

One mother, Cynthia, a very formal, serious woman who was relatively strict with her daughters, was having difficulty with her daughter Perrin. She worried she wasn't true to her real self.

> I do feel she's not true to herself. In her desire to please others she will do things that I'm not sure she enjoys doing, because she thinks I want her to do it, and I'm really worried about that. Like that's a very hard message, you know. Are you playing squash because you want to do it? I let it be. I figure if she hates it, it'll surface, but I guess I don't want her to get in the habit of doing things to please other people.

Cynthia's language shows the extent to which natural feelings are seen as ascending from bottom to top when they surface, and insofar as they are thought to be part of the true self, she thinks they will eventually "surface." This is different from the outer, false layers of the self, which are more easily sloughed off.

Often a split between school and home was spoken of, with the child tending to follow the norms of the group at school while being indulged at home. One preschool teacher talked to me about how often children act differently at home and at school. Children tend to "act out" at home more than school because they feel more comfortable there. Being social is seen as somewhat exhausting and somewhat unnatural, as something that can suffocate the real self rather than evoke it. Linda said:

> The closest thing I can compare it to is how you would behave at home with your family versus how you would behave at a cocktail party. If you were tired and crabby at home, you would act it out. You may even not want to be around anybody. You may say, "Leave me alone. I'm tired." At a cocktail party you would get dressed up, if you needed to, and you would be very pleasant and social. What happens with a lot of the children in our school is they're fine all day and they go home and fall apart. Because they've just behaved so well at school that they just lose it at home or they need to take a nap because they've [focused] so much on being successful at school. But one of the most important things as a parent is to realize that the place for your children to act out is at home.

Another woman, April, in talking about her nine-year-old as being "out of it" in terms of missing social cues from peers, was worried that her daughter didn't seem to need much social stimulation and didn't seem to want a lot of play dates. April told this to her own therapist, who then reasserted the importance of not doing things simply for other people and not worrying about social acceptance if the child herself wasn't worried. She told me her therapist focused on the healthiness of resisting group norms and said that the worrisome part would be if her daughter had an overly strong desire to please—if she just did things for other people.

Among the upper-middle-class parents of Parkside, self-expression is limited by class constraints to being controlled, kind, and mannerly. One mother, Beth, a filmmaker, spoke about how liberating it must feel not to care what the group or other people think. She talked about how she'd love to have more of a feisty, cocky attitude but that this didn't seem realistic in her social sphere:

> Like a Madonna-like personality, I watched her in a television interview and I think, "How can she do that?" [she says with awe]. . . . She's completely self-confident in herself. Whatever she feels she's like, "Fuck you. I don't care what you think." In an interview she was asked, "What's your favorite recipe?" She said, "I DON'T BAKE!" Well, I don't bake either, but it wouldn't come to me to say [that]. I'd say, "Well, hmm, I guess I don't have a favorite recipe," not this like offensive attacking.

At a parent guidance workshop, one woman, Janet, told a brief story about her daughter, Danielle, three and a half, not wanting to say hello to the people in her building. In the following section I quote Janet's discussion with the counselor:

> Janet: My husband and I had a discussion about this, that up until last year, Danielle wouldn't say hi to the neighbors and I was always prodding her to please say hello when someone says hi to you, and he said to me, "Why are you pushing her to say hello? If she's uncomfortable connecting with semi-strangers, don't force it." And I said, "You know, you're right. If she doesn't want to say 'hi,' I don't want her to be rude." I taught her how to just kind of smile and that way she didn't have to talk, but at least she wasn't being rude, 'cause I want her to be socially appropriate. I think it would be a shame if I forced her to do something that she didn't want to do, because then she's not being true to herself and she's going to feel awkward and uncomfortable. I think that's important. I want her to know that it's ok, to not have to talk to this person, but at least not be rude.
>
> Counselor: I think probably what you heard was when your child is shy and somebody says, "Yey there, little girl," and the girl goes yuck (and pretends to spit), you say something like, "You know, I guess Jessica isn't ready to talk to you because she doesn't know you."

Hence, emotional expression of one's real feelings was fine, as long as they fit within a general range of being kind, mannerly, and civil to others.

One mother talked about "battling bad manners" and wanting her children to learn to be "good citizens": "I think that things that worry me or upset me for this generation in particular and especially kids growing up in New York City, is being too spoiled, being unaware of other people's needs and a lack of sympathy for other people." This balance between honoring the child's feelings and making sure they came out in socially appropriate and polite ways was a difficult challenge for Parkside parents, who worried about the delicacy of their child's self and the way in which blocking expression of their feelings might hurt their child's self-confidence and individuality. Self-expression was quite important in order for the delicate child's self to flower, and yet the child should not be rude, aggressive, violent, or obnoxious in the process. This proved to be a tough balancing act for Parkside parents.

Privacy, Creativity, Communication

In Parkside, the process of unfolding a true self that was protected, reflected, and rationalized through the language of individualism involved cultivating creativity, privacy, and the ability of the child to communicate her true desires and feelings through words. Privacy was the physical and psychological space needed for the self to emerge on its own, in its own unique way. It was important as an open arena in which the feelings and thoughts of the child could unfold and the sense of self as distinct from the group could be defined. Creativity was an outlet, a way for the real feelings, the "true self" to come out. It was an expression of those interior feelings, an exercise in unfolding. Communication ensured that these feelings were heard and gotten out in the open in the clearest way possible. It was important insofar as the child learned to articulate her own needs and feelings accurately. Creativity and privacy especially were viewed by many parents as necessary aspects of the child's life and as key components in a child's development.

Privacy: Respecting the Psychologized Self

Interestingly enough, most Parkside parents referred to privacy not as a physical privacy of the body, needed when the child reached puberty or began to be aware of her sexuality, but as a psychological privacy. For most parents, psychologized space was viewed with awe and trepidation, a space that should never be trespassed. Comments such as this father's about his child's privacy were common: "I think it's wonderful to watch—it should be encouraged; it should never be challenged, ever, ever be challenged, absolutely never be challenged."

In talking about kids' private spaces one preschool teacher said, you need to "act as if it's almost trespassing, that you check to say, 'Is it OK if I come in now?'" One mother distinguished between two kinds of intrusion on space, one much less harmful than the other. She spoke of how it wouldn't be so bad if she barged in on her daughter when she was taking a shower or using the toilet; it was the *psychologized* space that needed to be protected and the boundaries obeyed. "My oldest daughter has a diary. She's never kept it locked. I would never, ever open it. I think that if you really believe you respect children and treat them with respect, that to not allow them a sense of privacy is totally just opposed to everything else you could say." One father, Ronald, who frequently used flower metaphors to describe the growth of his three-year-old daughter, Lida, said, "She plays by herself. You can be in the same room; you know I don't start eavesdropping on her. I listen for 20 seconds and listen and chuckle and then walk away. . . . I'll knock. I wouldn't just barge in, but I'd say, 'Lida, what's going on?' and I tell her I'm coming in." One preschool teacher spoke of the sanctity of the child's cubby. "That's theirs, their own things, and nobody is allowed to go in their cubby at all. That's sacred, I mean big time. If somebody goes into their cubby, it's a big issue. It's private and it's never been a problem; the kids are pretty sensitive about it."

A few parents said they would not open their child's birthday party letters or go into their child's room without knocking. One of the mothers in the Parent Guidance Workshop was worried that she didn't give her daughter enough solitude. Another woman responded to this by saying, "I was actually told by a psychologist that they should have their own room, and even better to have a lock on it, so they can have their own time."

Privacy was thought to help develop and construct individuality (that particular conglomeration of unique tastes, desires, and feelings that every child has to get in touch with), as well as confidence and assertiveness. One father, John, talked about how privacy helps construct an individual. "He has to be able to talk to himself and, as his godfather says, 'process, process, process,' and I think that it's part of constructing an individual, that one has a place to go, physically as much as mentally." When I asked one mother what would happen if her children didn't get any privacy, she said, "I think they'd miss out on some part of development. I don't know what, but they'd miss out. I think having privacy helps you be a little more independent. When you have time to yourself you can think your own thoughts. Then you can go out and share them if you choose to, but you do have them to yourself. You can investigate things."

One father said of his three-year-old daughter and her need for privacy, "It's all part of becoming an individual and thinking for herself." Another mother, Allison, talked about how privacy was crucial insofar as it allowed the child to conceptualize herself as an individual separate from others.

> You cannot have respect for an individual and not respect their privacy. You can't do it, I don't think. It's allowing them to see themselves as individuals separate from their parents. I think privacy goes along with respect. If you think of children as lesser, then you don't treat them with respect. I would never consider listening in on some conversation with one of my children or trying to overhear one of their conversations.

Because privacy was seen as so crucial to development, I began to ask what would happen if the child did not get any privacy. One mother emphasized the more passive, victimized, unhealthy qualities the child might take on. She replied, "Oh, I think they would just be basket cases! They would have no sense of self worth, they could be victims easily, in every way. They wouldn't be able to stand up for themselves, they wouldn't be very healthy people."

When I asked another mother how she thought her daughter would act if she never had any privacy, she replied by mentioning how it would stop the outward movement of the self unfolding into the world. No privacy would make for a more timid child. "She'd probably be overly modest or unwilling to try things or do things." One mother said, "It might affect her confidence in self . . . it's a self-confidence within your own environment of doing what you would like to do and without being aware or wanting to be aware of what anyone might think about what you're doing that is an important part of development of self." One father said, "He'd be a little more stressed out, [it would] force [him] to be a little more group-oriented. Therefore, they might not be as individualistic in their thinking and in what they're interested in."

Privacy allowed the child to solidify his or her self-concept as a unique individual, distinct from the group. In speaking about privacy, many Parkside parents invoked a public/private dichotomy, in which the self needed a respite from the public domain or "the group." When the child needed privacy, "she can go in her room and recover, from the group." It was a time when the child could express himself without the limits and constraints of the group, school, or family rules. When I asked why her daughter needed this space, she said that it was a place away from authority telling her what to do, a place to learn about herself.

> She has this place where she can go and be with herself and her own thoughts. She doesn't need me directing her or telling her what to do or helping her read or write. She's self absorbed, she's learning about herself, she's doing her thing . . . I think that it's very positive because then she comes down refreshed and renewed and she has the ability to be with her sister again, because sometimes she's a big pain in the butt.

However, most children needed to learn how to ask for their privacy and that they had a right to it. This constituted a crucial part of the Parkside socialization process. The outward unfolding process in the child's development included knowing you need space, knowing you have a right to it, and being able to ask for it assertively. One mother proudly talked about how her daughter was aware of her need for privacy. "She's aware of it, and it's something she'll know to ask for . . . it's that she wants to do, something without my egging her on or urging her on . . . when she says, 'Mommy, don't look at me,' I think they need it; it's their time of creating the surprises or when they're mischievous, to do something that they want to do they know mommy or daddy won't let them do." When I asked if that's important, she replied, "Sure, just like we want privacy, why shouldn't they be able to feel like they can have some uninvaded time? . . . She says,

'Mommy, don't look,' or 'Mommy, don't turn on the light all the way yet,' and 'leave me alone.' I'll always respect that."

One teacher at a preschool spoke of how important it was for teachers to be aware of children who are sending out signals that they need space or privacy.

> I am especially sensitive when I'm hearing that a child was wanting space from another friend or whatever. I will zero right in on it. It is important for our mental health, for healthy development that children have the sense that they can have space if they need it. In the classroom because there were some complications when children were sitting with their rug and he's too close to me and he's too . . . that we put names down on the rugs. It has changed things tremendously. When there is an issue of space, I think there needs to be a pretty good amount of structure, because once people start feeling crowded, it's not a great thing. So we've put names down on the rugs, and so now they just go and sit and they've got an allocated amount of space and everything is fine with that.

The teacher needed to be watching for this so she could step in and teach the child how to learn to ask for her space. She went on to tell two stories about teaching children how to learn to defend their own space. In teaching the child this, the teacher used empathy ("I feel that way too sometimes") to alert the child this feeling of needing space was a valid, normal feeling and should be acted upon. She told a story in which she worked with a child on becoming comfortable with the concept of space:

> Just yesterday there were two friends playing together, who have played together all year. One little guy was saying, "I don't want to play with you." I heard that and knowing it was not like, "I don't like you and I don't want to play with you," it was like, "I don't want to play with you. I need space right now." It was very much that. So, I went over and without being suggestive I asked, "What's happening?" because the other guy's lips were curling and his feelings were really hurt. He said, "I just don't want to play with him right now." I said, "Do you want to play with anyone right now?" and he said, "No, I don't want to play with anyone." I said, "Do you need a little space right now?" and he said, "yes." And I said, "I know I feel that sometimes too." I said that to the other child, "You know there's times where you just need a little space. He loves you. He's a dear friend of yours, but he just needs a little space." As I said, when I hear that, I'm very sensitive to it.

Privacy was so important that children needed to learn the skills to be able to ask for it, even when the child *did not himself know* that he needed privacy. She went on to tell me another story about the importance of not encroaching on another child's personal space.

> Space and sensitivity toward children who need space is just crucial. That's one other thing that a teacher needs to keep an eye on. Today we had a child hugging another child, really strong hug. The other child knew that it was a

sweet thing but looked a little uncomfortable. So I went into that situation and I said, "How did you feel when he was hugging you? Did you want him to?" He said, "No, I didn't really want him to." Then I said, "Then it's really important that you let him know that. I know you care a lot about him and that was really sweet that he hugged you, but you've got to turn and let him know." So he turned and he said, "Please don't hug me like that."

Another preschool teacher said, "They're fully entitled to it. They need it and sometimes you need to tell them that they need it, like 'George, you need to ask for this sometimes at home, if Sarah is around and you can't stand it.'"

Another mother of two daughters, Jane, also spoke of "empowering" her children through privacy and teaching them how to ask for their own space:

I absolutely think they need privacy. It's part of mutual respect; it empowers them; they have the right. Chauncey is going through a stage where she's so adorable it's hard not to hug and kiss her all the time, but I want to teach her to be able to say, "No, I don't want to be kissed now." She'll say, "Don't touch me, Mommy. I don't want to be kissed." People go up to kids and do things to them like "goochy, goochy" this or that and do things they'd never do to adults. Timothy said to someone when someone put their arm on her, "Don't touch me. My mother said I don't have to have anybody touch me." [She laughs with pride.] It does give them something, to have the power, because we create so many of the rules, to have what power they can have safely is important. You want them to obey, but nor do you want them to be a Nazi.

Some of the parents mentioned accommodating their child by enlarging their own space (usually their bedroom) so that the child could have more space.

We're big believers in your own space. Since I've had kids my space has gotten larger. When you have kids on you all the time, you have to enlarge it a little bit. My parents, when I was growing up their bedroom was off limits to the kids. That was their private spot—nobody, you didn't go in. I always resented that, and so now our bedroom is the center of everything. We read in there, we eat in there, we watch TV in there. I think that kids need a space where they can go and just do their own thing . . . the things that she holds dear and sacred and she doesn't want to share are in her room and she doesn't have to share them. They are her things.

Creativity

Creativity was seen as extremely important as an outlet for emotional expression. Given the importance of the unfolding and puffing out of the emotions and feelings of the self, creativity became prized for the way it was an outlet for the child's subjectivity. Creativity was a perfect channel for the release of one's true self, a catalyst in the individuation process. If creativity is encouraged, a stronger self emerges, one that has fully explored its own domains and knows what it wants and needs. It is hard for a child to unfold without knowing what he wants. Creativity is an assertion of the child's unique personality through color, light, paint, voice, song, design, and so on. One mother said of her three-year-old, "It's almost like a stream of consciousness, or her subconscious, a full expression of whatever is inside of her and if it's given enough strength now, I think it will help protect her individuality throughout education or her work life or anything that will tend to squelch that."

Many of the Parkside preschool teachers spoke of art as the unique expression of the child's personality. Art, said one teacher,

> allows the children to express themselves, to be who they are, through their art. If you can look at some of the paintings on these walls, it completely lets themselves express who they are, like dressing themselves. Sometimes through their art, it's completely discombobulated and then if you look at them, that's how they are, everything is all over the place, or sometimes it's really tight and they're very, you know they carry a lot of stress; that's a real way for them to express themselves. You have to really keep it open ended so that they can do it the way they want it and how they see it, like when I gave them the three shapes for a snowman. You can make snowmen, but they could have been sideways. I mean Charlotte made hers not connected and she's not a connected child, she's not. Chrissy, that's so her, she's totally tilted, and that's how she views the world, and sees herself like that. Look at Camilla, her person on the wall. Isn't that great? She's a really happy kid, and here she is. She has happy parents and she's so creative, and look, she made herself happy.

Thus, in contrast to the father in Queenston who resisted such psychologizing of the self, in Parkside, art was often highly psychologized. In doing creative art projects with the children, very rarely was any piece not viewed as an expression of the child's personality. The structure, line, and color of something were not random but the unique elements of the personality put into shape and form. The head of this same school, in describing the set up of the classroom, told me about the importance of the dramatic play area as a channel for the child's feelings; a place they could act out, through drama.

> Everyone has a housekeeping dramatic play area which at least in the beginning of the year and certainly for the three-year-olds is a mini-house area to replicate what they have at home and to act out all kinds of things that happen at home. Play helps them figure out their world, and so their dramatic play. They are acting out all kinds of things that happen in their lives that they see on TV, sometimes working out issues—kids having babies, kids working on sibling issues will be beating up the babies or be very tender and sweet with them, and then the block area is both used for constructing buildings and the dramatic play as well. They use the materials to act out.

Some of the parents in Parkside would hire a private art teacher to come and teach their toddler creative projects using painting, crayons, magic markers, and colorful stickers. I got to know one of these art teachers, who worked at a fancy toy shop on Madison Avenue. She supported herself by teaching about five students (two to four years old) art lessons for a very high hourly rate. She would go to the family's apartment and teach the child in a playroom. Most often the parents would leave the child and teacher alone for about an hour, not wanting to disrupt the creative process. She told me occasionally their pictures were made into Christmas cards, which the family proudly sent to their friends.

Creativity was also thought of as being good for self-confidence and independence. One mother, Anne, a filmmaker, talked about her four-year-old son: "I would say that it is feeding their sense of 'I can do it, my ideas are good, I am effective, I can put my ideas out there and my feelings.'" Another parent tied creativity to expression and self-confidence. "It's very important to make the child feel that they can do something and it has a lot to do with developing self-confidence. I think that you can get to everything through it because you're developing imagination and confidence."

One parent said, "Creativity is promoting independence in a way that they can do things and they can handle a situation on their own—leads to being better problem solvers and critical thinkers because you're not just gonna let somebody else tell you what to think. You figure it out for yourself, so I think it is very important."

Another father emphasized self-confidence and independence: "Creativity supports individualism, provides an avenue toward self-confidence. They've done something that will be acknowledged more often than not, positively, and that makes them feel good about themselves."

For many parents creativity was not necessarily something some children had and others didn't. It was all a matter of how in touch the child was with her emotions and unique tastes. One mother said, "I think children are naturally creative if they are allowed to feel who they are, and if they're allowed to express it, then they're naturally creative." If privacy allowed them to get to know their feelings, creativity was an objectification of them through light, color, sound, rhythm, and so on. Pieces of artwork done by the child, far from being interpreted as random, were seen as unique acts (though often unconscious) of self-assertion and expression.

And so we find that creativity was important for Parkside parents insofar as it was the vital channel through which feelings exited the self. Many parents viewed it as an "outlet," once again emphasizing the importance of the outward expansion of the self into the world at large. The more the child could engage in this, the freer the self would be. A certain tightness or "density" of the self associated with keeping feelings in—repression, too much group activity—was actively avoided. The "looser," more open the self was, the better.

Communicating Emotions through Words

Like creativity, many Parkside parents spoke of the ability to communicate the child's feelings as of utmost importance in the child's development. Interestingly enough, communication did not refer to nonverbal modes of communication but solely to the use of words. (See also Tobin, Wu, and

Davidson, 1989.) A couple of times on the upper east side, I'd see a child throwing a tantrum or hitting a sibling, and a parent would interject something along the lines of, "Use your words, Annie. Use your words." This mantra was repeated in Parkside preschools. Communication was one way to ensure that one's feelings were heard and expressed. To liberate feelings from the body was to communicate them to others. Communication was the happy medium between acting out a feeling in an inappropriate way (hitting, screaming, tantrums) and hiding or repressing it and keeping the self too dense and tight. Communication was the verbal assertion of one's individuality and rights in a socially acceptable and calm way.

The director of one preschool said,

> Their ability to use words, to hang in there with something, to keep going, in saying, "but that really hurts me," and "I really don't want you to do that," and to be persistent and consistent with that. We expect them to be gentle with their friends when they're upset, and we want them to use words and to talk it out with them. We try to get them to use the words. We get them to model what we're using to help work it out. But, the key thing is always getting them to use more words, always getting them to try to work it out with words, especially for three-year-olds, because the first impulse is you want what you want and you want it now and you're going to get it. And one way to get it is to pull it, to grab it, or to hit someone or whatever.

Another preschool teacher said,

> I think they need to be aware of emotions. I think that the most important skills that you can teach young children are open communication[s]. I encourage my children to say that they're angry and to act out anger, but to do it in a constructive way. I think that if you don't allow children to express anger in a positive, constructive outlet and you don't allow them to express other emotions, you are not helping them develop their communication skills. If they don't develop it when they're young, it's going to be much harder when they're older.

Some parents spoke with pride specifically about times their children "used words well." In response to my asking her to tell me a story about a time they were most proud of their three-year-old daughter, one mother answered, "It seemed like an overnight leap that she took with her communication, sentence structure, being able to really recant a story. She was two and a half years old, telling a story to me, linking sentences."

Another mother said she was proud of her son Todd. He was on a play date and was upset because the other child was unable to share his toy, "but Todd was very patient through the whole play date until the very end when he was frustrated and started crying and screaming, so I was proud he was able to just use his words, saying, 'He's not sharing,' and 'I feel angry.'" She went on to talk about one of her favorite characteristics of her son. "His precise way of expressing himself . . . like about a play date he said, 'Mom, a more ruder boy I have never sawn.' [She laughs.] So his grammar, his ideas about grammar are all . . . he's thought about it. He thinks about what he's going to say."

Typically, the use of words was tied to a certain amount of achieved self-assertiveness in the child. A father, Robert, said of his three-year-old,

> Language is an absolutely wonderful gift that should be developed at the earliest possible age, and that is reading, writing, listening, speaking. Words are important, sentences too, the ability to communicate, in the written word and standing up in front of a group of people—your views. That's a very important characteristic, so underdeveloped and underutilized.

Among these parents and teachers, communication was tied to talk about the importance of getting the child's needs met, protecting one's space, claiming one's rights. It was a way of ensuring the protection of one's space and needs. Communication was the last stage in letting the child's feelings flower and unfold. While privacy allowed the child time and space to explore the psychologized territories of the self uninterrupted, communication implied the feelings were conscious and objectified enough for the child to "stand up for them" through the act of speech.

Individualism and the *Flowering* of the Child's Self

Unlike the Queenston and Kelley parents, one of the main objectives of the Parkside parents was not to toughen the child's self from the outside in but rather to puff the delicate layers of the child's self out, so that the child could open out into the world and realize her full potential. It was one of assisting the child in emerging, unfolding, flowering—helping to actualize his or her unique qualities, thoughts, and feelings. The philosophy was not one of "my child against the world" but of helping the child to open out *into* the world. Thus, the self of the child was not to be tight, dense, vigilant, and ready for obstacles but loose and willing to pour itself into the world, to be as unique as it has to be in this environment. It was a delicate process insofar as any large, clumsy, or harsh interference might stunt the unfolding of the unique self. Thus, images of "softness," warmth, receptivity, delicacy, and unfolding were used in contrast to the fortress metaphors of the Queenston parents and the sports metaphors of Kelley parents depicting hardness, tightness, or density. Individuality in thoughts and feelings exists only as a potentiality; hence, the extreme measures taken to bring the process to some sort of fruition (e.g., when the child knows herself, can speak her mind, and has a good sense of herself) help her develop authentic emotional energy that better propels her toward success.

The parent has to take care to unfold the layers of the psyche gently, without getting in the child's way. One of the most common metaphors used to speak of this unfolding process was that of a flower. Images of growing, blooming, blossoming, and flowering were often invoked. The flower image so often used was the perfect metaphor to reflect the delicacy of the child's ego.

I interviewed one father, Ronald, at his home, which he worked out of as a computer consultant for banks and firms in Manhattan. He was a very shy person who spent a great deal of time alone. Most often he spoke with a great deal of hesitancy about his daughter, Lida, four years old, who was quite a talkative, confident, stubborn and outgoing child. He seemed almost in awe of her and quite resistant to getting in her way. "I don't have any desire for my characteristic preferences to be imposed on her. I think of her as being an emerging flower and I'm so happy with her."

Another father said, speaking of creativity, "If they don't foster it now, it'll never have a chance to bloom and blossom." One woman, in talking about preschool teachers, said of her three-and-a-half-year-old daughter, "I just want them to enjoy that child and appreciate that unique little thing, and let them grow." Another mother, the wife of a Columbia professor, said while watching her child, "It is so amazing to watch them develop; they're just like little flowers."

Images of the parent providing a tender, encouraging environment for the unfolding process to occur in were common. As the child's self unfolds, the parent stands around with gentle, open arms. In speaking about his three-year-old's great stubbornness and will, Christopher, the vice president of a large New York bank said, "We're not going to be able to do much about it. Quite frankly, I think what we can do is provide enough of an environment so that he has choices."

One mother said of her four- and seven-year-old daughters, "There are a lot of things we do constantly and put up with a lot of crap, and we put up with a lot of disruption in everything, and messes and things for them to express themselves, much more than most I think. I think it's healthier that way, although at times I want to rip my hair out."

Another mother, Jane, in speaking of her son and her attempt to let him "act out," talked about what you have to let the child do at home. Using a hydraulic metaphor to suggest that the release of emotional expression should never be blocked or shut down, she said,

> One of the most important things as a parent is to realize that the place for your children to act out, even though none of us want to deal with it, to whine, to throw tantrums, to do any of that, is at home. If we try and shut down on that as parents, then what we're really striving for is to stop their thrust for independence. The child starts striving for independence when they're a year old.

One mother, Judy, a successful sports photographer who worked out of her home, prided herself on her receptiveness to her children. She was quite happy that she was able to be home when they came back from school and that they could unload the day's troubles, worries, or excitements. She exemplifies the attentiveness and sensitivity many parents felt was needed in raising children. She said, "I took a course at PET, Parent Effective Training, and it really teaches you to listen, and if you don't have time to listen, you have to find time. If you don't have time to listen, you miss out on the cues . . . you have to be ready when they're willing to talk."

Another parent spoke of trying "to do the best for them, eliminating as many distractions as possible, like TV is out." One father spoke of giving his child as big a canvas as he could in which to excel.

> I don't think there's anything wrong with excelling—to excel at something— all of us have that capability. Giving a child with a capacity a big canvas so that you increase his odds that he will excel at something that he chooses, that is the ultimate goal—to make the canvas as big, so that that child has the highest probability of excelling at something that he chooses in an environment where he knows himself . . . so the child can actualize his own in whatever he chooses based on what he knows of himself.

It is this authentic emotional fuel, which was felt to come through having a good sense of themselves, that gives the children the "highest probability of excelling at something." What we find here is an incredible effort to create an environment for the child in which they can grow, whether this means eliminating distractions, providing art lessons, ensuring privacy, or giving a child a "big canvas" or a "warm environment."

Stubbornness, Charisma, and the Child's Will

Some of the Parkside parents described their children as stubborn, willful, and felt that raising their children was tough because they were for the most part assertive, unique, creative, and spirited children who didn't back down. However, parents felt these traits "would work well for them." Time after time, indirect references to how their children would be successful in the world were made in reference to the child's particular stubborn assertion of will, impulse, feeling, personality, etc. In contrast to some of the comments made by Queenston and Kelley parents on the problem of having a fresh kid who talks back too much, stubbornness and willfulness were even described as healthy in Parkside.

One mother described her three-year-old daughter with a sort of exhausted exhilaration, a tired pride in which she ultimately was quite pleased with the personality traits her children had.

> My daughter is Attila the Hun, very charming, impulsive, creative [she sighs, looking exasperated but pleased at the same time]—it'll work well for her. They are not amenable children, they're wonderful, empathetic, but they're stubborn as can be, strong willed. Then again, that's what we sort of wanted. We got it. In the long run I think it's going to be a good thing because they're strong and yet empathetic.

In describing her daughter again, she said, "I have two girls, an almost nine-year-old, a sensitive, loving caring and funny Attila the Hun, ADD, but doing really well, but difficult, from the word go, very impulsive and creative. I mean it's going to work well for her." Another mother, a filmmaker named Beth, in talking about her son, age four, said, "Even to the point where I think Frank's ideas about what he wants are stronger than I'd like them to be and I think he should be more pliable, I think in the long run that that will serve him."

April, a recently divorced woman, talked about her son. She seemed insecure about the whole child-rearing process, always a little paranoid that she wasn't doing enough, or the right thing. She also spoke of the simultaneous difficulty and joy of having a unique and "charismatic" child.

> Willy is my child who over the years has given me the most trouble and concern and a lot of it is he's been going to a pottery class suggested by his therapist. The woman is a therapist and he loves it. It's not like sitting in a psychiatrist's office, and he's producing all this stuff and he's been in heaven. And he's really special, wonderful and charismatic, but difficult, a difficult child to raise, but has such charm that he's worth the trouble.

Another father, Leo, spoke about his stubborn child, "It's much healthier emotionally, but it is tough parenting."

Another mother spoke of her three-and-a-half-year-old daughter's courage and risk taking. This was a trait that the parents had looked for and were quite pleased with when it arose. She, like many other parents, wouldn't dream of stunting these traits. "She's a risk taker—she'll test and she'll try. I think it's a personality trait that in the end will serve her well, somebody who's willing to try new things."

Christopher was extremely excited to see me and readily talked about his children. The moment I showed up he quickly ushered me in and shut the door, beaming with pride, itching to talk about raising children. Seeing the stubbornness and will in his daughter was beautiful to him; it was like watching a life force that would take her through the world. It was a sort of guarantee that she would probably be ok in the throes of a competitive world, that she had a certain indestructible momentum. "Charlotte picks fights with anybody; she's going to go right for the neck, which is great to see a will! A lot of times that's misinterpreted as the terrible twos. I think it's wonderful, it can drive you loony, but here is a little person with a point of view!"

One older father, Lenny, a man who took pride in doing a great deal of the child rearing, spoke slowly and methodically. He told a story about his two children in which he felt the healthier child was the more defiant child who asserted her will and had a strong sense of what she wanted. He sounded somewhat similar to the Queenston parents in that a stubborn child would not just go with any crowd, would not be converted or persuaded to follow the wrong crowd unless that was what she wanted.

> Teddy and she are two different kids. I actually prefer . . . I actually think that Christy is healthier—you're not going to be able to talk Christy into doing

something. She's not going to go with you when you say, "Come with me." She's going to say, "Who are you, and why should I follow you?" Teddy is very likely to just go along and they do get frustrating . . . I get really angry with Teddy but I try not to show it. It does show, though. They know that I'm angry. . . . I have to say my more defiant child is my healthier one, and the one who was never fresh was passive aggressive. She is really saying, "Hey look. This is a good way to be." I wish I had been more assertive than I was. It's much healthier emotionally, but it is tough parenting.

Reducing the Power Differential—Empowering the Child

For the Parkside parents, individualism also bound itself to an egalitarianism that extended to the child. Part of the process of helping the child unfold and emerge was to make the child "less victimized" by reducing the power differential between parent and child. Although there were certainly some Parkside parents who believed in the more hierarchical approaches ("because I'm your mother and you'll do what I say"), and even laughed at the "ridiculousness" of treating a child more like an adult, among many parents there was often a sense that because of this power differential, being a child was difficult. Often parents would step into the child's shoes and try to see themselves from a child's point of view. One mother, in speaking about her three-year-old daughter, said, "It's very tough being a kid! Everyone is bossing you around, telling you what to do."

One of the articles handed out by the parent guidance counselor in the parents group was written as if from the child's point of view: "On Being 12, the Age of Anguish and All Parents Can Do Is Try Not to Be a Total Nerd." Here the child is depicted as laughing at the shortcomings of the parent. One woman, Anne, in response to hearing about how another mother, Susan, got angry at her child for not saying "thank you" for a birthday party she threw her, said,

> If I did some of the things [to my daughter] you all are suggesting when she didn't say "thank you" for a party, she would be so struck with a deep sense of guilt that I wouldn't want to do that to her. We have such power over our children, especially at these ages when they are so vulnerable, that I'm very nervous about doing something that they'll remember twenty years later as the worst thing my mother ever said to me.

In short, the same egalitarianism that was extended to all adults should be extended to the child, except in times of danger, when the parent's power should be asserted in order to save the child's life. Many of the parents spoke of their discomfort with being too authoritative with their child and very often attempted to treat them as they would an adult. One mother, in speaking of her difficulty in issuing authoritative commands to her child, said, "I usually apologize after."

Certain techniques were used to give the child more power and reduce the hierarchical parent-child relationship. These ranged from empathizing with the child, identifying with his or her position, giving the child ample choice in order to allow them to gain a sense of control over the situation, consulting the child on how to solve a problem, empowering the child to handle a tough situation on his own, letting the child teach the parent, asking the child, "How can I help you get what you want?" and saving face in front of the child.

One father who was perhaps the most extreme in this hierarchy reversal said of his three-year-old daughter, Lida,

> My basic feeling about it is that I have no right to discipline her, but when she does things that are absolutely unacceptable, I don't want her to do that. I really think of her as having equal rights to me. If that's really true, then I have that power edge. It's easy to say that when I do have the ultimate power. Yeah, it's critical to explain to her, and Mary and I always try and give her warnings. . . . I guess I'm conscious of the power differential, and I don't feel just because I'm bigger and stronger and know more that I have the right to push her around because we disagree on something. Sometimes if I'm really upset if she hurt Luke or disobeyed me, disobeyed is a little too stern but. . . .

Another parent said about her daughter, four and a half, "Well, she's the boss—one very tough little cookie." Parents spoke of "empowering" acts in which they let their child name the newest child in their family. Another mother, Jennifer, talked about how she was trying to "empower" her son Simon, three and a half, to equip him with the tools to deal with his father on his own. Simon was afraid of the dark, and Jennifer said the father criticized and belittled their son about this. She told the parent guidance group that she said to her son, "How did it make you feel when daddy said he didn't believe you?" The son replied, "It didn't make me feel good." The mother then said, "What do you think you could do next time when daddy says that to you? Maybe you could say, 'Well, daddy, I really am afraid of the dark.'" She went on to say, "I want to learn how to give Simon the tools to deal with his father's belittling and berating."

In response to a question about what she wanted in a preschool teacher, one mother of a four-year-old boy talked about the importance of empathizing with the child.

> A magical understanding that these children are people too . . . when a teacher has this ability to look at a child as a person, that they understand that they have feelings too and they're real feelings and they're very serious feelings. And this morning my son was upset 'cause he was very angry at his daddy, and knowing that he was upset and he's a second child, I said, "Did you wish your daddy got hurt and was dead?" And he went, "Yesss!!" And I said, "You know what? Magical wishes don't come true, and in fact, we can call daddy and I bet he's fine." And he was so happy. So a teacher knows that there are some things that are different about children than adults; they should learn magical thoughts don't happen. On the other hand, they're allowed to be angry, they're allowed to be happy, they're allowed to be people, and acknowledgement— that's a good teacher.

Some of the parents implied that it was somehow demeaning to treat the child in a childlike way, as "a doll" or as "adorable" or "cutesy." It was also demeaning to treat the child as simply part of the group, as simply "a girl" or "a daughter" or any other wider social role the child had. One teacher said that if a situation is handled right, the children "aren't just herded and treated as 'the herd.'" One mother, Susan, a dance teacher, in talking about her three-year-old daughter, spoke of how treating a child as merely a member of a group was demeaning. "I think she has a right to be looked at as an individual, not as a group of three-year-olds or a group of girls, or a group of young children."

Respect for the child as a unique individual sometimes took the form of interacting with the child in a "serious" manner. When I asked one mother what were the most important characteristics of a good preschool teacher, she replied,

> I think a good teacher relates to a child not in a childlike way, to the child's level, but she speaks to the child as [if] the child is a person. It's not all about having a great time, and let's do this and let's do that. There is a focus, there's some learning about it, there's a seriousness that I think kids like. If you have high expectations and treat them in a mature way without being crazy about it, you can get a lot accomplished.

After proudly showing me her son's separate bathroom and bedroom, one mother, Celia, said, "Children have a very fundamental right to be treated as a human being, to be shown the same respect for their intelligence, their ability to maneuver through life on their own as any other person. I try to speak to them like normal human beings, the same way I would speak to my husband. That's a fundamental right that they have." After showing me her apartment, she said proudly, "See? My children all have grown up rooms; they're not treated like children. He moved in here when he was two—no diapers. He has his own macho bed." Later she said emphatically, "I don't make separate rules in my house for kids and grown ups. We have the same rules, general standards of civilized behavior at all levels."

Another mother emphasized how she wanted her children to know that she appreciated and respected them as individuals, as human beings, just as she did adults.

> I think that the fact that children are not only physically smaller than adults means they are often treated with no respect by adults—the fact that a person who has never met my child would walk up and pat them on the head. I mean, maybe they don't want to be patted on the head or cheek—I mean the way they treat children like we treat a puppy or a cat. I think to empower children is to allow them to realize that even though they're small in stature and even though some people may treat them with less respect or less respect for their individualization and how they feel about things, that as an individual adult, I, as a teacher and as a parent, try and get my children to understand that I see them as individuals and have respect for them, their wants, their needs, their wishes, their ideas.

One preschool teacher spoke of what she called the children's bill of rights, "the same rights as adults, 'cause they're people and they can't be trampled on.'"

Another teacher at the preschool, who was interviewing people for a new teaching position that had opened up, stated,

> The respect part, and it's very interesting because as I'm interviewing teachers, there are people who walk in here and [from] the first sentence that they say to a child, I know whether they are really genuinely respectful toward children or not. Though it has to do with whether you think children are cutesy and adorable or whether you really sort of understand them and empathize with them and feel and remember your own childhood.

I asked her to give an example of being disrespectful to the child. She replied, "Sort of laughing at the way a child responds to something. Like, 'oh he did this,' without sort of knowing he did that. Or a little bit condescending or something as opposed to . . . because we've got the years on them, we've got the knowledge on them or whatever."

When I asked one mother, a journalist, what she did to foster self-esteem, she replied, "I treat her like an adult too much I think [laughs], something my husband believes, like telling her the truth no matter what . . . he is always very straight with her. It gives her a certain status in the family, makes her feel like she's on an equal footing, her feelings are important as anyone else's."

In this interview Jasmine, three and a half, was often consulted about the answers to questions I had asked. The mother would turn to Jasmine and ask, "Well, what do you think, Jasmine?" trying to make her feel like she was one of us, at the same intellectual level as the adults. This never occurred in any of my Queens interviews. In response to a question about what rights her child had, the mother answered,

> What she wants is important. If we were to move or something, her opinion would be very important. She's a part of the family—her desires should be considered. She should have a chance to express herself when she's angry or something, given the chance to talk. Obviously, they can't make all the decisions themselves.

Another way of "empowering" the child was to give her a great deal of choice. One father said of his daughter, Lida,

> I'd like to see her grow and expand in the directions she likes. . . . I think Lida would make choices whether I offered them or not [laughs], if she didn't get that option. I think it probably certainly reinforces her sense of power and ability to control and steer her life, to have options. I have absolutely no interest in taking that away from her. Maybe I could be better about offering it, but she's pretty articulate. She'll throw options out there.

In response to the question about how much choice was important , one mother said,

> As much as possible . . . give a child as much choice as possible and they feel in control of their environment, because it's very tough being a kid! Everyone is bossing you around, telling you what to do. In as much as possible, I try to give as much choice as possible. . . . She has as much control over her environment as possible. . . . I respect Danielle a lot; I give her choices. I leave them alone in the morning, and I do my thing in the house, and if they want to . . . that's a big phrase around here—it's up to you, you decide.

Another mother said, "You do want to give them a certain amount of free choice because it's good for them to learn how to exercise control and it makes them feel like they're important and they're a big shot."

In one scenario described in the Parent Guidance Workshop, a mother had an argument with her daughter Perrin, nine years old, over whether Perrin and her friends could take food out of the kitchen. The parent guidance counselor then praised the mother because she gave the child respect, choice, and control over the situation.

> See, I think the reason Kate is a helpful model—she's very clear and consistent. I think what you did was treat her with a lot of respect, too, . . . if you say, "Well, here's some information and here are some choices." You see, what you did that I thought was really quite commendable was you took her aside, which also saved her dignity, and you said, "Here's what you can expect." In a sense you gave her a choice by saying, "If you do this, you will be embarrassed." You know, you have some control over this, because control is the issue that is the most frightening. I think we have to give them the feeling that they have some control. "I can't let you out on the street at night, because it is just not safe, but here are some things that you can do." That is not ramming it down their throat.

In reference to the importance of choices for her child, one mother said of her three-year-old, "I think it's real important—it gives them a little control. So much of the acting out and the stubbornness or whatever comes from mommy and daddy making all the rules, and this way, they get to choose some of the things that aren't important. Then they feel like they're developing a sense of responsibility, that they have some power." I then asked, "Is it hard with a big power differential?" She replied, "Yeah, I think it is. Everything that happens is what mommy and daddy want, so if they can pick the book at night, or if I lay out a couple of outfits in the morning and she gets to pick, or playing a game and she gets to choose the game, then that's good for her." Another father said, "Choices are very important!! Maybe the ability to make choices and inherit the results of those choices in life is empowering and the beginning of taking responsibility and strength of character, very important! Being able to actually, to know what you want to try, to do it and see what happens, the essence of living in a sense, and taking responsibility."

Another father talked about his three- and seven-year-old daughters and how choice empowered them.

> We give our children the right to choose what activity they want to do, if they want to play. Just about every decision we make with them we try to incorporate and include them in the process, so it's not, "I'm going to read you the book about such and such," but "why don't you pick a book that you'd like me to read?" It lets them have some ownership of the situation and that's good.

Let The Child Teach You

One way of giving the child a sense of power and control was to have them play the role of teacher to the parent. One mother in the Parent Guidance Workshop, Jane, talked about how her daughter was having trouble with the daily routines,

> I'm here for Timothy. She's a tough nut; I love her dearly. I'm so much an internal mirroring kind of person. Timothy is now taking a socialization course at Churchill. That teacher is so extraordinarily behavioral, it's incredible; she will never mirror even a feeling. I'm having difficulty with daily routines, changing from one activity to another. That's an area I'd like to work on, eliciting more cooperation from Timothy. She's impulsive, she's unwilling to let go of what she's doing. She is a pleasure, she's fabulous, she's a caring, empathetic, funny, wonderful person in many ways. She's just difficult on the ordinary daily routines.

The counselor replied,

> You can say, "Well, that's wonderful, Timo. I'm really impressed with that, but I'm not clear on what it is. Could you tell me what it is?" And I would just jot down what she says and then if it doesn't work, I would just say, "Well, let's look at this. You have this wonderful plan. Something seems to be getting in the way." I mean, let her teach you what she's got in mind, and then say, "How can I help you implement it when it's not working?"

The counselor suggested to the parents in the group that when a parent finds some behavior unacceptable, they should go to the child and tell them. They should then ask the child how they might solve the problem, giving them a feeling of power. She suggested saying, "Well, when you talk to your children about it, I would say to them, 'Is there any way that I can help you with this, 'cause this is something that I really find unacceptable.'" The parent then acts as the assistant to the child, helping the child implement the plan that she or he has devised.

One mother, who was also a preschool teacher, spoke of her seven-year-old child acting as a consultant, telling her what to do with her preschool class. "She comes home every day and tells me what she does at school, and before I even say a word, she says, 'Now, the way I think you could do that with the children you work with. . . . '"

The director of one preschool told me a story about how she consulted with the children at the preschool about the lack of space in one of the rooms. She wanted to build a loft, so she said to the children, three- and four-year-olds, "'I need your help. I want to brainstorm with you about this loft or about finding more space.' Then we started talking about building up and so on. Then the children said we could build a loft. So I hired this person to build one. The children did the drawings with him; they went to the lumber yard. We had children who helped with children's hammers."

Saving Face and Saving Voice

For Parkside parents, part of ensuring the most relaxing, comfortable, "nice" environment possible for the child to unfold involved saving face and voice in front of the child. This involved both vocal control and molding one's emotional temperament. In the Parent Guidance Workshop April said, "My children very often say they don't like it when I'm angry, and I'm not feeling angry, but I have a tone of voice that comes across as angry, and I'm now quite aware of it so I work on it."

A father said in response to this, "I get really angry, but I try not to show it. It does show though; they know that I'm angry."

The head of one preschool spoke of the importance of keeping a teacher's emotional balance. "I think it's most important that they be stable people, that they be emotionally well balanced, happy people, that they be fairly confident. The ability to leave problems outside the classroom is very important. These are little people; they really can't deal with people being unhappy."

Part of saving face involved presenting a kind, gentle, and understanding voice to the child. One preschool teacher, who was also at one time an actress and singer, spoke of the importance of voice. She said that you need to talk to them in a way that

> makes them feel that they really can learn and understand, not to talk down to them but to be clear and be willing to repeat as necessary, not to embellish so that it gets lost, to have a tremendous amount of patience and vocal control so that the voice is not sending a different message from the message the teacher wants the child to receive, so the voice becomes a conduit. That's terribly important.

She went on to talk about a sheet the teachers got the other day about all the ways you can say something is good "without too much, but just where everything sounds positive or encouraging but doesn't cut it off as if it's over now. I think there is almost no let up in the need for that language." In speaking about voice she said, "It's not about words but about emotional content. That's why acting and teaching get into relationship, 'cause the voice, especially young children, pick up what's in the voice, every bit as much as they pick up the words themselves."

When one mother in the parent's group, Jennifer, said that her child had asked why people smoke, the counselor modeled to the group how to respond to the child in a very polite, slow, respectful, and gentle manner.

> Whenever your child asks a question like that, see if you can say, "That's a very good question." And then you can say, "You know, a lot of people have been trying to figure out the answer to that question . . . scientists and philosophers have been asking that for years. Do you have any thoughts on that?" You know, it's kind of a lovely way to treat a child with respect, and they also come up with some very interesting answers.

The need to "save voice" was also very prevalent in giving the child praise. Here the parent or teacher must sound authentic and not simply give the child empty, hurried, or overly general praise. Empty praise was praise given in a voice that is devoid of emotional content and sincerity. Both the preschool teachers and the parent guidance counselor modeled in extreme detail and complexity the way parents should speak to the child. One preschool teacher spoke of the importance of voice in giving praise.

> Praise without any feeling behind it—just words—children know it has no meaning, whereas if you get somebody angry, you can feel it's a visceral response and even that can be more satisfying if somebody says, "Oh, that's very nice, dear." And then you go on to something else and you throw the milk on the floor and say, "What do you think you're doing!!?" So praise, the very word sounds as if it might be exaggerated or something. It's [she says in a perky and interested and almost awe-struck voice] "How did you do this?"—praise that has more emotional content than specific meaning, "You buttoned that yourself?" [She says this again in a very sincere voice full of awe.]

In response to one woman in the Parent Guidance Workshop who felt that her child was too concerned with getting her mother's praise, the counselor said she should give her "authentic praise." Authenticity is shown to the child through an attentive enthusiastic voice. The counselor said,

> In a way what you're doing is you're saying, "That's nice, dear." So all she's going to do is up the ante, and I think maybe it would be better if you were very enthusiastic for two minutes and then stop and said, "You know, I wish I had more time right now, but I've got to do something." But instead of giving her the praise with one foot and holding on to the other foot, if you could say to her, "Oooh!! That's original!" or "I never saw it that way!" It's a very different way of expressing it. Don't say, "That's great." Say, "I never thought of it that way," or "tell me some more about that!" So you don't have to be effusive, but if you're going to say something to her that is a compliment, do it to her and give it to her completely rather than with the breaks in the accelerator.

Many other parents also distinguished between types of praise. They spoke of praise needing to be sincere, saying that kids could see through insincere praise. One mother said, "You need to be very specific about it. It seems more genuine and frees them up."

We have seen that Parkside ethnoconceptions of the child's self promote a loosening and freeing up of the self, an opening of its boundaries into the world where it can reach its fullest potential. The metaphors used in describing this self are of opening, emerging, and releasing rather than storing, holding, toughening, or tightening as we find with many of the Queens parents. The goals of this kind of soft individualism are the promotion of privacy, creativity, self-expression, and choice and the reduction of the power differential between parent and individual. The child then learns that self-assertion, uniqueness, and individuality constitute legitimate rights in themselves—rights that should not be infringed upon by other children or by the adults who take care of them.

Chapter Six

Queenston and Kelley Preschools

In all of the preschools I observed both sociocentric and individualistic values were being socialized. For most parents preschool was the time for the child to learn how to be a member of a group. And yet the Queens (mainly those in Kelley) and Parkside preschools I observed were very different both in the kinds of "hard" and "soft" individualism they promoted, as well as in the different ways they socialized more sociocentric values. Perhaps the most striking difference was that the Parkside psychologized individualism of feelings, rights, and uniqueness was not nearly as prevalent in the Queens preschools. Rather, what was emphasized was a nonpsychologized individualism of self-reliance and resilience: learning how to cope with difficulties without help, not expecting a lot from others in the way of praise or sympathy, dealing with things alone, not calling too much attention to yourself. In the Queens preschools, a child's independence was highly praised most often if it were enacted within the constraints of a particular order or routine within the school day schedule.

This same difference in the degree of psychologization of the self was present in the socialization of sociocentric values as well. Group life for the Parkside preschools was often taught by emphasizing how one's selfish act was hurting other children's feelings. Empathy, listening, and learning to articulate one's feelings in words were extremely important skills for the child to learn. In the Queens preschools (and again mainly in Kelley) conformity to group life was taught more through practices such as teasing, public shaming, blaming, promotion of a sense of competition between children, and use of threats. All of these had the effect of "toughening" the child up, thickening the child's skin, making her more resilient. This thickening did not necessarily involve "talking back" to the teacher but rather an ability to move on silently and not be crushed by what would be seen by Parkside teachers as harsh words or nonverbal signs of frustration or anger from a teacher.

Another striking difference between the preschools (and as we have seen also a difference among the parents) lay in what was seen as damaging to the child's self. The processes of handling and crafting the self of the child had distinctly different qualities, namely of loosening (Parkside) and blunting and tightening the self (Kelley, Queenston). In Parkside "soft" individualism, the teacher had to approach the child gently so as not to impede the delicate process of the unfolding of feelings and allow for enough space for the self to "flower." In Kelley "hard" individualism, a more "dense" self was encouraged—the child was often expected to be self-reliant and quietly independent within the status quo. Through teasing, threats, blaming, and competition between children, teachers engaged in practices that butted up against the self of the child. This "friction" toughened the borders of the self, blunting the edges so that, unless asked for, the child's unique feelings and thoughts opened out into the classroom less readily. Thus, the "hard" individualism of Kelley emphasized a more stoic individualism, a quiet and tough belief and reliance on the self that would persevere despite hard knocks, discipline, or teasing.

Kelley Preschool Classes

In keeping with hardening the boundaries of the child's self, among the Kelley teachers a different type of behavior was used in socializing and interacting with the child, behaviors that the Parkside teachers and parents would have considered cruel, demeaning, and disrespectful, and would have seen in general as blocking the unfolding of the child's self. The first weeks I was a participant observer in two Kelley classes I saw many forms of discipline that struck me as harsh, and I sometimes left feeling sorry for the children. By the time I left Queens, I myself had been toughened to a certain degree and didn't find the socialization practices nearly as surprising as I did at first. By the end of my field work, much as I tried to be "completely objective," I still found myself vacillating between finding the practices refreshingly upfront, emotionally honest, and direct, on the one hand, and, on the other, still feeling jarred by what struck me as harsh yelling. Much as I found myself reacting critically to some of the Kelley teachers, I never once thought any of them were purposefully mean. We simply had very different notions of what a child emotionally and verbally needed. Some upper-middle-class readers may think some of the Kelley practices "too harsh" and cruel, but it is important to remember that most of the teachers did not seem to feel the child needed such softness and delicate handling in the first place. It is the Parkside teachers, then, who might deem them as too harsh, not necessarily the Kelley teachers. Kelley teachers seemed to have more confidence that the self of a child was resilient, sturdy, and durable, that there was a certain plucky inevitability to its development. The teachers I observed did not view the children metaphorically as "flowers" they were mowing over in order to toughen and thicken them up. Rather, they were more like *weeds*: healthy, spunky, inevitable, and resilient. It was from this more sturdy ego base that they began teasing or what struck me sometimes as yelling. They never assumed these would ruin the child's ego, but thought they would merely cause it to rebound with even more strength. Teachers were helping the child adapt and grow, starting from what they felt the children *could* handle.

Many of the teachers in the Kelley preschool walked, moved, and held themselves in a way in keeping with the hard individualism and toughness they would then localize in the bodies of the children they taught. These women's bodies were not bendable, soft, or approachable. They did not try to surround themselves in a halo of smiles like some of the Parkside teachers. Nor, with the exception of Miss C, were they treated as gentle mountains that the children could crawl all over, hug, or cling to. They wore practical gym suits, sweats and pants, as opposed to the softer flowery dresses and skirts at Parkside. They certainly laughed a great deal among themselves and the other school administrators, but sometimes, especially among the school kids, they also moved through the halls in a rather rigid walk, often with a fairly flat and stern expression on their faces that nonverbally hinted at their authority. When an adult came down the hall they would suddenly smile and engage in pleasant conversation, but they were often very strict and authoritative toward the children in the hallways.

Queens school children at P.S. 1 and 2 were used to a relatively lower level of sympathy, praise, and attention, a deficit that the Parkside teachers would have considered neglectful. On the whole, in school, Queens children asked for much less attention from adults and required and sought less hugging, verbal reassurance, and affection. At the age of three or four, they were already well on their way to becoming less "psychologized" and emotionally demanding than their Parkside counterparts.

The classrooms of the Queens preschools themselves were quite similar. They were extremely crowded rooms: cubbies stuffed thick with coats and boots; old Easter, St. Patrick's Day, or Christmas projects on the walls; tattered books piled high in a corner bookshelf. Most often the room was humid and filled with the smell of milk, paint, and crayons. In the middle of the room were about six desks, each of which sat four children. These were assigned seats and the children were supposed to go and sit down at the appropriate seat when they came in to school each day. To one side of these desks was a small rug area where stories were read with the teacher sitting in a chair in the middle and the children sitting on the floor at her feet. Every morning the class gathered together on the rug. They learned day, year, and month, as well as that day's weather. The answers to the teachers' questions were given as a whole group. At Parkside, part of circle time involved giving each child a chance to say something about his day while the whole class listened; for the children at P.S. 1, this was not part of circle time. After learning the date, there was roll call as the teacher asked who was having hot lunch. Following this, over the rusty and nearly inaudible intercom came a child's voice, saying, "Good Morning, today is April 3rd, 1994." The whole class would then stand up and the child on the intercom would give a quote for the day, but this could never be heard insofar as the intercom was perpetually broken (although bits and pieces of it sometimes came through). The children then stood quietly with their right hand on their heart, waiting for the intercom music to come on so they could recite the pledge of allegiance. After the music ended, they sat down at their respective seats and took on some sort of art or coloring project.

Interestingly enough, a great deal of (what Parkside teachers would perhaps see as "empty" or wasteful) time was spent at their desks waiting for the teachers to get materials together. During this time the children chatted amongst themselves, put their head down if sleepy, or simply sat fidgeting in their seats. There was no harried sense that the children had to be entertained every second of the day. Teachers did not seem to feel the least bit pressured to hurry up and get things together so the children wouldn't have to wait. If anything, this was a good chance for the children to sit and relax, learn how to be quiet, and entertain themselves. The rest of the day consisted of snack time, time outdoors on the playground, story time, project time (in which they were assigned a different game or puzzle to work on with three other children), and, whenever the children were too restless or rowdy, a group "drill" such as Simon Says to get them to focus, obey, and pay attention.

One of the Kelley preschool teachers was an older woman who had grown up in Kelley. She was known as Miss C. She was the most lenient and grandmotherly of all the teachers, with the other two younger teachers trying to get her to be more strict. She had a hearing problem and at times it was quite difficult to talk to her. The children learned they needed to speak very loudly to her or else simply figure out a task themselves. Although Miss C was more lenient and somewhat more motherly than other Kelley teachers, she was somewhat sterner, stricter, and less attentive toward the children than Parkside teachers. The assistant teacher, who in actuality really ran the class, was known as Miss D. Miss D came from Queenston. She was extremely down to earth and unpretentious, quick, and witty. She wore bright pink and purple gym suits, had short dyed blonde hair, a gristly cigarette voice, and an extremely weathered and wrinkled face from years on the beach. She often walked into the room after a cigarette break like a military sergeant with the plan of whipping the children into order, but did this with a sense of joy and fun, hiding a smile underneath her orders. Miss D had a wonderful sense of humor that she used on the children in various forms of teasing. I remember feeling quite awkward around her at first. My hesitance, what must have seemed annoying over-politeness, and timidly phrased questions were often met with short, "of course" matter-of-fact answers that implied I was being too worried about my interference in the class. At times I wondered if my presence annoyed her. I felt like Woody Allen, neurotically worrying about everybody's feelings and trying not to be a bother, while asking her if sitting here or there was ok. During these times Miss D and I had a way of accentuating each other's cultural and symbolic capital, and suddenly my own psychologized individualism seemed exaggerated, if not silly and overdone. When I worried about the hurt feelings of this child, that parent, about offending someone, or about getting in the way, she offered me a resounding "RELAX"! I realized I was no longer sitting in the field of "flowers" that I had been in at the Parkside preschools. I also learned that I could ask about particular children and Miss D would tell me about their background, not thinking me too nosy or that she had to protect the child's privacy. This type of background information I only received from some of the Parkside teachers once I got to know them fairly well, and even then, they were much more guarded in what they revealed and how they judged certain parents in front of me. There was one young girl in Miss D's class I felt incredibly sorry for. She was a loner, often arrived late, always seemed on the verge of tears, and was quite tired and unkempt. Her hair was braided in unbelievably tight braids all over her head and a skin infection was growing in the spaces between. When I asked about her, Miss D said, in language too soft for the child to hear, that she came from a "bad family"— that they weren't responsible and didn't take care of their kids, and that the mother had a problem with drugs. Miss D commented that she came in wearing the same clothes almost everyday, saying "I don't even think they change her. It's just horrible," and that the skin on her scalp was still bad. She made a motion of disgust at the unfairness of the situation, as if she could not understand parents who didn't take proper care of their child.

The other teacher, Miss B, who ran her own class next door, was the youngest. I spent half of my time observing her class and the other half observing Miss D's. Like Miss D, she was quite strict and was not afraid to shout in anger or frustration, and the children knew not to mess with her. I never saw either Miss D or Miss B touch the children in any way as a sign of warmth, support, or love. The thought of having one of them sit on their lap was ludicrous. Children did not come to school to be babied and mothered. They came to school to grow up, become a big kid, and prepare themselves for kindergarten and first grade. I always felt that Miss B was letting me in her class because the principal had asked her to and that once my time was up, she'd just as soon have me gone. She ran a tight, organized class, with little room for the children acting fresh, silly, or funny. Her strictness and loud orders were rarely buffered by any sense of humor. When she had the children line up, she was not humorously playing a drill sergeant, as Miss D sometimes did; she was one. Even with the classroom doors closed, you could often hear her yelling quite loudly at the children in the hallway, "David, get back in line. I never told you to get out of line. Get back there!" Nor did this type of yelling ever seem to cause a sense of alarm in the other teachers. Hence, for the most part I stayed quietly in one corner of her room and we very rarely interacted. Whereas Miss D and I developed a joking camaraderie and she often talked to me at length about the families each child came from, Miss B and I never spoke more than a few sentences. I often wondered why Miss B was teaching at all since to me she seemed so angry and frustrated, yelling all the time. And yet I learned that although she was quite strict and verbally tougher with kids than the Parkside teachers, she also cared very much for them. The loudness and "harshness" in her and Miss D's tone of voice, which I assumed would be draining and exhausting day after day, seemed more their neutral base verbal territory, their comfort zone, so to speak. For them, the Parkside teachers' soft hesitance, indirectness, and "neurotic" worrying about hurt feelings *would* have been exhausting. After all, neither teacher seemed to be acting in a way that they thought was *damaging* to the children, or uncaring and overly harsh. In both Miss B and Miss D there was no apparent sense of conflict between their love and care for the children and the type of "harsh" yelling, public shaming, and teasing they practiced.

The child's self was further toughened by restricting the amount of praise and sympathy they were given. The type of praise I most often heard was when a child did something showing his independence *within* the confines of what he or she had already been told to do. Miss C said, "Did you clean up your cubby by yourself this morning? Yes. Ooh, that's very good." Or, "Everybody give Carmine a hand; he did the class puzzle all by himself." The "stoic" individualism of coping with the difficulties of an already prescribed task were encouraged and praised. For example, Miss B said, "You see what Tommy Jones did? He came right in, hung up his coat, and started his work. I didn't have to tell him what to do. He just did it. That's the sign of a big boy who's ready for first grade." Or, "Look at Nathan. He hasn't griped once. He figured out what to do all on his own. See his picture? Isn't that nice?" Or "If you want to be picked, you gotta show me, not ask. Emily didn't ask and I picked her, since she did what she was supposed to do." An independent act was often viewed as mischievous or subversive if it came out of turn, out of schedule, or seemed to challenge the teacher's authority. Most often it was only praised if it did not threaten the established hierarchy, the school rules, or what the teachers had said to do. Independence in the form of challenging the rules a teacher had set or moving outside the given exercise was frowned upon as being "silly," "wrong," "spiteful," like a "smart ass," or like a "big shot," or was given the negative labels of "clowning around," "showing off," "daddling," or "being silly." For example, Miss D said, "See, look what Peter Maldanado did. He finished his painting all by himself, with the colors nice and neat, while the rest of you were runnin' around like crazies, showin' off!"

I soon learned that unlike Miss C, who tended to "baby" the kids, Miss D and Miss B were not there to accommodate the unique and "idiosyncratic" impulses and moods of the child, nor was this the role of Kelley preschool. Unlike the Parkside teachers, neither Miss D nor Miss B necessarily greeted the children when they walked in, but this was not seen as necessarily hurting the child's tender feelings. Nor did they bend down to talk to them on the kids' own physical level or tolerate as much noise as the Parkside teachers did (in an effort to "let kids be kids"). Teachers throughout the school often addressed the children as a whole group (saying, "you kids," "you guys," "kindergarteners," and "the natives are restless today"), or by gender ("boys line up, girls come line up"). Addressing them in a "lump sum" rather than by their first name was not, considered disrespectful. Furthermore, teachers were addressed by the children as "Miss —" rather than by their first names, as with the Parkside teachers.

Statements in which the teacher was frustrated because the child had not adjusted to her standards, time plan, or vision were also fairly common. The child was then encouraged to come to the level of the teacher rather than unfold in his own delicate and unique way, in his own sense of time. Statements such as, "Hurry up, John. Tell us about your picture. We have other things to do," or "Mary get outta the bathroom. You've been in there long enough," or "Peter, I'm gonna throw you out if you don't behave" taught the child he would not be catered to but rather must work toward keeping up with the teacher's schedule.

Whereas Parkside teachers went to great efforts to help with the gentle unfolding of the child's budding self, Miss B and Miss D often expected the child to accommodate their own adult needs, bodies, and time schedules. Every so often Miss D would randomly call on a student to perform some task that she could have easily done but chose not to. In this way, the child practiced obedience. For example, Miss D was correcting homework books when a paper fell out from one of the books. She yelled for a child across the room: "Matty, come here. Pick that up please," she said matter-of-factly. At other times she would take a child out of a circle in which they were listening to a story to have them pick something up for her. "Isaiah, go get me the other papers over there. Get up and get those papers." At another time, Miss D dropped Sally's still-wet painting while trying to move it from the easel. She then called Sally over, gave her a mop, and had Sally clean up the paint marks on the floor.

Saving Face in Front of the Child

Perhaps the most interesting and most pronounced difference between the ways teachers in preschools from Parkside and Kelley managed themselves lay in Kelley teachers' relative lack of concern about saving face in front of the child. Facial expressions and tone of voice associated with negative emotions were nonchalantly woven in and out of everyday conversations and interactions between teacher and child. When a teacher was disappointed, disgusted, impatient, bored, irritated, annoyed, or angry with the children, this was not necessarily hidden underneath a gentle and sympathetic face and voice. The child was not catered to in this way. Rather, the range of negative emotions was shown in the body and the face without any feeling that this would hurt the child. After all, frustration, annoyance, disappointment, sarcasm, boredom, and anger are part of life. Seeing them in the bodies and faces of the teacher won't shock or tragically hurt the child, so why go to great efforts trying to hide it? Wouldn't that present a false reality? Why present a CandyLand to the child if this is not an accurate picture of life in general?

Between Miss B and Miss D I was struck by what seemed to be a certain "naturalness" to their teaching that can only be achieved by an adult who is not monitoring her behavior in front of the child so as to appear (only and always) warm, sweet, gentle, and happy. When teachers were done yelling, they did not later mark their outburst as a cruel one that should not be repeated. A constant facial glaze of warmth or kindness would be considered false and unrealistic, like living in fairyland, which Parkside preschools sometimes felt like. Parkside teachers' efforts to be positive, warm, chipper, and what struck me as immensely enthusiastic were so pronounced that the teachers sometimes seemed like actresses in a play. I remember returning from these Parkside days feeling exhausted because of the amount of exaggerated facial posturing, verbal praise, and enthusiasm I felt I was required to show in relation to almost any aspect of the children. This facial exhaustion is something I did not experience after Kelley and Queenston days, where I felt I could hang out with the preschool kids with a more "neutral" facial expression.

On a couple of occasions in Kelley children cried and the teachers seemed quite impatient because they did not know why. Justin, an overweight boy who was known as a crybaby, as too "soft," and as a child who received too much freedom at home, was crying during circle time. The head teacher, Miss C, looked troubled and asked "What's wrong?" The child didn't answer but continued to cry. She asked him again, "What's wrong?" while still sitting at her chair in the center of the room. Getting a little annoyed, she persisted. "Justin, tell me what's wrong. Did something happen at home?" Justin still said nothing. Miss C had an annoyed look on her face, then said, "Why don't you go to the back of the room? Tell Miss D what the problem is." Justin moved reluctantly and slowly to the back of the room, sniffling as he walked. Miss D stood shaking her head, as if to say, "Here we go again." Rolling her eyes with impatience, she put one hand on her hip and tilted her head to the side, drumming her fingers on her leg as if to pass the time, showing Justin and the class she was bored and tired of waiting. She then took him out into the hall.

In another scenario Miss B was taking the kids outside to work on their parents' day dance. The school and playground at P.S. 1 were perched on the edge of Jamaica Bay, with the water in full view, Manhattan in the distance, and pigeons flying everywhere. It was typically cold and very windy and none of the children had coats on. One child asked in a somewhat whiny tone, "Miss B, can I go get my coat?" Annoyed and irritated that she was being interrupted, Miss B replied in a fed up tone, "Would you shush? Stop complaining!" She then rolled her eyes and took on a look of disgust to show the child how sick of her complaining she was.

At another time during free play a child was sitting at her desk blowing air through her lips, making a buzzing sound. Miss D looked annoyed and took on an irritated expression. She said crossly, "That's annoying, unless you all want to stand up and we'll all do it—it's silly, annoying." She then looked away and continued grading books. When any child interrupted her from her task, she'd give a short, brisk answer, showing the child she had a lot to do, she was in a bad mood, and that they should leave her alone and figure it out themselves. The child would then leave quietly and deal with the problem himself.

Occasionally, when Miss D played Simon Says (to get the children to focus on her, be obedient, and pay attention), she went through the motions in a sloppy, jaded, bored way, as if to imply with her body and face, "I'm so sick of having to do this." Her motions were flaccid, as if she was worn out, tired, and fed up with kids. Her words slurred and dragged a little. Later on in the day, Miss D played a series of songs on the record player to keep the kids from getting too restless. She sang along with the tune to encourage the children to sing as well. In general, her words were listless and dragging. She showed her boredom without any sense of guilt or remorse. In one song she sang, "I've been workin' on the railroad, all the live long day. I've been workin' on the railroad, just to pass the time away." She then started laughing and said sarcastically to the children, "Yeah right, just to pass the time away. That's what we're doin." Miss D was obviously not sure the children understood what she meant, but this didn't seem to matter. Often something that was stated out loud in front of the children wasn't tailored to the child's level of humor or intellectual development but was meant only for herself and other teachers.

At one time a child needed to blow his nose, and Miss B responded with disgust and impatience. "Will you get something to blow your nose? Ugh, how gross. Blow it, blow it. I've asked you three times!" She then said to me with the child right there, "If that child were mine, I'd just squeeze it out, but since he's not, I'm gonna move since I don't want to look at it."

Often Miss B and Miss D would get openly angry with the children, shouting loudly, pointing fingers, and getting red in the face. They got most angry with them during the dance practice sessions in the gym when they were trying to control 20 or more children. For example, at a dance practice for grandparent's day, Miss D was screaming at the children, fed up with how bad they were. One child, John, clapped a couple times by mistake after the children were supposed to stop. Miss D turned to him, pointing her finger and yelling, "Oh, and you clapped again?! Just to be spiteful?!" Then in a very loud voice in rapid fire she yelled at child after child and then to the group as a whole:

> You're still talkin', Fatima—you still haven't learned your lesson from yesterday!
> Get away from there, Peter Crowley. I didn't tell you you could be over there!
> Amanda, hurry up. You've been dawdlin' all day.
> Everybody, I want to hear you speak. You're flat. You don't sound like you love your grandparents. Get up. You're all wrong. You're movin' your chairs and messin' everything up!
> Stop doin' that. You're aggravatin' me.

The kids responded to this quietly and without complaining. They learned not to challenge or get in the way of these outbursts but to be quiet, stay to themselves, not get noticed, and do what they were told.

The teachers also expressed disappointment. At one point Dawn had paint all over her smock. Miss B shook her head in disappointment, put her hands on her hips, and said in a whiny voice, "Oh, Dawn, why do you always get it all over you like that? You can't paint without getting it all over you like that."

Thus, there was not a sense that the dominant expression on the face should be one of gentle, loving sympathy. Negative emotional outbursts were slipped in and out of quite easily without a sense of guilt or disapproval from other teachers. Most often a teacher would walk by a child being (what would appear to Parkside teachers as) sternly disciplined and not interfere, knowing full well it was the child's "fault" so to speak. Miss Delanty, the P.S. 1 principal, walked by Miss D, leaving her alone to discipline a child as she saw fit. In Parkside, however, I once saw the director display a concerned face, as if worried that the child might be incorrectly disciplined or unfairly represented by her fellow teacher. She stopped and tried to "help" her fellow teacher with the situation by talking to the child herself for a bit, lending some advice as to what the child might need and how they could make him feel better.

Teasing the Child—Blunting the Edges of the Self

During my participant observations in Parkside, teasing was something that never occurred insofar as it might inhibit the growth of self-esteem and would possibly damage the child's ego to the extent that the process of unfolding and flowering would be inhibited. Teasing for the Kelley teachers was a way of both blunting the edges of the self and bringing about a certain healthy retaliation on the part of the child. In their teasing, teachers attempted to spark the defensive part of the child's self, to ignite it just enough so that it "talked back." Whereas talking back was most often not tolerated, in instances where it was invited, such as in the case of teasing, it was actually encouraged.

Teasing was an act of riding over the edges of the self with certain challenging, offensive, shocking, mocking, or critical statements. The child's response to this usually involved a solidifying of the borders of the self, a sticking up for himself. If the child didn't respond, nonetheless, he or she had still gotten used to an act of butting up against the self. Teasing constituted an open invitation for the child then to answer back or defend him or herself. Often it took the form of a question, egging the child on, asking for an answer. In this way teachers subtly encouraged a certain amount of contained self-defense on the part of the child. In responding to teasing, the child then must harden the boundaries of the self, become strong, and stick up for him or herself. Often teachers would tease a child and then get an excited look on their face, waiting with anticipation for the way the child would talk back. After butting up against the child with this teasing statement, the teacher would then smile, and sometimes look over at me or another adult, to bring us into the act of waiting for the reply. They sat waiting with a look of excitement, of let's see what he does, let's wait for the comeback.

One teacher, Miss D, in particular teased the children about what they were wearing, how they looked, and what they drew. To one child, barely sitting up in his chair, wanting desperately to fall asleep, Miss D said, "Matty Ultsch, what time did you go to bed last night?" The child didn't respond but continued to sit and look sleepy. Miss D grinned devilishly, implying that she knew he looked tired and didn't get enough sleep but just wanted to tease him about it. "You're not tired?" She grinned again. "No," he said stubbornly. "Oh, I thought I saw you yawning." Again, she smiled.

Another child, Peter, had worn the same shirt to school for three days. After finishing her grading, Miss D looked around with a devilish look in her eye, as if looking for a child ripe for plucking. She scanned the room looking for things she might comment on. Finally, she stopped at Peter. "So Peter [she laughs], you gonna start wearing that shirt to bed or what?" Miss D looked at me, smirking. We both waited for his response. Peter squirmed a little in his chair and smiled, knowing he was being teased. Miss D finally gave up, knowing she couldn't get anything more out of him.

A couple minutes later, Miss D was over near the sink cleaning paint-brushes. Stretching her foot out, she kicked the garbage can near one of the boys, Tommy, who looked up a little startled. With a devilish smile on her face she said, "Tommy, you want this garbage can near you? Don't fall into it!" and laughed.

During free play, when the boys and girls were playing at things they had either been told to play with or chosen themselves, Miss D, with time on her hands and in a playful mood, had fun with the kids, trying to change the gender stereotypes they were used to. The girls were playing house and kept giving her cups of coffee and giggling when they asked her to pay them $2.00 for one cup. She laughed back, "You girls don't have to cook! Make reservations!" The girls laughed. She then yelled to the boys, "Boys, get over there and cook me something, and you girls get over there and be engineers. [Smiles at a young boy.] Carmine, cook me up a pizza." Carmine blushed and said he couldn't. Miss D said, "Come on girls, out of the kitchen! Carmine'll cook ya up something, won't ya Carmine?"

It seemed that most of the children who were teased were boys who were thought to be "soft"—ones who cried too much or seemed spoiled or were known to get a lot of freedom at home. Justin, a chubby child who often cried and whined, once came over to the teachers and Miss D said, as he came forward, "If there ever was a whiner!" She laughed at him and in mock sympathy said, "Oh, Justin, everybody is your friend. Everybody loves you; you're just a chunky kind of guy. You should be on Saturday Night Live just like the whiner. What are you whining about now?"

In another scenario, a couple of boys were painting at an easel. This was an excellent example of the simultaneous teaching of both conformity and teasing in which the child was provoked in order to get him to stick up for himself. Initially, during free play Miss D went around the room fed up with the mess, telling the kids what to do. "Johanna, you painted yesterday. Come over here and build me a big bridge and a little bridge." To a group of girls playing with beads she said, "We're not swinging these around on a string. That's not what these are for." To a group playing bingo she said, "First of all, this is some mess of a game here—who's cheating? You can't go through life cheating." She then said to Carmine, who was painting, "Don't give me mish mosh now and don't put your paint in the same color." She then wandered around the room once more, seeming almost bored. Then with the same devilish look on her face that was usually the preamble to teasing, she said to Carmine, "How we doin' Carmine? You don't want to overkill that," she laughed. She teased him again, joking about how he'll be Andy Warhol and make her rich. She'll be an agent for him. She waited expectantly for his comeback, but Carmine acted shy and continued to paint quietly. Another boy chimed in, trying to get in on the teasing, and she quickly put him in his place. "Did I ask you to talk? Turn around and do your words." She then said to another boy, Peter, that he could have his turn to paint. She told him as he was putting on a smock, "The purple goes in the purple, orange stays in orange. Keep the colors apart." Later she asked him, "What are you makin?" He answered with a lisp, "Bart Simpson." She then teased him by imitating his lisp, "Bart Simpthon? Where's Bart Simpthon's hair?" Impatient and disappointed, he didn't make a comeback. She told him what to do. "Wipe your brush off, Peter. You should make the hair a different color—pick up a different color, do his eyes, nose, ears. Watch it; you're drippin'. Make the eyes, nose—make me a pattern. No, no, no. Take the brush like this, so you have some sort of picture or something, not all." I then joked to Miss D about how in the Metropolitan Museum of Art they wouldn't be able to tell his stuff from others. Peter chipped in and said he had a toy turtle. Because his response was not appropriate to the joke I made, she said sarcastically to the boy, "Yeah, that fit right into the conversation." What was interesting here was the way talking back to the teacher was invited through teasing, but talking back still had to conform to the general theme of the joke set by the teacher. Even after a cue for the child to talk back and defend himself, the response must "make sense."

The practice of teasing encouraged sticking up for oneself. And yet this was coupled with a strong emphasis on respect for authority. The child was both subtly taught to toughen the self and yet not get too full of himself. Teachers urged children to talk back in the act of teasing, knowing they themselves always had the upper hand. Children learned to walk the tightrope between acting too soft and wimpy (being a sissy, cry baby) and being a smart-ass or big shot. Learning this delicate balance was what constituted most of the interactions. Children needed to learn strength, pride, self-assertion, self-reliance, and self-determination alongside the values of respect for adults and group conformity. In teasing, self-defense was encouraged. Teachers jokingly egged the child on with comments of greater and greater annoyance, shock, or criticism, trying to get a response that hardened the self into a stance of defense. In these brief teasing encounters, certain components of hard individualism were encouraged and the pride, self-respect, and self-determination involved in talking back were practiced within limits.

For teachers at P.S. 1 values such as respect for authority, group conformity, knowing one's place in a hierarchy and living by the rules of the school institution were taught through use of public shaming techniques, threats, and direct commands and through highlighting the teacher's position of power. These teachers often drew attention to the power differential between teacher and child and were not at all uncomfortable with using it to obtain obedience or teach lessons. Occasionally teachers would highlight the fact that they were the adults and the ones in charge, and usually very little explanation was given as to why the teacher was inhibiting the child's wishes. For the Parkside teachers, it was believed these types of lessons deserved explanation insofar as the rights and power of the child were being blocked. The blocking of these desires in Queens children was not seen as hurting them, as stunting their development or decreasing their self-esteem.

Verbal Discipline

One of the ways of teaching the child the rules of the classroom and the power of the teacher was through direct commands. In school, children learned to follow the orders of the teacher, to respect them because of their age and status. They learned their place in a hierarchy in which the teachers were not equal but had total power and control. Acts that would be judged creative or unique among the Parkside teachers, and thus allowed and even encouraged, were more often sternly disciplined and corrected in Kelley. Not only were they not allowed, but they were interpreted as challenges to the teacher's established authority in the classroom. The following are examples of the distress Miss D and Miss B sometimes felt when the children did things for which they did not receive a direct command. "You come to school to listen and do what you're told." "You're not here to have fun." "You have fun learning, but you're supposed to listen to the teacher."

In getting the kids to play Simon Says, Miss B got aggravated when they didn't settle down. "Hello? Is anybody out there? All right, about face. Oh no—no way. I did not tell you to go. All I said was about face. Now quietly go inside."

Such statements were often said while the teacher was angry because the kids were doing something the wrong way. Often all the teacher would have to say was, "Ah, excuse me?" in an incredulous tone, implying "why are you doing something I did not tell you to do?" Other statements that would have made Parkside parents shudder were:

> Matty, who told you to wash your hands? You can't put your jacket around your waist. I can tell you that Miss Delanty [the principal] doesn't like that look. You can't do it.
> Don't touch those scissors. No one told you to touch those yet. What's this? Stop it. Did I tell you to bang them? No, I told you not to touch anything.
> All right, forget it. Heads down. I am not speaking with people interrupting me. If I wanted you to speak, I'd ask you.
> I don't know who gave you permission to start chitter chattering.

Miss C said to a child who had moved out of his place in the circle, "Get up here. Who moved you? You were supposed to be over here. You better listen to me. Who moved you?"

To a child who didn't want to do his math, Miss B said, "Yes you do. You don't say 'no' to me." Similar statements were heard throughout the day: "I don't want you all over the classroom. Sit down, sit down. Write something;

don't just sit there. Excuse me? I don't like the way you're sitting, and I asked you to write something on your own, and you didn't do it." And, "I clap for most of you. A couple of people have acted silly. Most of you do the right thing though. That's really good. It shows you're growing up, so give a clap for yourself."

One form of discipline was to verbally deny what the child was doing. Teachers would simply override what the child was doing with a statement like, "You are not doing that." For example, when it got too loud in the classroom, Miss C said to the children, "If I'm up there talking, you're not at your seats talking." At another time, Miss B said to a child who reached over another child to grab for the glue, "What're you doing? You're not going to reach over like that. Take your body and move! Where's your head?" When one child was sopping his paper with paint, Miss B said "Don't saturate it. When it's done, it's done. You're not painting that anymore."

Sometimes Miss D would go around the room issuing loud commands in rapid succession to different children. "Take that out of your mouth. Sit up. Take your shirt out of your legs." She also practiced certain "drills" that involved following her orders. Simon Says was a favorite one. She would also say "All right. Put your paper on your lap and do what I do." She then put her hands on her head, then nose, then ears, as the children followed. If the class was out of order, the teacher might stop everything with, "I want all pencils down, and look up. Sit up [and] turn around. Jean, look up."

Settling Fights between Children

Another example of the difference in socializing group cooperation was reflected in the ways some of the Kelley teachers, when confronted with two children fighting, did not ferret out the rights and claims of each child or insist on each child being heard. Having each child's side of the story told was not given any priority since repressing the truth was not seen as damaging to the child. Time was not spent trying to figure out whether the child was being unjustly accused of hitting. Nor did teachers insist that each child understand how the other would feel if they were hit. Rather than verifying if the "tattletale" were right or not, they often immediately punished the one who was being complained about. An exhaustive airing and unfolding of the child's feelings was thus not practiced. Often the teacher would rely on what she knew of a child to settle the fight by saying to a child who complained of being hit, "Robbie's not a hitter. Stop complaining." Thus, her knowledge of the child's personality took precedence over the child's tale of what happened. In Parkside, the teacher would be more apt to say, "You're not a bad person, but you have done a bad thing in hitting someone," thereby distinguishing between the self and the act. This kind of characterological characterization of a child (as a whiner, a baby, a hitter, or full of himself) seems more reflective of the Queens conception of the child's self as being (and becoming) sturdier, more contained, solid, and perseverant. In Parkside, teachers seemed to work with different, more fluid metaphors of the child's self in which children's moods and feelings could change as quickly as the weather. This is not to say Parkside teachers didn't also say to me in private, "He is so spoiled!" Or "Isn't she just amazing!" (when referring to one girl's seemingly permanent sunny disposition), but this characterization very rarely seemed to permeate the discipline associated with settling fights.

In Kelley, teachers responded to fights in the following ways:

One girl went up to Miss D and said that a boy hurt her finger. Miss D said, "Robby, come here. You broke the pencil, smashed her finger. What's the matter with you? Sit down over there."

To another child Miss B said, "Oh, come on, Barbara's not a hitter. That was an accident. Say I'm sorry. She's not a hitter."

When a child came up and complained that she couldn't play because of another child, Miss C said, "That's too bad. She's sitting there and you're gonna have to work around it. Play together; learn to play together."

In another scenario, a boy, Kevin, was on his way up to tell Miss B that Jill hurt him. Jill barged past him and told the teacher, "I said, I'm sorry." Miss D looked at Kevin, irritated, and said, "She says, she said she's sorry, so take it." The two of them walked away.

At times, rather than show her concern for airing the children's feelings, the teacher would show her annoyance at the fighting. One child, John, said to Miss D, "Kimberly squeezed me." Miss D said angrily and annoyed to Kimberly, "Why? Stop it. Leave him alone." She then made a joke referring to how Kimberly was bigger than John. "Besides, Kimberly, you're bigger than he is." Miss D laughed.

Another time, a girl, Shaquana, went up to Miss C and said something to her about what Matty did to her. Miss C went over to Matty's table, "What's the problem?" Matty mumbled that it happened by accident. Frustrated, Miss C replied, "By accident. I don't want to hear by accident. You say that every time—'by accident.' I don't want to hear it anymore."

The act of ferreting out feelings so they could then unfold and develop was only practiced when the child seemed sick or injured, and even then, sympathy and patience were not always common. Blunting and containing a feeling was a common practice. For example, one child, known as a crybaby, was crying at his desk. On seeing this, Miss D said to him, "Whatever it is, it's not worth crying about. That's it. The tears don't help anything." Hence, the feeling is contained rather than legitimated, encouraged, or empathized with.

Shaming

Socializing the child to do what the rest of the group was doing was often brought about through public shaming or through the use of threats that successfully blunted the "flow" of impulse or feeling from the child. Shaming was a regular part of the day, with the child's self blunted and showcased rather than buffered, coddled, and hidden from view. Most often shaming occurred when the teacher was working on a dance project or play with the whole class. These plays and dance concerts were then performed at parents' night and the teachers seemed very invested in their productions. Kelley celebrated holidays with great relish. For Mother's Day, Father's Day, Christmas, Easter, Grandparents' Day, St. Patrick's Day, and Hallow- een they always seemed to have an elaborate pageant in the gymnasium, where each class performed something on its own. Parents and older kids in the elementary school came to watch and it was usually a fun, joyous occasion. Some of Miss D's comments seemed to imply that parents wanted to see a good show, that they weren't just going to think the kids were cute and sweet no matter what, and so that it was important they really had their act together for the final show. The teachers did not want the children to make fools out of themselves. They had pride in their classes and felt the children should, too.

While Miss B was showing the children the dance steps to a song they were practicing for Mother's Day, she said, "Thank you, Sean, for ruining my song." Addressing the whole group she said, "See Sean? I think I'm going to have to call his mother—he's clowning around, acting like a big shot."

Again, when one boy was not dancing in the way the teacher had demonstrated, she said sarcastically, "Nice Eddie Murphy. You do that and you're gonna make a fool out of all of us. Nice!" Later, to different boys, she said, "Johnny you want to embarrass the whole group?" and "That's it, Michael. You're not going to ruin this show for everybody else."

While the children were practicing for a dance performance, Miss D said to Justin and Sean, two boys who were very enthusiastically dancing, laughing, and at times falling out of line, "I don't like Justin there thinking he's great and he knows what to do and thinking how he'll do something himself not with the rest of the class, full of himself. Justin, you have to dance with the rest of the class." They continued practicing. Justin stepped out of line. Miss D stopped the class and said, "Get outta there. How dare you? Why don't you dance behind Sara?" She sent Justin off to the corner and spoke to the class. "You see what they did?! He not only didn't dance with his partner, he went all the way around and danced around everybody. Your mother's going to be very proud to see that you're messing up the dance, and Sean just stepped in front of his partner."

She put them both in the corner and yelled to them from across the room, "You guys can dance and laugh in back by yourselves and hopefully your mother will have a video."

One morning one of the children came in looking quite disheveled and sleepy, with bags under his eyes, a runny nose, and messy hair. He was one of the children whom the teachers felt was neglected. As he was walking down the hall, the teachers were standing outside the office. They said loud enough for him to hear with a look of shame, "and we have to look at this all day?"

Encouraged Competition: Bumping Up against the Selves of Other Children

Among the Parkside preschools group cooperation was taught through teaching the child to understand what it would feel like not to get heard when you were telling your story at circle time. The rules of the group were taught through promotion of a philosophy that everyone in the classroom was your friend. A strong egalitarianism was encouraged in which, rather than compete with each other, children were taught to listen to and encourage the articulation of feelings in each other. Kelley teachers (and one of the Queenston teachers), however, when socializing the child to conform to group activity, follow school rules, or do what the teacher told them to do, used another technique that toughened the child's self: the promotion of a certain amount of competition between children for the praise and compliments of the teachers. In bumping up against the selves of other children, they learned how to toughen themselves while simultaneously learning the more sociocentric lesson the teacher was promoting.

When Miss C was teaching math to the children and one of them, Sean, was paying attention and giving the right answers, she said, "See, John, I think I'm gonna give Sean a star today for bein' so good. You could get one too if you just paid attention." She then went around the room and commented on different children's behavior. "Sean looks like he's working very nicely, Samantha is working very nicely, I like the way Philip is sitting. The rest of you, until you sit quietly like Philip, I'm not going to put your name up on the board." At another time, after reading a story to them, and asking them questions, Miss B said to one child, "Very good, David, but Samantha and Anna were playing with their shirts. I'm going to get my stickers for some people. I like the way David is answering, and Sara too. That's why they're getting a sticker." After explaining to the children what to do on an Easter basket cut-out, Miss C said, "The kids who listened and can tell me how to do this, I'm gonna put their names up on the board and I'll give a prize out later. Now let's see who listened. I bet you Emily F. knows what to do. Can anyone else show me how they listened as good as Emily did?"

Children were often seen comparing themselves against others, to try to one up the next child in knowledge, manners, or answers. Getting their name on the board for a prize meant they had to be better than the next child. This competitive spirit in the classroom was not seen as hurting the feelings of the children around them or squelching the legitimate rights of the weak, but as healthy training in survival of the fittest, in which the best deserve what they get. Teachers often looked on with amusement and joy as children scuttled to get in line and become more quiet and more attentive than the next child. They seemed to feel there was a certain healthy feistiness in this process. Children who lost in the game needed to learn to accept it without whining and move on.

The bumping and colliding of self against self meant the child learned how to toughen himself against the strivings of other children, to defend his place in line, his piece of artwork. There was a competitive rubbing of self against self that was not promoted in the Parkside preschools insofar as it promoted a lack of empathy and concern for the other child's ("friend's") feelings. In Kelley preschools children were taught that blunting or stumping the self of the other through healthy competition was ok; it did not damage the self or development of the other child.

These children learned to walk a tightrope between the hard individualism of the self-reliant, tough child who quietly and independently performs a task and, on the other hand, the obedient child who does what he is told, follows the schools rules, doesn't cause trouble, and is not so full of himself that he is drawing attention and thus disrupting the flow of an activity. The individualism fostered here was a quiet, stoic, and blunted individualism that contained itself, so to speak. Psychologized space (feelings, desires, preferences, emotions) was contained and not allowed to dominate a classroom. The self was encouraged not to loosen but to become more "dense." It was not an individualism of celebrating one's special uniqueness but of dogged, silent self-determination in a prescribed task without help or encouragement from others. The children achieved a balance between complete blind obedience (being spineless, wimpy) and freshness and willfulness (being spoiled, a smart-ass).

Queenston Preschool Classes: Introducing the Pedagogy of Self-Expression

Unlike Kelley, Queenston had only one teacher, Rose, who was middle class. Her classroom assistant, however, was working class. Rose was getting her master's in Early Childhood Education at a local Queens College and wanted to go on to get her doctorate. Sometimes she would chat with me during class time when she wasn't overwhelmed and talk about what school was like for her. She spoke in a more academic language than the teachers at Kelley, saying, "I'm more into socialization than anything else, like modeling their speech. . . . When you're coming out of school *now,* you're more into process than anything. I'm not product oriented. I don't care if there are 25 pictures on the wall." Rose was in many ways more similar to the Parkside teachers I had observed. She was much more apt to focus on encouraging the kids in their behavior and projects, making an effort to praise paintings and clean-up jobs. She softened her directives with question marks ("Laura, will you give me a moment to come to you?" or "Do you want to put that toy back in the box?"). She tried disciplining indirectly with added praise ("We're all smart, but we also all have to take turns") or the use of "we" ("That's not how we sit"). She used a tentative tone of voice qualified with buffers such as "*I'm not sure* he'd like you doing that, Nathan," as well as limited her expressions of anger and frustration with the children. I also noticed that she used phrases that blamed not the child but the behavior he was engaged in: "Christopher, you're not using your listening ears today." And she practiced a lot of physical closeness with the children through hugging and rubbing their backs.

At P.S. 2 I spent a lot of time reading the classroom walls as well as the walls of the pre-K Parent Room. This was because they were covered with posters like "Family Affirmatives List," "Anger: Tips on Parenting When You Feel Like Lashing Out," and "The ABC's of Helping Your Child," which all seemed aimed at the working-class mothers who came in as class helpers every so often. Perhaps the idea behind parent helpers and the pre-K Parent Room was the hope that parents would absorb some of the upper-middle-class socialization practiced by Rose and read the posters, which were obviously not meant for the children. The irony of these posters made me somewhat uncomfortable insofar as they seemed to be socializing the parents to treat the children in a sickeningly sweet way, without addressing the real problems most of these mothers were having. One of the few posters that did acknowledge the frustration and difficulty in parenting was one about anger:

ANGER: TIPS ON PARENTING WHEN YOU FEEL LIKE LASHING OUT

Take three steps back.
Breathe for ten seconds.
Phone a friend.
Hug a pillow.
Eat an apple.
Write it down.
Take a hot bath.

But how many of these mothers could respond to their anger by taking a hot bath when their child was tearing around the house?

FAMILY AFFIRMATIVES LIST

Infants: I'm so glad you're here. You're wonderful.
Toddlers: I love watching you grow, I'm glad you're who you are.
Preschool: I'm glad you have your opinions. I love how curious you are.
School Age: I love who you are becoming, it's wonderful to watch you make your own decisions.
Adults: I am a wonderful parent, I'm glad I'm who I am.

For each of these affirmatives, I thought of the other things many of the Queenston mothers said and perhaps felt when I was in their presence. Mothers were exhausted, needed time to themselves, didn't want the child to be too fresh and disrespectful, and most certainly didn't seem to have a high sense of self-esteem. I remember reading a poster about social learning objectives and thinking, if this seems sterile and formal to me, what must the working-class mothers think?

SOCIAL LEARNING OBJECTIVES

1. Children will cooperatively interact with others of varying cultural backgrounds.

2. Children will work cooperatively and independently.
3. Children will use language to resolve social conflict.
4. Children will demonstrate positive self-concepts and self-care by choosing to share their products, volunteering their ideas and making choices.
5. Children will demonstrate responsibility to the group by sharing in-group tasks, maintaining the environment and honoring group rules and routines.

Despite these attempts, there were also ways in which Rose was different from the Parkside teachers. For example, unlike the Parkside teachers who introduced me to their class, explaining what I was doing there so that the children wouldn't be disturbed by my presence, Rose never introduced me to the kids, perhaps thinking they would not be as ruffled by my presence. I also never saw any crying at drop off times in Rose's class. Children came in alone or with a parent who would stay only briefly (compared to one Parkside class where kids cried a lot and had to be comforted by a teacher when the parent left). Children did not call Rose by her first name, but rather Ms. so and so. And at times she would make statements more similar to Kelley teachers ("I won't call you 'til you sit down. You're not doing the right thing.")

One of the most striking juxtapositions of hard individualism in a classroom covered in posters advocating soft individualism was manifested in one child, Amanda. Amanda told me how her brother "smacked her on the back" so "she punched him back." Then her mother "smacks him for smacking her and then her mother smacks them both," she said. Amanda was four years old, very plucky and perhaps my favorite of the children because of her colorful nonverbal behavior and theatrics. I remember being truly astounded at how sophisticated her negative facial expressions were. She had already learned how to posture a somewhat jaded, cynical, snide look, and seemed to take pride in showing me her facial antics. During free play with a rumpled apron tied around her waist, she would clean house and laugh at how pathetic the other children's play was, as if they were naïve and clueless and hadn't wised up. She'd look over at me, as if acknowledging our status as fellow outsiders, and make an exaggerated snide look on her face, as if all of this playing house stuff was too quaint. She stood with one hand on her hips, dustpan in the other, and mimicked a tough, bitchy expression on her face. Other times, I noticed she was snide to the other children, laughing at them, making faces at them, as if to imply they were losers. Another child would say something to her and she would roll her eyes with a look of disgust, making her hand into the shape of a fist as if she'd like to hit the child. She did all of this quite skillfully beneath the notice of the teachers, knowing she had to work underneath their gaze or she'd get in trouble. She had accepted their authority and knew not to get caught threatening it or disturbing the peace of the classroom. She had perfected the art of tough individualism within the established hierarchy of the classroom. Self-determined, she moved quietly underneath the eyes of the teachers, only showing her cocky and defensive stance toward the other children and to me, not letting any child push her down or get in her way.

Field Trip to the Planetarium

One day the children took a bus to the West Side Planetarium in Manhattan. I had asked if I could go along, hoping I would be able to sit with Mrs. Costado, the woman hired to increase parental involvement at the preschool. Mrs. Costado was an upper-working-class, very energetic, down-to-earth woman who was incredibly easy to get along with and had a great sense of humor. Of all the people I met at P.S. 2, she was undoubtedly my favorite. I admired her greatly and basked in her warmth, jokes, and ability to ride with the punches. She seemed to have a great rapport with the parents, laughing, joking, and even teasing them, always jetting around talking to them during drop off or pick up times, trying to rally parents into a field trip or project. She seemed to enjoy the parents and really like some of them, as they did her. She certainly did not seem a threatening or aloof figure to them. I remember envying her rapport with them, because the parents seemed much more shy, private, and defensive around me. Mrs. Costado saw herself as part of the "new ways" that were being taught in schools now. She felt that for the kids to be successful, they had to have a higher sense of self-esteem and have their parents more involved in their schooling. She mentioned that another, more working-class teacher should go back to school because "she was teaching them too much of the old stuff and it's a new world, mixed races . . . it's important to keep up with the changes." At one time she worked for Head Start, which she liked better than P.S. 2, because they were more organized and they monitored her more—"I want to learn and get criticism, but at P.S. 2 they don't do that for me. The principal sends me a form and says, 'Fill out this observation/monitor form and I'll sign it'. . . . I'm disgusted by that. How will anyone learn?"

We sat for a long time on the bus, amid the screams of the children as the bus barreled along. She spoke of how "bad the Board of Ed." was, how she would never send her kids to public school. She was very proud of her own children, both of whom went to college in Queens. One of them was going to be a chef, and one of them fought in Desert Storm. He had been hurt, but ended up ok. She had his picture up at work. He had been on TV and in the paper. The reason her kids "are successful and hardworking is because she spent a lot of time with them, teaching them and sent them to Catholic private school, 'where they are kept track of.'" She then jokingly said she "wanted to write a book someday on how the kids coming out of this public school system won't get anywhere or learn anything."

On this bus ride she seemed to need to vent to me about some of her frustrations with getting parents involved in the pre-K program. We talked about how discouraged she was with the relatively low parent involvement this year. I tried to make her feel better by saying that influencing just one parent was an immense accomplishment. I realized once I said this that I had betrayed my bias and wondered if that was partly why she opened up to me so much that day. I know that even before this remark, however, simply because of my college education she thought of me as on "her side"—the side of those trying to implement changes into the low-income preschools.

She had been at P.S. 2 pre-K for seven years. Of about 75 parents then in two classes, only about 10 were active in the parent program. She was able to talk quite frankly about the children's parents, since the noise drowned out any fear of being overheard. The idea behind her job was to get parents involved from pre-K on, interested in their kids and their kids' classes, so that they would stay involved throughout their child's schooling. Today was a field trip to which parents were invited, and Mrs. Costado made sure to amply praise and encourage the few parents who had come. She went up to the few parents who were going to stay for the trip, telling them how pleased she was that they had come. As we boarded the bus, I overheard various mothers telling their children to be good. Cindy, wife of a policeman, whose son was very proud of his father's status, told her friend "if he's not (good), I'll smack him upside the head," and she laughed. Cindy seemed very close to her son and extremely proud of him. He cheerily boarded the bus, waving, seemingly unaffected by the comment, which to a Parkside parent would perhaps seem cruel. This same type of talk of smacking seemed to be one of his favorite topics, not something taboo.

During the bus ride, Mrs. Costado told me about how she tries to get parents to tell their kids to put on their own coat, to do things on their own more. She said, "Some parents try to keep them babies," but she tries to get them to "feed themselves." She tells the kids in kindergarten, "Since no one's going to put on your coats for you, you need to learn it." She also tells the parents that at home they should give the kids more choice on what to buy or wear, "not unlimited, but limited choice—say out of two things, they can choose one." And yet some parents expect too much from their children. Because some of their three- or four-year-olds are physically so big, they make the mistake of expecting too much responsibility.

Mrs. Costado also spoke of how she discourages the parents from hitting and yelling negative things at the children. She tries to get across to them that the children's:

> self-esteem is really important and it will be low if they tell them they're stupid or hit them in the face. If they tell their children they did something wrong, they should also tell them they did something good yesterday. This doesn't make the child feel so bad. I ask the parents, "How would you feel if I sat here telling you that you were stupid?" . . . They'll just go out, or they'll not do anything cause they'll feel so bad about themselves.

One of the ways she tries to increase parent interest is by having the parents do the same projects the children are doing. She teaches them "health stuff and how to make cheap things, recycling, shopping for less." She said the pre-K and parent involvement program go hand in hand. Without the family office, the pre-K isn't funded, so if she doesn't get enough parental involvement, pre-K could be eliminated. She also invites them to come and make baskets, have rap sessions where parents talk, "but the attendance is so low, and it is so discouraging. The parents now are younger, many single-parent families. Some just want to stay at home and watch the soaps. They aren't involved not because they work, but because they watch the soaps. Some of them could care less about what their kids do." She also found that the parents who were already involved with their kids were the ones who came for activities, so she felt like she was preaching to the converted. "I can't get the others out of their house. They want time away from their kids. I ask them, 'Do you like this pre-K free program and all they're doing? Well then, show me. I don't expect you to be here 24 hours a day, but just give me one hour a week.' And they actually say to me, 'If I can come in and watch my soaps, I will.' But they can't miss them. . . . This year attendance is lower. It's like pulling teeth getting them to come in."

When I asked Mrs. Costado about the best way to go about getting interviews, she said that she would put in a good word for me, but that "they might lie to you, embarrassed of real problems and how they actually treat their children." Mrs. Costado had sent a pre-K questionnaire home to parents about how they feel about their kids, and "They lie. They say their kids are angels when I know that they come in being driven crazy by them and fed up."

I will never know if the parents actually did lie on these questionnaires, or their reasons for lying, or if they watched soap operas to the extent that Mrs. Costado implied. I do know she said all of these things from a place of warmth and a genuine desire to help. If they did any of these things (which appear taboo only if looked at from a Parkside perspective), I'm sure they had good reasons. Nonetheless, I did witness the gap that Mrs. Costado was speaking of, the gap between upper-middle-class teaching styles hoisted onto parents who obviously practiced another more working-class style. Just in watching the parents load their kids on the bus I heard what struck me as very loud authoritative commands filled with a visible frustration they didn't seem worried about hiding. Amanda's mother yelled at her daughter, saying, "You be good. Stay with your partner!!" and then looked at me with a joyous smirk as if to say, "Isn't my kid a little devil?", while another father shouted, "I *don't care* if you're angry—you either behave or you don't go!!"

Chapter Seven

Parkside Preschools

Unlike the one Queenston preschool, where upper-middle-class psychologized individualism was introduced to parents and children who had been raised in a more hard protective individualistic fashion, Parkside preschools seemed to mimic the soft individualism socialized by Parkside parents. Things such as threats, topic switching, insults, sarcasm, and irony, found among the Queens parents (or, as with Miller's work, among the south Baltimore parents), were not practiced in Parkside preschools. In the practice of *soft* individualism at Parkside preschools, efforts were similarly made to help the child's self unfold, to allow for feelings and thoughts to flower in their own right. Certain practices were engaged in that contributed not to the blunting or toughening of the child's self but to its unwinding and loosening—acts such as saving face in front of the child, using questions/suggestions to discipline instead of direct commands, giving the child ample time and space to explain himself, and interrupting a fight so that each child's feelings could be heard. I often wondered if the preschool teachers made extra efforts to intensify their soft individualistic focus when I was around, because at times I could not believe how much praise the children were given, how much choice, what they let the child get away with, how much they interfered so as to ensure the child could voice her feelings, how much they saved face and voice to cover their true feelings in front of the child. Many times their approach seemed excessive and almost funny to me, and I found myself longing for some of the feisty honesty and tell-it-like-it-is qualities of the Queens teachers. And yet, sitting in my little child's chair in the corner, slumped over my field notes, it really seemed the Parkside teachers were most often quite unaware of me. It seemed to take all of their attention to handle the ten or so preschool kids they were in charge of, without enough left over to "perform" for me. Furthermore, many of the teachers had been there for quite some time and didn't seem afraid that they might lose their job if I talked to the director about their teaching style.

Other behaviors were felt to contribute to the unfolding of the self. A child was *always* addressed positively when they arrived late to school. Praise was given much more frequently than in the Queens preschools and it often "piggybacked" the normal or mundane routines that were part of the day. If a child put his book away, the teacher might say, "Thank you very much, Daniel. You're a good helper." If the class lined up, the teacher said,

"Great line up. Give yourselves a hand." If a child went to the bathroom and closed the curtain, "Good job, Nathan." Also, a more nurturing motherly role was taken on by the teachers—they often sat holding or hugging the children and at times even asked the children to come over and sit on their lap because "you look like you need a hug." Furthermore, a much higher noise level was tolerated than in the Queens preschools. Noise seemed to mean the enthusiastic exercising of the child's own voice; thus, a great deal of it was tolerated. If the child interrupted two adults, often the teachers would immediately turn their attention to the child, not making him wait. Efforts such as this were made to make the children feel special, to show them that what they had to say was important. Unlike the Queens preschools, children were also allowed to vote over what they wanted for snack time, and they were always given a free choice of what activities to do during free time.

Parkside circle time (which consisted of roll call and an occasional show and tell in Kelley) occurred first thing in the morning. It was a time when each child was shown that he was important and had something to say that others found interesting and would like to hear about. The teacher went around the circle, asking each child if they had anything they'd like to say. During circle time the most important thing was that each child be given as much time and space as they might need to say anything. Here the teachers looked on even more lovingly than usual, giving the child a lot of nonverbal facial encouragement. Their bodies leaned toward the child, and an expression of warmth and acceptance came into their faces. Rushing the child never occurred, except for an occasional verbal interruption to help the child get a certain idea "out." The child's speech was allowed to roam, flounder, repeat, and unfold in any way it wanted. When the child finished, the teacher would incorporate praise into her response in some way. "That's very good storytelling, Lucy. Did you know that you just told a very good story? Do you know that? You started at the beginning of the morning and then told us until school!" The children were somehow praised regardless of what they said or whether they simply sat and squirmed. Whatever unfolded from the self of the child was warmly accepted. The teacher also tried to help the other children understand the child who was speaking. In this way she encouraged listening and empathy in the other children, while the child who was speaking was encouraged to open up, to feel they had a right to speak and that what they were saying (whether a sentence or a paragraph, about their dinner or their sister) was special.

An effort was also made not to jolt or surprise the children emotionally in any way that might upset them. Unlike the children in the Queens preschools, they were told when any strange adult or new child would be in the class. Thus, they were told about my arrival before I came, and I was formally introduced the day I did arrive. After telling the class that I was here to observe, the class, the teachers, and I all had a discussion on the meaning of the word "observe." The director of one preschool said that group playtime was so important for the children that she did not allow any adult interruption during this period. Even she didn't go into the room during this time. The other director of one preschool told me that during gym time, "teachers are supposed to sit away and on the outside of the gym. Otherwise, it disturbs their playing, it distracts them, they start to focus on the teacher. We want them to focus on each other, to play among themselves, to do their own things."

Efforts were also made to reassure children that whatever emotions they were experiencing were ok and that they didn't need to do something that might feel uncomfortable. One day the children were looking at a hermit crab that was in a box on the floor. One child, Catie, was a little afraid of it. The teacher said, "You don't have to hold the hermit crab if you don't want. Some people don't like to pick it up and that's OK, 'cause you know in our class we don't make anyone do anything they don't feel comfortable with. See, Catie, you get as close as you feel comfortable with. It's your right not to get too close." Later she repeated this, "If you want to hold him, you can. If not, you certainly don't have to. If you want to hold one but are a little concerned about it, hold this one. He's a little more shy—some people like holding them, some don't, whatever you want." When Catie recoiled from the crab, later the teacher reiterated, "It's OK, Catie. You don't have to pick one up if you don't want. Lots of people don't even like hermit crabs."

There were three teachers I observed in Parkside—all of them women, all of them with master's degrees in early childhood education. They tended to wear fun, "child-oriented" clothes that were bright, colorful, and practical, yet feminine. It was very common to see these women holding the children on their lap, hugging them, and touching them with tenderness and sympathy. The children called them all by their first name: Dana, Kathy, and Ellen. Dana had been a preschool teacher for ten years. She was a long-time New Yorker who lived on the upper west side with her two young children. She was extremely dedicated to the preschool children and spoke fervently about how much she loved her job. She was fascinated by child psychology and continually emphasized the importance of respecting the child. She often invited her own children into her preschool classroom if they had no place to go after school, and when they went home for dinner, she asked them for advice on how to run her class.

Kathy was a recent college graduate who was much less in awe of the children but still spoke about how much she loved kids. She was fascinated by the families the children came from, often treating them like one big soap opera she needed to catch up on daily. She loved to gossip about the lives of some of the "rich and famous" and kept pumping me for any information I might have gleaned during interviews. She spoke about how exhausting the job was, but there was still a sense that this was exactly what she wanted to do. She was the toughest of the teachers, not as gentle, warm, and forgiving as the other two. She seemed less worried about whether certain forms of verbal discipline would harm the child and sometimes showed the children her anger, impatience, boredom, or exhaustion. She loved to talk about each child's personality and often predicted certain behaviors and future career paths based on the type of personality she had given one child or another.

Ellen was much older than Kathy. She was an actress/singer turned preschool teacher who very much loved her present job. It was a real delight for her to work with children. She emphasized the importance of voice and body language in the socialization of children. She tended to be quite theatrical in her dealings with children, using a tremendous range of voice, facial expression, and body gesture in an effort to capture the child's attention or show a full degree of empathy. She made a point to always seem quite interested and fascinated by what each child had to say. There seemed to be some tension between her and Kathy insofar as Ellen felt Kathy could be a little too harsh with the children.

Ensuring Each Voice Is Heard: Feelings, Empathy, and the Mediation of Fights

One of the main ways soft psychologized individualism was socialized was through the teacher's careful arbitration of fights and arguments that occurred between children. (See also Tobin et al., 1989.) If the sound of a fight could be heard across the room, teachers would routinely call over whoever was involved in the fight. Most often, however, because the children knew the course of action by heart, they immediately marched over to the teacher so the fight could be mediated. Teachers took on a very serious facial expression and tone of voice in this process to let the children know they took their complaints and thoughts seriously. The voicing of each child's rights and feelings was an important matter. Each child had to be heard. This was no time for joking. The delivery of words and the conveyance of feelings was not to be interrupted but highly respected. Teachers would often squat down so that their face was on the level of the child's. They would first make sure each child had expressed what they felt had happened, giving equal time to each child. While one child was vocalizing what had happened according to his side of the story, the other child had to sit and listen quietly. In all of these encounters, the emphasis was on the sacrality of personal stories and the importance of silence as a way of respecting the other child's story. The teacher did not speak for either child. She verified what happened and made sure both children were listening to each other as well as understanding how the other child felt.

Asking the children to focus on how they would feel in a given situation often enforced discipline. If a child was throwing sand and it hit another, a teacher might say, "How would that make you feel if someone got sand all over your design?" Or, "Excuse me, if you were going potty, would you want someone to open the curtain and peek at you?" This not only encouraged empathy but got the children comfortable with reflecting on their emotions, feeling they were valid, and articulating them to themselves and the teachers. Punishment also involved a focus on feelings. Often the child was separated from the group so that he could focus on how it would make him feel if someone else hit him. Discipline was based in part on empathy, on the child knowing and reimagining the intensity of a negative emotion.

In one scenario Katie and Chaz had a fight. Katie went to Dana and said Chaz had pushed her down and said, "I don't care. I don't like you." Dana replied, "Well, then, should we ask Chaz to come over here and talk about it?" Katie nodded. Chaz was summoned. Dana said, "Chaz, Katie says you hit her and pushed her down and said 'I don't care, I don't like you.' Did you say that?" Chaz said "yes." "Well, then, I think you should go over to the corner for the rest of the time, then, and think about how it would feel to be Katie." This gave Chaz a chance to really think about how he made Katie feel. Solitude was needed to reflect, empathize, and focus intensely on an emotional state. Thus, empathy was strongly encouraged, to the point of separating the child so that he could really imagine how it would feel to be the other child. Displays of empathy on the part of the children were highly praised. For example, at one point a child, Courtney, had a bloody nose. A couple of the other girls crowded around to see what happened, looking concerned. Ellen then said to them, "That's very nice of you girls to be so concerned."

Another time, four-year-old Chaz was complaining about how he hated circle time because he felt it was boring. The teacher said to the other children in the circle, "Excuse me, children, but could you tell me how it makes you feel when Chaz says that? Would you like it if we talked about space and trains everyday like Chaz wants us to?" The children all said, "No!" At another time, when one young girl, Molly, wanted to be the line leader two days in a row, the teacher asked the rest of the children for their feelings. "Excuse me, would the rest of you like it if Molly were the line leader everyday?" The class answered, "no," and Molly went to the back of the line.

One child, Jane, went to Dana and reported on how Michael was hitting her. Dana replied, "Well, did you talk to him about it?" She then had Michael come over and had both of them tell their side of the story. Dana then instructed Jane to tell Michael how his hitting her made her feel. "Would you want someone to make you feel bad, Michael?" He shyly said, "No." The teacher then said, "Then, what do we say to our friends when we hurt their feelings?" He then said he was sorry. The teacher looked over to Jane to make sure she was satisfied with this. She was quiet. The two of them were dismissed.

Often during the negotiation process of these fights, statements emphasized the need to respect someone else's rights by listening. "Checking" and even "double-checking" the children to make sure they were listening to each other was common: "Are you listening to Ben? He's expressing a right.

Listen." "Excuse me, Timothy, did you hear her? What did she say to you? If someone asks you to stop, then you need to listen and stop hurting her."

At one point one of the children, Chaz, was running around during circle time, pointing and yelling at kids. Dana said, "Chaz, are you listening to your friends? They're asking you to stop." All the children yelled, "Chaz, stop!"

Occasionally, the teacher would intervene in a fight or interaction even when the children did not seem distressed, had not asked for the teacher's help, or had already solved the problem on their own. The teacher would do this to ensure that both of the children's needs were met. Even when the children themselves had not established an interaction as a fight, a teacher would treat it in such a way in order to emphasize the importance of respecting each other's needs.

For example, in one scenario two children were having a lot of fun pinning each other down on the rubber mats in the gym. Ellen walked over and said to one of the children who was now on top of the other, "Martina, you need to make sure Desiree likes what you're doing to her." Ellen then said, "Desiree, was that all right with you?" "Yes," said Desiree. Ellen replied, "All right. Ok, I'm sorry to interrupt."

But what if a child who was accused of being mean did not admit to doing something, even though it might be quite obvious that he was lying? Unlike the Queens preschool teachers, in instances such as this where the child was not in any danger to himself or others, Ellen did not feel she could question their authority. To do so would challenge the child's knowledge of her own feelings and what she knew to be true. Hence, the teacher did not feel she could say, "I don't believe you. You're lying." This would diminish the child's authority and right to speak for himself. And yet, certain nonverbal cues were given to suggest to the child that the teacher did not trust his answer (raising her eyebrows suspiciously, pursing her lips). In one instance one child mentioned he had to go to the bathroom. Three other children then chimed in that they had to go, too. It was obvious that they were saying this just to follow along with the other boy. Dana rolled her eyes at me as if to imply, "Yeah right. You have to go to the bathroom," but to the children, she said, "all right, line up!"

Tobin (1995, et al. 1989) and Lewis (1989) provide us with an interesting contrast through their descriptions of Japanese preschools. After showing Tobin's *Preschool in Three Cultures* video (Tobin et al. 1989) to my classes over the years, I have found that the students are most shocked by four-year-old Hiroki's behavior, when he purposely stomps on his classmate Satoshi's hand, making him cry, and the teacher does not intervene. When asked by American teachers why she didn't intervene, she responds, "Of course, there are times I do intervene, depending on whom Hiroki is fighting and under what circumstances, but in general I let them fight because it is natural for boys of that age to fight and it's good for them to have the experience while they are young of what it feels like to be in a fight" (1989:32). In a statement that most Parkside teachers would find shocking, and perhaps more reminiscent of Queens teachers I interviewed, Catherine Lewis tells us of one Japanese teacher's explanation of children's fights. "When I see kids fighting, I tell them to go where there isn't concrete under them or where there are mats. Of course, if they're both completely out of control, I stop it. Fighting means recognizing others exist. Fighting is being equal in a sense. . . . I tell children to cry if they're being hurt, because the opponent will bite or pull until they cry" (1989:78).

The Subtleties of Discipline: Avoiding Direct Commands

Among the Parkside teachers, unless one of the children was in real physical danger, discipline was almost never in the form of a direct command. Rather, a somewhat hesitantly phrased, polite question was used in its place, giving the appearance of giving power to the child to decide what he wanted to do. Use of a question also created a situation in which the adult was seemingly following the command of the child, a command given in answer to the teacher's question. Nonetheless, most children could see through the pretty wrapping, and these questions were still interpreted by the children as commands. If children were doing something wrong, such as throwing balls up into the stage area in the gym, the teacher would say, "Ah, excuse me, children, but where do we throw the soccer balls?" Children often didn't even answer this but rather simply stopped throwing the balls onto the stage. They knew it was not a real question but rather a command in the form of a well-phrased, polite question.

Asking a question gave a sort of superficial power and authority to the child. "SIT DOWN!" became, "Would you like to sit down now, Jenny?" The voice was not stern and flat, but somewhat hesitant, soft, and approachable, allowing for negotiation. In getting the children to greet each other, Ellen asked them, "What do we say to each other in the morning?" Addressing the group with a question was also common. "You know what I am noticing? Has anyone noticed it, that people are talking without raising hands and interrupting?" The teacher was then "forced" to wait for the child's answer. She could never rush this time, and in this way the child was given a more active role in the discipline process, a period of time when he controlled the situation in silence. Until the child had formulated an answer, the teacher respected this space.

Often considerable time was spent with a child in this question-and-answer mode in which the teacher was trying gently to orient the child toward the "right" answer without issuing a stern command or interrupting his attempts to come up with an answer. This involved using several questions over and over. If a child was using a hammer to pound in a tack when he could use his finger, Kathy asked, "Do you think that's the best thing to use? [Silence. Long pause.] It's up to you, but do you think you should use that? Can you think of anything better to use?" The child shrugged his shoulders. "What do you think might be better to use?" Through this process the child seemingly discovered the answer on his own. Hierarchical direct commands were changed to a question-and-answer format such that the child seemingly disciplined himself through the answers he gave to the teacher.

Qualifiers

Very often, asking a child to do something he or she didn't want to do was cloaked in qualifiers to try to soften the blow. In this way the teacher's power was diminished and equality between teacher and child was attempted. Instead of saying, "Be quiet!" teachers would say, "Now, today is the only day I'll ask you to have to be quiet." The word "might" was often used to soften a suggestion. "Laura, you might try some red paint on that." Suggestions were also softened with, "I'd really appreciate it if you could . . ." If a teacher made a mistake and misjudged what the child meant or was doing, she often apologized, emphasizing that it was her fault, backing off from the child's activity or conversation so as not to get in her way anymore. Perhaps the most apologizing was done when the classroom was hectic and noisy and the teacher called a child by the wrong name. One child said, "Ellen, you called me Darby?!" Ellen replied, "I'm sorry. I apologize. Thanks for letting me know. I wasn't looking. I'm sorry." Calling a child the wrong name erased the child's uniqueness and made her seem like just any child. This was fixed immediately. At another time, when the children were made to wait while the teachers filled the cups with juice or practiced a dance step so they could show it to the children, they might say, "We're gonna get this done. Bear with us." When a child obviously needed help in arriving at an answer, the teacher might gently ask them if it would be all right to help them arrive at the answer. "Can I give you a hint? Can I just tell you something?" If the child said no, that was her right to engage in the process alone. Teachers would then have to take a hands-off stance and let the child come to the answer themselves. Very often teachers said, "Excuse me" to get the child's attention or to interrupt an activity. Furthermore, if the normal routine were being interrupted, teachers would tell this to the children. "Normally during free play we let children choose what they do—today I'm going to tell you."

Classroom Architecture: Feelings, Words, and the Fluidity of the Self

In subtle ways, respect for the *fluidity* of the self's emotions was encouraged. Teachers emphasized that many shades of feeling arise in the body and change from situation to situation and these were to be respected. The self was not static. A child could be angry one moment and totally afraid the next and this was not condemned as inconsistent or fickle behavior. Any shade or type of feeling that arose in the body at different times of the day was to be respected because it was a feeling, and feelings had rights unto themselves insofar as they comprised the seat of the child's individuality.

The architecture of the preschool classroom was designed to accommodate the changing *flow* of the child's self and feelings. Usually a corner of the room had pillows and blankets where the child could go if she felt she needed to take some time out from the group. This was the child's prerogative and usually wasn't questioned unless it became excessive. "Overloading" by the group was not considered healthy for the child's self. Thus, the corner was considered a haven where the child could rest and have space. As Ellen told me, a child could go there at any time to rest and be quiet and get some space. Or the child could go sit in her cubby (they were actually large enough to fit a four-year-old child), which I was told some children did when they needed to feel safe. In one preschool a weekly 15-minute chapel "service" was also emphasized as a sanctuary where the children were always loved and safe. Although in chapel the word "God" was used to teach kindness and sharing, the school itself had no particular denomination and it adamantly defined itself as nonreligious. They described themselves as a school with no particular religious affiliation, emphasizing Christian concepts of sharing and kindness. In this school, the addition of going to chapel as an activity did not seem to make a difference in their practices of individualism. In chapel God was described as loving, kind, and gentle. Angels were said to watch over the children. It was a place where "God takes care of us and holds us." God was made part of the giant canopy under which the delicate self of the child could unfold and be nurtured.

Children could also go into one of the play areas, which were intended, through household play rituals and role-playing, to help the child work out, or act out feelings that might be emerging at home. (See also Tobin, 1989, for other examples of this.) If a child needed to be cuddled, she could go over to the teacher and crawl on to her lap. This could be done at any time during any activity. The child learned that the architecture of the classroom was designed to accommodate the fluidity of the child's self throughout the day. The child learned that the self was not one solid block all day but changed in temperature and tone, and particular feelings were worthy enough to warrant their own architectural and human space. The child needed to learn to be in tune with these changes so that he could accommodate them in the appropriate architectural space. Hence, in an attempt to accommodate the child's psychological fluidity, classroom setup was more "diverse" than in the Queens preschools, where the self was encouraged to be more consistent, contained, and solid. In contrast, Kelley children had assigned seats and shared cubbies. There were no designated play areas or quiet reading nooks where a child could be alone. Rather, the whole room was transformed into a space where all of the children could do the same activity at a time the teacher had decided. Kelley children, especially, learned to change the self to fit the prescribed activity, whereas Parkside teachers designed a room to fit the moment-by-moment needs of a *fluid*, changing, "temperamental" self.

Perhaps one of the best examples of how children learned that feelings were important, legitimate, and valued was when one preschool had all of the children's "Feeling Books" hanging on clotheslines around the room. On the cover in bold letters it had the name of the child and then in dark bold letters, "MY FEELING BOOK." Inside, each page had a sentence written by the teacher that said, "I feel happy when . . ." and then a blank space where the child could tell the teacher the answer and the teacher could fill this in. On the following pages it said, "I feel sad when . . ." "I feel angry when . . ." Exercises such as these were an attempt to get the children comfortable with naming and identifying their feelings. The lesson was that feelings arise and must not be repressed. They must unfold and speak. Children were told to listen to their own feelings, to name and articulate them.

Words, Words, Words

As with Parkside parents, the importance of words in self-expression was emphasized in Parkside preschools. (See also Tobin et al., 1989.) Often the first thing said to the child when she reported that another child had hurt her was, "Well, did you both talk about it?" The teacher might also say, "Are you listening to her words? What did she say? Please listen to your friend's words from now on."

On another day in chapel one of the teachers told a story about two children, Bill and Melissa.

> Bill and Melissa were great friends and took turns going over to each other's house. They had a teddy bear and they argued over whom it belonged to. Then one day, Melissa said, "OK, it's yours," and threw it into the corner and stomped off. They didn't play together for days. Melissa then said she was sorry, that she wanted to be Bill's friend again. Bill said, "that's OK."

The teacher then said, "When we get angry, it isn't good to fight. When you're angry, go up to your friend and *say*, 'I'm angry. I'm sorry, I'm angry with you. God loves us. God wants us to be friends with each other and to try hard not to fight.'"

In chapel on another day a teacher spoke about anger. "When you get angry, you feel like hitting someone, but I saw someone who didn't hit." She tells a story about a boy who used his words, "loud words," instead of hitting. "He could express all of that anger without hitting, so when you're angry, *talk* about it! You can say it. Everybody has had an experience of anger, so let's thank God for *words* to use, so we don't hurt God's children. Amen." One child then went up to a board and placed a hand with a red cross through it on a large piece of wood with other symbols from previous weeks' lessons. This hand symbolized no hitting.

Accommodating the expression of a child's negative feelings was so important that words became vital insofar as they were expressed and out of the body in a peaceful and socially acceptable way. They let the child express a negative emotion without the negative consequences involved in the act of hitting. Words were the happy medium between acting out and repression. They let the flow of feelings and thoughts exit from the body in a way that was not harmful to others. Teachers tried to get the child accustomed to staying with and owning a feeling rather than being frightened by it. The child could own whatever was passing through the body by voicing it and even celebrating and being proud of it through art (e.g., the "Feeling Books" and songs).

Art, Personality, and Self-Esteem

Perhaps more than anything else, in the process of making a piece of art it was very important for the children to label their drawing or painting with their names. Even before they had painted something, the teachers made sure they all had their names on the pieces of blank paper. Art was seen as a reflection of each child's unique personality, and thus the naming of one's work was paramount. Pieces of art over the course of the year were seen as reflections of the child's development. Each child had a portfolio consisting of a self-portrait, a standard work that all the children had done: a teacher-selected piece; and a child-selected piece. Throughout the year teachers might also include quotes of what a child had said alongside the artwork.

In talking about a boy's portfolio one teacher said that she wanted to put in the piece of work he did with colored glue. Imagine James's (the Queenston prison guard from Chapter 3 who resisted the psychologization of children's art in portfolios) response to this analysis:

> He kept piling the glue on until it was one inch thick and then hurling sticks and stuff into the glue till it was all covered and then he started over with another layer of glue and covered it all—it was so Michael. It couldn't have been more Michael because instead of thinking, "All right, maybe I'll place a button here and a color there," he's all over the place—his energy isn't really focused. I couldn't have chosen or made a piece which better represented him. No one else could have done that piece of work.

Free choice was highly encouraged during times when children were making art. Children could use anything they wanted for their project. This was a time to revel in any color, size, shape, or fabric they liked. Works of art were displayed on every inch of free space in the classroom. If there was no more space on the walls, artwork would be hung on a string that went from one end of the room to the other. On this string were handmade books made from colored paper that said, "MY WORK, by [e.g.] John" in big letters on the front. Hanging these books and other pieces of art in clear view was a way of instilling pride in the children, teaching them to be proud of their own projects, their own feelings and selves. It brought feelings proudly out into the open, emphasizing the looseness and opening up of the self that was sought after by these teachers.

Often, lessons about a child's specialness were incorporated into artwork. Creativity became a chance to reinforce a positive self-image, combining words about uniqueness and self-confidence with color, shape, size, and pictures. An art project might involve painting a child's family for a book called "What Makes My Family Special," or drawings of different self-portraits, which showed different things that the child liked about himself. In one book, called "Why I Like Myself," children drew pictures of all the things they did well and why that made them special. In this way, often artwork was piggybacked with lessons on self-confidence and pride in the special quality of the child's self or family.

Saving Face

Part of the unfolding process in Parkside preschools involved helping the child open up through pleasant facial expressions, comments, voice content, or body language on the part of the teachers. Efforts were made to present a very kind, gentle, accepting tone of voice and a loving expression on the face. Given the constraints of the classroom (hectic, busy, high noise level), this could not be achieved all of the time, and yet the "lowest" verbal response ever reached was one of disappointment or inattentive flatness in which the teacher was busily engrossed in something else. Emotions such as anger, frustration, disgust, or hatred were never shown to the children, and yet teachers would make faces or comments in which they showed disgust, anger, and impatience with the child to me. Sarcastic or bitter remarks were made to me about a child, revealing how the teacher was sick of them. The teacher then swiftly returned to the child with a fairly kind and understanding expression on her face. It was then that I started noticing the ways in which I sometimes became the back stage to which the teachers briefly turned and vented before returning to the front stage audience of the child.

At one point a child who was felt to be the most spoiled and obnoxious by all of the teachers said to Dana, "My mother is paying you a lot of money to play with me, so play with me!" Dana said back to him, in a very calm expression, "No. You come to preschool to learn to play with other children, not with me." Dana then turned to me and said softly, "It would take a lot of money to get me to play with this kid all the time." She hid her annoyance from the child, revealing it to me as she turned her head over her shoulder, sneered, and whispered this. At another time one teacher yelled to the children, "Please stop screaming in each other's ears. Cut it out!" She then looked over to me and said, exasperated, but softly so the children couldn't hear, "What a bunch of lunatics!" In contrast, this was something Miss D in the Kelley preschool would have said directly to the children when they became too loud.

At times the children were crowded around Kathy reading a story, screaming, "Let me see. I want to see. What is it?" as she showed the pictures to them. The children were so close to her that her feet were stepped on and she could barely move her arms to open the pages of the book. She did not tell them to move away but made great efforts to adjust her body to accommodate their excitement. Any time a trace of strain crossed her face, it was replaced with a smile and look of warmth.

Equal but Different

Establishing a sense of equality and friendship among all of the children was very important in the Parkside classrooms I observed. Often, statements were made that attempted to erase differences suggested by the children about their peers. This was situated beside an elaborate discourse on uniqueness and how each child was equally special in his or her own way. The teachers taught children that they were all different, yet difference did not mean better or worse treatment. One song was, "We're all a family under one sky. We're all people, with animals, birds and flowers." Another song the children sang was all about loving each other and showing affection. When children called each other nasty names, again, the fact that everyone was the child's friend was emphasized. "Alex is our friend. We don't call our friends annoying. All of us are friends." Or, "The book is everybody's in our classroom. We learn to share with our friends."

Teams were also sometimes discouraged. One teacher said, "We don't have teams here. We're all friends." Competition was also discouraged. One child insisted, "I am the teacher's helper." The teacher responded, "No, every child in the class is a teacher's helper." The child said, "No, I'm a better one, a good one." The teacher said, "No, everyone is a really good one." This went back and forth with the child wanting to be seen as better and the teachers insisting on equality. Practices that discouraged favoritism or bias on the part of the teachers were observed. When the teacher was writing a story with the children, she said, "Ok, just so it'll be fair, I'll close my eyes and point to one of you to do the next part, ok?"

In one instance, a child came to school with a fake tattoo he was very proud of. When another child said that he didn't like tattoos, the teacher immediately asserted the rule of equality and the right of difference among children. "Different people like different things and that's fine." She also turned this lesson into a chance to praise the child with the tattoo, to ensure that his feelings had not been injured in the process. "You know, Willy, it's a good thing you're here to remind us of how we're all different, but special people." And so, the message of difference within equality was given to the children and the children learned to view difference in nonhierarchical terms. They learned the complex lesson that with each difference comes its right to exist as different, in an equal way. Given this emphasis on equality in virtually every domain of the classroom, the only area where difference *was* encouraged was the domain of feelings. Hence, feelings became the one way the child could assert herself as different.

In chapel, it was also emphasized that children had more than one family, that they needed also to view the people in their school as their family. This was one way of getting the children to view the other children as equal and special. "We're also a member of the world family and God's family—God's family comes in different shapes, sizes, and colors. You know that even twins don't look exactly alike?" Or, "All of us are very, very different. All of us look, dress, talk different, but God loves all of us because we're all part of God's family." When the children prayed with the teacher, they said, "Help us love all of God's family."

Chapter Eight

Balancing Psychologized Individualism with Societal Constraints and Uncovering the *True* Self

In Parkside, parents were faced with the difficult task of trying to insert sociocentric values into the sacred pillars of the rights of expression. The parents began a juggling act, attempting to do both, more often leaning toward the side of the expression of feelings and the practices that promote this (privacy, communication, creativity). Perhaps I became most aware of how important Parkside parents felt it was for their child to express themselves when I sat in on a weekly Parent Guidance Workshop and watched parents struggle to find a balance between raising a polite, well-mannered, cooperative child and one that still expressed her own moods, needs, desires, thoughts, and feelings. It is important to keep in mind in reading this chapter that Parkside talk of individualism often existed alongside talk of the importance of the group. The ultimate goal of these parents was to fit such psychologized and expressive individualism into the more restrictive elements, which were required by society. The truly successful child would get nowhere without an ability to get along with the group and a developed sense of what was socially appropriate. No child was an island, nor did parents want them to be. Thus, lest it seem that the group was viewed in a completely negative fashion, keep in mind that social values existed alongside the promotion of the individuality of the child. To say these parents all wanted outgoing, completely uninhibited children is going too far. When I asked these parents what was most important for the child to learn in going to preschool, most of them answered "learning how to get along with the group."

The Parent Guidance Workshop consisted of about ten Parkside parents who gathered in the living room of one of the participants along with a nationally renowned parenting expert. During my field work, all of the parents were mothers, except for one father, who came regularly and was very proud of his large role in raising his children. Each session was two hours and parents met regularly for ten sessions (at $40 a session). The counselor had a degree from Bank Street College of Education, had written two widely read books on parenting, gave lectures throughout the United States and abroad, and wrote for and edited various parenting magazines.

Parkside parents discussed problems they had been having with their children and asked very specific questions on how to handle certain situations. The counselor and other parents talked about these issues and gave advice. Each parent came hoping they would learn how to be a better, more effective parent. Many of them came to the group wanting to be reassured, and there was a certain confessional, anxious nature to their stories. Parents seemed to feel a little guilty about not handling an interaction with their child in the right way. The retelling of a story in which they were confused about the proper response, coupled with the understanding nods of other parents, was quite healing.

During the workshop, the counselor provided a structure to the discussion but also tried to follow the lead of the group in addressing concerns. Role-playing often occurred, with a certain scenario between parent and child that had happened that week reenacted in the group. Often this was done to promote a child-centered philosophy, so that the parent could feel what it was like to be in the child's shoes. Sometimes mock situations were given to the parents to role-play. For example, two parents were told to play the mother and daughter in a situation in which the child was very rude to an acquaintance. The parents were encouraged to be "spontaneous and natural," just as they would at home with their children. A few times the counselor also brought in copies of articles she or other experts had written in various well-known parenting and family magazines (*Working Mother, Parents*). Most of the articles dealt with rudeness and freshness and how to handle it while still encouraging the expression of feelings and respecting the privacy of the child. One article talked about ways parents could strike a balance between firmness and respecting the child's privacy by disciplining the child at home, *after* the rude remark had been made in public. Instead of embarrassing the child in front of her friends, the parent could take the child aside after the actual event occurred. Parents could discipline more subtly in the moment by sending the child a warning signal, a family signal of parental displeasure such as a raised eyebrow or an "I beg your pardon." Public restraint, however, should be followed with private discussion.

Most of the parents' children were from one to ten years old. This period was thought to be a delicate, influential time of emerging and unfolding, and parents often acted as if they were walking on eggshells when they talked about discipline. A certain amount of guilt and anxiety arose in the parent out of a sense of the extreme importance of this time in the child's life and the parent's inability to handle it well, to do the right thing at the right moment so that this process would not be hindered. Parents were very aware that socialization of *soft* individualism must coincide with socialization of cooperation, politeness, empathy, and other more prosocial "selfless" values. Their challenge was to work within the constraints of group life (good manners, basic politeness, kindness to others, and the importance of a certain amount of group activity in the life of the child) while still helping the child flower to her fullest. This was a tough balancing act for many of the parents to achieve, and most of the sessions were devoted to discussion of how to attain the one (*soft* individualism) within the constraints of the other—this theme of achieving full expression within limits was the core concept parents wrestled with.

As parents taught their children not to be rude, or how to be polite, they also had to give them privacy (space to unfold), respect, empathy, and ample choice. As the counselor said at one point, "What we want to do is help children feel comfortable with who they are but then set limits on the way they express it, which is a difficult process." Parents were faced with how to impose a morality and discipline on feelings and impulses that were legitimate simply because they were seen (tautologically) as the unique property of the child, "because they were hers."

In one meeting, parents brought up stories of their child's rudeness and were concerned about how to handle such rudeness in the best way. What followed was advice on how to discipline the child so that the feelings of the child could still be validated and empathized with, but the rudeness avoided.

April: Is there something you could say when the child goes [makes a crabby face]? What I do with Katherine, and I'm not sure it's the right thing to do, is recently she got quite aggressive, and one little girl she went up to and kind of punched her one day, and I made a big point of having and then she got hysterical when I told her that that was not the right thing to do. And I said, "You have to go to Susanna and apologize. Go up to her and tell her you're sorry, because that is one of our rules. You don't hit people." And she was hysterical, but I made her do it I really pushed it.

Counselor: We were brought up to say, "Now, say you're sorry" [she mimics in a voice of disdain], and even if we weren't sorry, we had to say it. So I'm concerned about having children feel one way and act another, but I would encourage her to apologize.

April: Maybe to talk about how she feels about what she did. Say, "Well, how do you feel?"

Jill: You can do more by even emphasizing how someone feels when someone does that to them, and mine sort of get that. And I just say, "I don't care how you do it, but somebody's feelings are hurting and you need to make it right." And then they can choose how they make it right.

Jennifer: I had a conversation with Simon [her four-year-old] and he said, "I don't care if I hurt some people's feelings." I said, "What do you mean?" He said, "Well, if I don't like them, I don't care." And I said, "You can't hurt people's feelings." But he doesn't care. He told me he doesn't care. What do you do in the face of that? What should I have done last night?

Counselor: Well, let's do it [role playing]. Simon has become rude. Leo, will you be Simon? [They then begin role-playing a scenario between Simon and his mother. Leo acts as the son, Simon, and Jennifer acts as herself.]

Leo: I'm not sure that I feel at all uncomfortable about Simon's not liking people.

Jill: Me neither.

Counselor: No, he doesn't have to like them. I want to hear just how you talk to him.

Jennifer: [Playing role of herself.] That was really impolite. I can't believe you did that.

Leo: Well, I did that, but I don't feel . . .

Jennifer: Well, I think you probably really hurt her feelings. This is a girl—you don't even know her. I can't believe you did that.

Leo: I don't care about her feelings. Why should I?

Jennifer: Because it's bad manners to hurt people's feelings on purpose.

Leo: What's bad manners?

Jennifer: Well, you're a nice person, and you should not hurt people's feelings on purpose.

Counselor: Ok, stop. What's the problem? . . . I think it comes back to because we're really between a rock and a hard place: We want children not to feel badly about what it is they feel. The problem is we want them to be able to express it in a way that isn't rude or derogatory or cruel. I think what's happened today that many of you have discovered for better or for worse is that if you encourage your kids to talk about their feelings, they express them. What we want to do is help children feel comfortable with who they are but then set limits on the way they express it, which is a really difficult process. So maybe a very short, clear response would be different. Would anybody respond differently to Simon's being rude? Let's try something else. Jennifer, you just be Simon for a minute. April is mother now.

Jennifer: Mom, I don't want this girl to be here. I don't want her here.

April: Sweetheart, we invited her over and she is a guest in our house, and as long as we have somebody as our guest in our house, we treat them kindly.

Jennifer: I don't want, I don't want her to eat my cookies. Let me go get them from her.

April: You're just going to have to accept it for now. She's here, she's our guest. If you don't like her having your cookies, then you can take a little time out until you're ready to be a little kinder.

Jennifer: [At this point he would start losing it.] No, she can have water, but she can't have milk.

April: Maybe you'd like to have a little time out in your room so we can calm down.

Counselor: Ok, stop. Jennifer, did you invite this girl over?

Jennifer: I did, yes. These are people who it is inevitable that we get together, so I arranged for them to get together in the park, but then it got cold, so then they came in and there was no way I could get out of it. It was one of those things. No, it wasn't ideal, but I knew there was no way I could get out of it. But he still has to be polite. He wasn't, but . . .

Counselor: One other thing you might have done is to take Simon aside and say, "I know this is a pain for you. You didn't invite her over, but she's a guest in our house, and for an hour I need you to help."

April: Yeah, yeah, 'cause then you're validating their feelings, that you don't have to like everybody. I think you have to respect his feelings, because you don't have to like all of your neighbors.

Jill: And it is ok not to like everybody. When you foist it on him . . . so to acknowledge his feelings might have helped him. I bet an hour is an intolerably long time at that age.

Susan: So helping them feel grown up like Nancy said would help?

Jennifer: We had a big debate yesterday and we have a rule in my family that Simon is not allowed to sit in the front seat if there is another adult in the car, and we just had this endless discussion, and I said, "That's it. That's all there is to it." And he was debating it and saying, "Well, why can't I sit in the front?" And these older women were saying to me they were in shock. They said, "I can't imagine having a conversation like that with my mother. I wouldn't have even questioned it." And they were so shocked that I was even allowing him to debate with the stuff I had said to him. The point is, when you set down a dictum, it was accepted. Our family rule is, this is how we do it, but still, I wish he would accept these dicta about manners and rules.

Jill: [Angrily, referring to the women in the car] That's their problem.

April: Yeah, one of my problems comes from the looks I get, the people who don't accept that, and that's very hard because I'd like to have people understand what I'm trying to do and to see that in the long run this may be healthier.

Counselor: Well, you see, this is where I think the ability to [she trails off] . . . is very powerful. I mean, he's not taking it sitting down. At the same time I think about what this woman said to me yesterday, that she was very afraid of her parents, but . . . was determined to do differently [so her kids were not afraid of her]. She was not happy, and I said, "Well, if you had to do it all over again, would you do it differently?" She said, "No, because my kids come to me and they talk to me and they know that they can tell me anything that is on their minds, and I never talked to my parents because I was frightened. I didn't trust them to care about how I felt, but they are fresh and so I think with this kind of thing, maybe just for the parent to acknowledge and say to them, 'you don't think it's fair.' You would like to sit in the front, and some rules don't seem fair to you, but that's the rule and we've decided on that, so it's really not worth arguing about 'cause I am not going to change my mind and say that's the way it is."

Later Jennifer returned to the topic:

Jennifer: Just to follow up, as we were coming out of the elevator this morning there was the whole family of the daughter Simon had been rude to and I said, "Simon, say good morning, please, and say good morning to Jackie." And he said, "Good morning, Jackie." "Say it a little louder, please." "Good morning Jackie." And she was so happy, and I think he had listened to what I said yesterday 'cause he wasn't reluctant to be polite this morning.

Counselor: Did you say anything afterwards, praising him?

Jennifer: I should have.

Counselor: I hope you'll get another chance.

Leo: It was probably hard for him to do that when he didn't really want to, so you might say that you noticed that it was hard for him. Say, "I bet that was something you didn't really want to do that much, and it was probably hard for you to do it, and I'm so proud of you that you were able to do it even though it was so hard." What you do then is teach them that it's ok for them to feel that way. You don't have to act that way. That's what I'm trying to teach.

In another scenario April was complaining about her daughter, who seemed to hate everything lately.

April: Lately, Katherine seems to have a much more negative attitude. She's four and a half, and she had a friend over and had already left, and I asked her how her play date was and she said, "Terrible. I don't like her." And I said, "Oh, that's too bad. What happened?" And she said, "She wanted Starlight [her stuffed horse]. She wanted to play with Starlight and she wouldn't let me have a turn, so I just don't like her." And then while we were talking about this I got her some frozen yogurt and put some raspberries on it, and she immediately went, "Uch. I hate this," and made this incredible face. And I just got to there with this whole attitude. I think I was mostly upset by my reply. I just kind of lit into her and I said, "Kitty, you know, I'm so tired of this. You're just always so negative about everything."

Counselor: The next time she says "I hate," instead of saying, "That's not a nice thing to say," I would say, "Can you tell me five things that you hate? You hate yogurt, you know." But this "I hate" is so appropriate and so normal and natural for a child at that age. They're not developed enough to say, "You know, it really makes me angry when . . ." And I think parents overreact too. What they mean at that moment is "yuck." It's an expression of an immediate negative feeling.

In these scenarios, as the counselor put it, parents were "between a rock and a hard place" in the sense that it was important that the child's feelings were acknowledged and expressed, but the children could not be rude in the process. What was taught was that no feeling is a wrong feeling. Whatever comes up is valid and can and should be felt. This is the right of the child, to own and express what he or she feels. It is what individuates the child from others and this very difference must be treated as a right in itself. In contrast to the older women, who were shocked by Simon's debate over who got to sit in the front seat, Jennifer, April, and Jane supported the notion of debating an issue with a child. And yet April was concerned that others might see her as too lenient. Ultimately, she decides it is more important to "hear the child out" than to care what other mothers think of her.

In a story about her children's sibling rivalry, April talked about her three children (two boys and one younger daughter, four years old) and their fighting. Again, emotional expression and validation of the children's feelings were recommended practices while she tried to get them to stop fighting. April continually felt uncomfortable dictating or issuing strict commands to her children. She wanted a more egalitarian approach in which they all worked together to come up with a solution.

April: Well, it's the usual problem with my kids fighting with each other—two separate incidents. There was sort of a fistfight and it was in front of other people, which always makes it twice as bad. That was one thing and yesterday returning from Florida at the airport in New York the two boys were teasing and she was screaming and I did something that I'm not very proud of. I said, "That's it. One more time and no allowance for two months." And I hate using threats. I guess what I'm trying to think about is how can I talk to them about this? I don't want discussions where I end up feeling like I have to take it to a threat. What can we all do? How can we all work together so I don't feel so pushed to have to threaten them?

Counselor: Have you discussed it with them since?

April: No, I haven't yet.

Counselor: There's something very good here, even though I know you don't like to threaten, and I agree with you that that's not a great practice. One of the things that's worse than threatening is threatening and not following through, and you know, two months is a long time. That's the biggest problem. Then you have to stick to it.

April: It really drives me crazier than anything when they all start fighting.

Counselor: But there was one good thing here. . . . They stopped. They take you seriously. They believed her. There are so many parents who threaten their kids.

April: I don't think I do it that much because I don't like to. I would much rather not do it.

Counselor: I would take away their allowance. You could say, "But there must be a better way." You could say to the boys about their sister, "I mean, obviously, this is something that is totally unacceptable. Now she is very annoying, I know. She is very tempting because if you just look at her sideways and it works, you're a lot smarter than her, and it's not an even fight. It's like putting a twenty-pound person against a hundred-pound person. If you saw a fight like that, what would you want to do?" You might say this to them when they're ready to listen or else one at a time.

April: To me it feels like it's cruel.

The counselor then recommended empathizing with how the children feel, letting them air their feelings.

Counselor: I would say, "Look, I can see how it's tempting because she does react every time, but it's not an even fight. She is annoying and I know she is very babyish sometimes, but the fact is that you are older and stronger, means that you're taking advantage of somebody weaker and it bothers me. It's not a nice thing to do." I would take that incident and I would discuss it with them and say, "You know, obviously, this is something that I feel very strongly about, and I know it is hard for you because sometimes she is very annoying. I know she is provocative, but I see this as deliberate cruelty, and I can't have this in my home, and I have a certain tolerance for this stuff and it gets to a certain point where I can't . . . " Maybe that's what I need to say to them. I mean, you can give them a chance to talk, give them a chance to air their feelings and say, "I know she's so annoying, and all you have to do is look at her and she goes off the deep end, and I can see that, but what I see is an uneven fight."

Susan: Do you think it's all right to tell your kids, "You're pushing my buttons"? "You're really—I'm almost at my level."

Counselor: As long as you're not playing good guy to their bad guy. I mean, that's not really fair.

April: Maybe we can help find a solution together. Maybe we can say, "Find a solution to help blow off your steam, find out what helps."

In another discussion, the parents talked about how sometimes the child would take anger out on them because they didn't know that they were actually angry with somebody else or about something else. One mother, Jane, then talked about the importance of putting up with a certain amount of flack and helping the child discover what was really bothering them. Perhaps the least strict of all the parents, she believed in excusing the child in most instances and forgiving them on the basis of misdirected feelings. She said, "My response would be to try and figure out what's really being said here. It's not appropriate. What is really being said is, 'I'm really so frustrated.' They don't know how to express what they're really feeling. Timothy has told me how she hates me because she was furious at her friends."

Naturalism/Realness and Hyper-Individualism in Parkside Psychologized Individualism

Parkside parents seemed concerned about the conflict between individualistic and more selfless values, whereas among the Kelley and Queenston parents and teachers these two discourses and forms of socialization existed side by side without any sense of conflict or discomfort. The fact that children needed to conform to the group, to know one's place in a hierarchy and withhold one's impulses was not perceived as inhibiting the child's learning of *hard* individualism. About one quarter of the Parkside parents I interviewed seemed well versed in the current pop psychological theories of the "true" or "real" self. Not surprisingly, most of these parents were also those parents involved in the Parent Guidance Workshop. I mention these parents not because they were representative of *all* Parkside parents but because the pop psychological references to the self that they make represent a *hyper-individualism,* perhaps the most extreme form of psychologized individualism.

Pop psychological conceptions of the true self depict the self as a layered entity, with more superficial or false layers on top of a core, unique, natural self. Getting in touch with this more real self is considered quite healing. Rosaldo describes this "Western" conception of real vs. false self in her article "Toward an Anthropology of Self and Feeling" (1984). An analytic framework that equates "self/individual" with such things as spontaneity, genuine feeling, privacy, uniqueness, constancy, the "inner" life, and then opposes these to the "persons" or "personae" shaped by mask, role, rule, or context is a reflection of dichotomies that constitute the modern Western self.

Running throughout these popular ethnoconceptions of the self were strains of what Deborah Gordon and Margaret Locke, in "Tenacious Assumptions in Western Medicine," refer to as the two major Western traditions of naturalism and individualism. Gordon and Locke note that among other values and assumptions, the tradition of naturalism promotes the following assumptions about the individual: that the individual is prior to society and culture, that nature is separate from culture, that nature is autonomous from society, and that nature is universal, autonomous from time or space. They write, "A conviction exists among some that underneath the cultural/social coating, a real, unique, 'deep' natural self exists, one that is 'given' to the individual. Society poses a threat to this 'real self.' To be socially determined is to be weak, trapped, limited" (35). The true self, real self, core self, and true feelings, such common themes in pop psychology, are seen as the unique and individual bedrock that is natural, true, and more real than the more epiphenomenal culture, which can be wiped off the self like frosting on a cake. (See also Turner, 1976; Shweder and Bourne, 1984; Curran, 1989; and Moffatt, 1989.)

Shils states,

> There is the metaphysical dread of being encumbered by something alien to oneself. There is a belief, corresponding to a feeling, that within each human being there is an individuality lying in potentiality which seeks an occasion for realization but is held in the toils of the rules, beliefs, and roles which society imposes. In a more popular . . . form the concern "to establish one's identity," "to discover oneself," or to "find out who one really is" has come to be regarded as a first obligation of the individual. . . . To be "true to oneself" means, they imply, discovering what is contained in the uncontaminated self, the self which has been freed from the encumbrance of accumulated knowledge, norms, and ideals handed down by previous generations. (Shils, qtd. in Gordon and Locke, 1988:10–11)

It is important to keep in mind, however, that, like other theorists I have mentioned who wrongly assume that these descriptions of self are representative of all social class identities in the West, they do seem to apply to some upper-middle-class American parents. Hence, one blatantly "psychologized individualism"–type question I asked in my Parkside interviews was, "What is a self to you?" or "What does the phrase 'real' or 'true self' mean to you?"

What were the ways these particular Parkside parents spoke about the self, or, if specified, the true self? Often parents and teachers spoke in terms of an inner core, a false vs. a real self, a child within, the true self being something real, natural, constant, and unique. Vertical metaphors were used to describe the true self's location on an axis that ranged from superficial top layers associated with culture, group norms, public persona, to a more real bottom core associated with creativity, naturalness, inner being, and immutability. One has to protect the true self from the outside world as well as work on expressing, finding, and discovering it. As we saw above, however, all of this authenticating of the real self must be done while *still* remaining polite and cooperative. Of course, not all Parkside parents liked the rendition of self that was current in pop psychology. One mother, whom I interviewed in her office at Cooper Hewitt, responded quite strongly against pop psychology and its portrait of the "true" self. I will never forget her response.

> I absolutely hate pop psychology and pop psychologists and I think they've done more damage, and it really almost gags me when I hear people say they're trying to figure out who they are. Maybe I have a rude awakening when I discover I'm not who I thought I am and I don't mean that there isn't a lot of searching in life and that its not difficult to establish priorities because it is, but a core self—I don't know how to separate that from something like personality. Or if a person believed in a spirit, then maybe that would be part of the core, but I don't think that life is a journey to discover the core self. . . . I don't want to imply there might not be something at the center of us, that somewhere along the line you say, "Oh yes, here I am again, and it's where I started out." That could be. I don't like the idea of spending one's life looking for one's core self. I think it's disgusting to be so focused on the self.

As I mentioned earlier, however, those who did resonate with the pop psychological conception of true self consisted almost entirely of the members of the Parent Guidance Workshop. Interestingly enough, when interviewing the working-class parents in Queens, I stopped asking the question, "What is the self? What does the term 'true/real self' mean to you?" insofar as it felt inappropriate and somehow silly even to ask this question. After a number of tries, either I felt embarrassed to ask questions about the self, or I soon learned that mention of the true self didn't really generate enough discussion to ask these kinds of questions. Sometimes, after sitting in on a Parent Guidance Workshop or interviewing a Parkside parent, I would wander through one of the many mammoth Barnes and Nobles bookstores on the upper east and west sides, looking at their sections on pop psychology. I would often browse through a current issue of *Parenting* magazine sporting a cover article like, "What a Personality! Ways to Nurture Your Baby's Nature," with a two-page graph on how to recognize and respond to various emerging natures and how to cope with them. I was reminded of Arlie Hochschild's discussion of the book *Born to Win* (James and Jongeward, 1971), ironically, a book people read in order to learn how to be *natural*. Such manuals for how to be natural, real or true to oneself, are all over the upper east and west sides, from Barnes and Noble psychology sections and New Age therapies to grocery store checkout counters displaying magazines like *Self, Glamour,* and *Mademoiselle*. In a section called "Private Time" in *Glamour,* young women are taught how to get in touch with their feelings through private retreats, walks in nature, candlelight baths, and warm cups of tea sipped while writing in their journal. The assumption is that they are at risk for becoming estranged from their inner, true feelings, and hence, the feelings must be recovered, touched, cherished, and nurtured.

Below are some responses from Parkside parents and preschool teachers when asked to speak about the self or what they thought of the term "true" self.

> Well, I've read a lot of child psychology books and they always say, "Is your child its true self or is it who you want it to be?" So that's one aspect of it, and the other aspect is when you meet a person who is clearly fake, and you know that they're not their true self, you don't know who their true self is, but you know that's not it.
>
> I think there's a center of gravity, which maybe is equivalent to the core, and that there's from that very dense and commanding control center there are a huge number of layers of lighter and lighter important variations and the chemistry flows throughout the system, so the core keeps the direction.
>
> I think it's the inner self, it's the inner thing that carries you, sort of like your spinal cord. . . . It's all the qualities that you sort of come out of the womb with. Children are born or predestined a certain way and then the environment gives them the next step.
>
> Yeah, I believe people have an essence. I believe in a lifelong journey to get closer and closer to your essence. I'm not sure anybody ever really gets there. It's a constant.
>
> I think there is a part of you that is like the honest, the real you that is there.
>
> I think there's a core self that's certainly almost impossible to change.
>
> There is that essence of whom we are that doesn't change from one stage of our life.
>
> I guess I would believe that you are yourself at all times no matter what environment you are in. . . . There may be certain environments where you are more self-confident or more relaxed, but that's not changing yourself.
>
> That little child that is vulnerable, filled with awe and seeking. . . . Hopefully, you want your life work to be connected to that little child, something real going on, or it's just meaningless.
>
> I think there is an inherent core self, expressed in different ways.
>
> You the individual, your ego, your id, the composite, your persona, what you believe in, who you are, your center, the unique aspects of an individual.
>
> The self doesn't change, but the arena changes.

When I asked one mother if people should present their true self, she said, "I think if it's at all possible they should. Some people for whatever reason, can't, but in our family, we put a priority on it. We have what we call a fake voice. We know there's something wrong. You have to allow your child to be whatever they are, within the context of whatever you consider to be acceptable behavior. Do you repress certain aspects of their real self? Probably, but hopefully not any key aspects of it."

Sometimes children were seen as having a more authentic and real self. One mother, whom I met at her office at Chemical Bank, said, "With the younger children there is more of this core self because they're just so genuine in their selves. They're manipulated, but they're just very obvious about, very sincere about their personality." Another mother said, "That's the beautiful part about kids. I love that part. They could be with Margaret Thatcher and they don't know. I love that."

One preschool teacher, in response to my asking her what a self was, what it consisted of, began to describe how she felt most connected to her self when she was in nature. She went on to say, "When I have felt most with myself, most who I am, it has been when everything else has been kind of cleared away and I'm by myself and everything is kind of, it's the essence of who you are as a person."

The false self was sometimes equated with veneers, top layers, acting, costumes, regret, exhaustion, and the external world. As one mother said, in referring to the top layers of the self, "The other parts are veneers, on top." Another mother said, "I don't have a lot of social clutter in my life." And another said, "When you're not being yourself, true to yourself, then it's a façade or a cover up." One mother, the first Parkside woman I interviewed, said, "I think there's a core self, and we put on costumes and we try out other things and situations, but you always come back to who you are." One preschool teacher spoke of the way being false or being around false people made her tired, so much so that she had to limit her time at dinner parties where there were often too many fake people.

When I asked the husband of the couple that hosted the Parent Guidance Workshop about having multiple selves all equally him, he responded with a sense of regret that he was not more true to himself.

> I guess and I say this with some fear and trepidation and sadness that multiple selves is true for me, I'd like to say I had a true self. It's really hard for me to do. It's like peeling layers of an onion to get to, so really I'm different things to different people. It's unfortunate. It's the way society is. I think there is a core [he then pauses and says regretfully], but I think that it is as far as true self goes I'm a bit of a charlatan. . . . I would hope that my child could be stronger and say, "That's not for me. I'm not going to do that."

One mother said, "I know how for me, I mean personally, when I get too caught up in the external world, business and activity I feel I begin to lose my centeredness. Nature, quiet time, being by myself, reading helps me get to my real self." One Parkside preschool teacher, Ellen, spoke of how well she had to know herself to be an actress, how she had to retrieve and look for feelings from a deeper part of herself. "In that respect I know things about myself that I don't like to know. You end up having to go find really awful, ugly stuff 'cause your role requires it." She also spoke of the importance of being authentic and truthful to herself. "I have a strong sense of responsibility for being truthful, not presenting versions of myself different places, not playing games. . . . I do feel that whatever I am, I need to be aspects of what I really am rather than versions that play well in the setting."

Sometimes, the growth and freedom of this natural core is seen as hindered and limited by "outer" sociocultural forces like peer pressure and the media (movies, MTV), a major topic of discussion in the Parent Guidance Workshop. One father said, "We all live a restrained existence. There are many things we all want to do if we hadn't got the restraint of the environment, but nobody really lives their true self. You're careful of what you say, do, and how you do it."

Hence, the liberationist call of these Parkside parents was often one that attempted to uncover the child's real self by removing the shoulds, oughts, repression, and parental and societal control, while still leaving the child polite and socially acceptable and cooperative. As one mother said, "I don't want her to do something just because others want her to do it." As Bourdieu notes in a somewhat cynical vein, in contrast to the puritanical view of the child's nature as dangerous, as that which must be contained, "the therapeutic ethic, with its psychobabble of 'liberationist' commonplaces (father figure, Peter Pan complex, etc.) credits the child with a good nature which must be accepted as such, with its legitimate pleasure needs." (1984:370)

Children, women and men, young and old are thought to feel better if operating from a natural place of truth and authenticity, and, hence, discourses around feeling good are also interwoven with this strain of naturalism. Another mother said, when I asked her if it was important to be authentic to yourself,

> Absolutely. I think that's what life is all about, what is the point. Either we have the choice to live life like some prescription that someone has handed out to you, or we're constantly trying to figure out what our lives are about. But specifically unique just as we are, there's work to be done. I can't imagine—I see here a lot of inauthentic stuff, a waste of time. I want my children to be strong enough to be who they are and put up with the flack.

One mother said, when I asked her if it was important for her child to learn to place a value on being true to herself, "Yeah, I think so, because I think that's where the good self-image comes from also. Otherwise, maybe you act differently all the time than your true self because you don't like yourself or you're afraid."

Some of the Parkside parents I spoke with seemed quite familiar with discourses focused on getting in touch with their (and their children's) real, authentic, true selves. Privacy and creativity helped in this process. In the magazine *Young Children,* art in the classroom is said to have the role of "helping children become more themselves instead of more like everyone else. Each child's inner existence calls for expression and takes pleasure in such expression . . . each person doing art is expressing his or her own feelings, making them come alive." (Sydney Gurewitz Clemens, "Art in the Classroom: Making Every Day Special," January 4, 1991).

One Parkside preschool teacher said, "Creativity to me. . . . It's digging down deep into yourself and coming out with it and not just doing something that is expected of you or something. That it is like going way deep down inside and coming out with that." Another mother said, "I think children are naturally creative if they are allowed to feel who they are, and if they're allowed to express it, then they're naturally, naturally creative."

One mother said, "I think it is important for every individual to have some time of privacy and some time of not, to let your hair hang down, be you without thinking about how others might be perceiving you." The search for self involves probing the depths of a place that is real and authentic. This requires the parent and teacher to stand back and let the child unfold with delicacy and gentleness. Without a certain amount of privacy, for example, a child can feel off-balance, exhausted, burned out, out of touch with who she really is. Hence, sometimes a Parkside teacher will recommend the child take some time out in a quiet, solitary, reflective space. One director of a preschool said, "Space and the sensitivity toward children who need space is just crucial."

When I asked what situations tend to bring out your true self, the answers of family, nature and alone time were often given. One father said, "Being with my family, being alone and having private time, those are probably the places where my true self comes out more than in more institutionalized settings." Another preschool teacher said, "I love solitude in nature. I have to add music, too. " One mother said, "For a child I think it's more at home than at school. They're willing to let their guard down and not worry about what other people are going to think. It's the time when their ego is most exposed, when they're most fragile."

True Self and Success

Some parents spoke of the importance of one's job or life reflecting one's true self. In describing the true self as a little child, one mother went on to say, "Hopefully, you want your life work to be connected to that little child, something real going on or it's just meaningless." Another mother said, "I would have to say that by the time you've decided what your true self is, you try and organize your life so that all of those elements fit as closely to your true self and reflect it as much as you can."

Knowing this core self will help the child become successful. One father spoke of a certain "authentic fuel" that comes through a child knowing himself and gives him the "highest probability of excelling at something." One Parkside parent said this when I asked what it takes for their children to be successful: "If the child can begin to understand who he is and where he's weak and strong, his development will be very, very outstanding in terms of himself." Another parent spoke of the importance of the child learning his likes and dislikes; otherwise, "It would be very hard for the child to develop a sense of self. It's part of learning to listen to their own emotions and needs. It keeps them at a very elementary level in regard to understanding and being attuned to their own needs and interests when they feel as if they have no options."

Other parents said: "Knowing what she wants . . . awareness of abilities and capacities," and thought it was necessary to "Develop an ability to know what she's feeling, to know yourself."

For these parents, it seemed that to not know how you feel often renders the child somewhat impotent and directionless, lost and unable to share, choose, assert, and stand out. To know how you feel and not have this coupled with a strength of conviction and confidence that it is worth sharing also renders you somewhat impotent. What rises to the top of this competitive creativity are leaders, self-starters, and stand-outs possessed with a certain dogged vision of what they want and feel. One father said, "It all comes back down to this creativity thing. The more individual she is, the more creative she's going to be . . . we want them to free wheel and do what they want to do." One young teacher in a Parkside school spoke of the importance of the child being true to herself and linked this with getting a job.

> That's what attracts people to people. "Oh, you're so unique." And that's how you get jobs, too. I am always attracted to very eccentric people, outgoing people. They're fun, they're interesting.

Hence, it seemed a certain momentum, energy, creativity, and power are associated with tapping into this natural place of true wants and desires, and, as one parent said, "If they don't foster it now, it'll never have a chance to bloom and blossom." As another father said, "Entrepreneurs, successful entrepreneurs are absolutely driven and single-minded and megalomaniacal, and in many respects they are children." Perhaps one of the most common phrases uttered by Parkside parents was that spoken by one mother, the hostess of the Parent Guidance Workshop, about her daughter, "She is very difficult, but adorable. I want them to know their feelings. I want them to know their anger, too . . . an adventurous spirit is something I shoot for, so I guess I'd say, we encourage an awful lot of expressiveness." At times, it seemed even ADD or ADHD was associated with a certain spontaneous, uncontainable energy and creativity that would ultimately work well for the child.

Hochschild notes that the authors of *Born to Win* quite simply state, "Winners are not stopped by their contradictions and ambivalences. Being authentic, they know when they are angry and can listen when others are angry with them." (James and Jongeward, 1971). A child who knows herself, who is authentic to herself, will do much better in the long run, insofar as she is not running on fake desire and staged likes and dislikes. To get somewhere, you have to tap into what the child naturally really loves. Being true to oneself is associated with taking risks and standing out and being unique and creative, all qualities that are more likely to help them excel in their future jobs.

Parkside and the Cultivation of Positive "Authentic" Feeling

In Parkside preschools, I could not help noticing what Joseph Tobin (1995) refers to as "The Irony of Self Expression" in which great importance is placed on letting the child express her true/natural feelings, and yet only certain feelings are allowed to be expressed and a great deal of co-construction and conarration goes into ferreting out the appropriate positive feeling. This was also done in the realm of discipline, where questions such as "Do you really want to be bouncing that ball so that it might hit others?" were posed that really acted as commands: "Stop bouncing the ball." One parent said Parkside preschool encouraged the importance of letting true feelings "shine" through. One day in Chapel a song was sung about letting who you are shine through. It went, "I'm gonna shine all day, I'm gonna shine all day, show what's mine, shine on through, shine in my neighborhood, I'm gonna let my shine come through."

And yet sometimes a child is not allowed to say, "I wanted to hurt Jimmy," without the teacher saying, "No. Let's think about this. That's not really what you meant. What do you feel? Do you feel *sad* that Jimmy took your blocks?" Nor is the child allowed to write in his Feeling Book, "I feel happy when my mommy finally leaves." In a world where people are *not* equal, where everyone is *not* your friend, and where sometimes people *are* bad, great efforts were made to get the child to feel and believe the opposite.

Hence, the metaphor of gently opening the petals of a flower or simply providing a warm canvas on which the child can comfortably open her unique self is sometimes misleading, insofar as there seems to be more solicitation, direction, coercion, and coconstruction than Parkside teachers are willing to admit in this process of self-expression (and it is a process, rather than a single act on the part of the child). Feeling Books also involve a process of learning what to leave out. Tobin writes about Books about Me and notes they are not allowed to contain sentences like, "I love the feeling of warm urine when I wet my bed," or "I like to watch my dog go doo doo," or "My brother keeps touching me between my legs," or "I sometimes imagine what it's like to kill someone," or "I like to say 'fuck, fuck, fuck' when my parents aren't listening." Tobin states, "In our contemporary educational settings, under the guise of helping children let their feelings out, we interrupt and then attempt to eliminate expressions of feeling which we find grotesque, parodic, silly, sexual, or sadistic" (1995:253).

In regard to the socialization of children's emotions and self-expression, the age-old question remains: What is too much and what is not enough?

What is the balance between a *Lord of the Flies* classroom where the id rules, and a heavily psychologized discourse of emotion that only allows the prettiest, tamest, and nicest of real feelings to "surface"? And who should decide this matter? And what children benefit from the decision? Directing, intensifying, and channeling certain emotions and types of self-expression is the work of culture, and it is a marvelous piece of work, colorful and adaptive. However, as we have seen, Parkside is adaptive to a very different class experience than the one children from Queenston (and less so Kelley) are equipped to deal with.

Conclusion

The Varieties of Individualism

Individualism adapts itself to local worlds. In this book I have tried to dehomogenize the monolithic individualism anthropologists and other social theorists generically refer to (and compare other cultures to) by describing the varying styles individualism takes in three communities in Manhattan and Queens. The spectrum of what we refer to under the umbrella of individualism is extremely broad, ranging from self-reliance to assertiveness to personal self-expression to hardihood, stamina, intellectual independence, a unique core of feeling, or a preference for being alone. (And even this list is not exhaustive.) And yet, not all communities practice, use, or socialize these various strands of individualism.

In my research, I discovered that communities of differing socioeconomic status wove different strands of individualism into narratives about the development of the child's self. Hence, individualistic styles were highly adaptive to these varying socioeconomic environments, each one preparing the child for dealing with experiences involving differing levels of poverty or affluence, violence or safety, possibility or protection. Each community style of individualism corresponded with the class-based parental trajectories that each parent and teacher envisioned for the child. Specific metaphors, images, and phrases woven into parent-teacher talk about the child's self in Manhattan and Queens were, as Clifford Geertz would say, "models of" and "models for" the socioeconomic conditions in which the adults (consciously or unconsciously) felt their children would inhabit. These trajectories were often not described as one among many the child could choose from but rather seen as normal and natural, the "of course," obvious choice that is generated by one's class habitus. (Of course she won't become a plumber. Of course he won't get a Ph.D.)

This book is largely an ethnography of three New York communities' different styles of individualism and the different strands each community emphasized. This is not to say that in some individuals various styles of individualism didn't mix. The types of individualism I describe are styles or orientations, not boxes that are rigidly separate from one another. One type of individualism does not necessarily preclude another, just as individualism doesn't preclude an emphasis on the importance of the group. For example, sometimes I would sense a strain of hard protective individualism running through an upper-middle-class parent, or a strain of psychologized soft individualism in a working-class parent. But mostly parents tended to lean toward one style or another.

I began field work in Manhattan and Queens hoping to contribute to the dehomogenization of the Western concept of self by exploring the complexities and subtleties of individualism, particularly among white American parents and teachers of preschool-age children from different social classes. My research pointed to the ways parents and teachers in Manhattan and Queens took up individualism and used its various strands in ways that correlated with the specific needs, values, beliefs, and ultimate concerns of their local worlds. Individualism was differentially woven into metaphors of opening or tightening up, of Superman or flowers, of delicateness or hardiness, fragility or resilience. In this way, the child was socialized into the various orientations of what I refer to as the "soft" or "hard" styles of individualism practiced in each community. These metaphors seemed to reflect the parent's conception of the nature of the child's self, be it delicate or hardy, as well as the offensive or defensive trajectory children should and would take as they developed. In this way I discovered two basic styles of individualism—hard and soft, within which various subtypes also emerged.

Hard individualism, the style most often found among Queens parents and teachers, emphasized a resilient, tough self that was hardy enough either to protect itself (as in Queenston), or project itself into a higher social class (as in Kelley). Queenston parents spoke more of surviving, defending oneself or one's family and staying put. Kelley parents spoke of hardening the self, enabling children to burst through to a higher socioeconomic level. In Queenston, a hard self should be able to deflect the dangers that came its way. Hence, individualism in the form of "not relying on or trusting anyone else," self-determination, privacy, and self-reliance was often seen as a way to survive the rigors of a bad system, a system that could not be trusted. For Queenston parents, individualistic values could not be extricated from a tough environment (gangs, drugs, racism, violence), a difficult past (child abuse, alcoholism, drug addiction, divorce), or a belief that the future held struggle and hardship. It was not uncommon to hear gunshots coming from the projects just one block away from the observed preschool. In the early morning light, as I walked down the street from the subway stop to this preschool, I stepped on garbage and broken crack vials. Every now and then a shivering, bruised prostitute appeared, guarding her street corner. Doors were shut, shades drawn. Many parents spoke of "the street" as if it were an enemy they must contend with, a force with a gravitational pull that they had protect their children from getting sucked into. Phrases like "staying put," "standing your ground," "minding your own business," "keeping up your pride," and "not letting others get under your skin" were common. Parents implied that these tougher boundaries of the self were better able to keep out the negative influences of the street (gangs, peer pressure, violence, alcohol, drugs).

In Kelley, a fairly safe and neat town with a great deal of pride, individualism does not bind itself as much to violence and poverty. Kelley parents viewed themselves as part of a close-knit and hard-working community that had made something of itself and was surrounded by very dangerous and low-class areas. In contrast to Queenston, where gunshots could be heard and prostitutes could be seen, in Kelley children played on the streets, mothers yelled to each other from their windows and babysat each other's children, and the American flag was displayed outside a number of houses. Projective images of stepping out, putting one's best foot forward, and building momentum were common insofar as a thick, tough skin was needed—not for protection from danger so much as for surviving the rough weather on the way up the socioeconomic ladder. Hard work, good grades, strong values, sports, and discipline would help the child break through to success and escape lower-working-class status. Here are the beginnings of pride and a more projective, offensive emphasis, which we find even more pronounced in Parkside. Hence, two different kinds of hard individualism emerged, projective and protective, both characterized by a conception of the self as being and needing to be tough, hard, or resilient, but for different reasons.

Upper-middle-class soft individualism, on the other hand, emphasized the delicacy of the child's self, the extreme care, resources, wide canvas, and gentle touch needed in helping this unique self "flower" and open up into its full potential. This individualism was characterized by highly psychologized discourses around the self and, in its most extreme form, resonated with some of the naturalist and essentialist strains found in conceptions of the true self in current pop psychology. Parkside parents and teachers brought to child rearing what Tipton (1982) refers to as "psychologized individualism," which stresses the importance of the child's cultivation of emotions and the development of a good sense or knowledge of the feeling self as crucial foundations for being happy and successful. Talk of autonomy, uniqueness, individuality, good self-esteem, and self-confidence were intertwined with talk of how important it was for the rights of the psychological self (emotions, feelings, desires, tastes, personality) to emerge and be the best it can be. For most Parkside parents, raising an individualistic child was akin to assisting the child gently in emerging, unfolding, flowering, and self-actualizing his or her own unique qualities, thoughts, and feelings. Thus, the self of the child was not to be tight, vigilant, and prepared for obstacles but to be willing to pour itself into the world. It was thought to be a delicate process insofar as any large, clumsy, or harsh interference might stunt the unfolding of the unique self. One of the most common metaphors used to describe this unfolding process was that of the child as a "flower" (a term used often both as verb and noun), in which images of growing, blooming, and blossoming were invoked.

In any book written about individualism, it is easy to de-emphasize the extent to which the group and more sociocentric values are also highly valued by Americans. This book in no way wishes to paint a portrait of America as solely an individualistic nation. Working in three socioeconomically different communities I immediately noticed that parental conceptions of the child's self did not reflect simplistic bipolar class constructs (a solely conforming working class and a self-directed upper-middle class), but that a strong strain of individualism permeated the supposedly "conformist" working class. Even among what Kohn (1969) would describe as the most self-directed, there was a fair amount of sociocentric socialization of children, just as there was a great deal of individualistic talk among the working-class parents. In all three communities, parents and teachers were concerned with socializing their children in values of individualism and sociocentrism. In writing a book on the subtleties of individualism I avoid freezing groups into single modes of orientation by pointing to the ways in which the supposedly conformist working class emphasizes individualism, and yet such an emphasis on individualism can also hide the extremely important role more sociocentric orientations take in various social classes in Manhattan and Queens. Keep in mind that Tobin et al., in their study *Preschool in Three Cultures* (1989), found that among middle-class American parents 68 percent chose sympathy/empathy/concern for others as one of the top three things for children to learn in preschool. Furthermore, in answer to the question of why society should have preschools, 62 percent said that one of their top three reasons was that it gave children experience being a member of a group.

When asked if I feel these styles of individualism would resonate with African Americans or second-generation and later-generation immigrants, I can only answer that they very well might, but obviously this is something I did not explore in this book. Again, this would depend on a great number of other variables. It would seem the general projective and protective individualistic themes would emerge, but the specific metaphors and images (of Nike ads, flowers, or Superman) would greatly differ pending on the rural, urban, ethnic, or racial landscapes. I have no doubt that individualism binds itself to other racial and ethnic aspects of local worlds, taking on the particular flavor or spice of a rural or urban, media-soaked or media-damp community. If individualism were not so agile and absorbent, it could not survive. Jay MacLeod (1995) in his book, *Ain't No Makin' It: Aspirations and Attainment in a Low-Income Neighborhood,* asks this very question as he considers how social inequality is reproduced in the United States. In many ways, MacLeod challenges social reproduction theorists such as Bowles and Gintis, asking them to explain why the working-class African American "Brothers" of Clarendon Heights have such different aspirations and achievement ideologies from their white working-class classmates, the "Hallway Hangers," even though they are exposed to the same schooling. How is it two groups of teenage boys from the same social class, living in the same housing project, and attending the same school can experience the process of social reproduction in fundamentally different ways? His book is an attempt to accommodate the interactions among ethnicity, family, schooling, work experiences, and peer associations.

He writes,

> The circular relationship Bourdieu posits between objective opportunities and subjective hopes is incompatible with the findings of this book. The Brothers, whose objective life chances probably were lower originally than those available to the Hallway Hangers because of racial barriers to success,

nevertheless nurture higher aspirations than do the Hallway Hangers. By emphasizing structural determinants at the expense of mediating factors that influence subjective renderings of objective probabilities, Bourdieu presumes too mechanistic and simplistic a relationship between aspiration and opportunity. This component of his theory fails to fathom how a number of factors lie between and mediate the influence of social class on individuals; Bourdieu cannot explain, for instance, how ethnicity intervenes in the process of aspiration formation and social reproduction. (1995:138–139)

Hence, MacLeod suggests that the ways in which these teenagers respond to the structures of domination is "open-ended. . . . the outcomes are not predefined" (1995:139). MacLeod critiques Bourdieu and social reproduction theorists such as Bowles and Gintis, pointing out the more active, creative, even resistant roles ethnicity and race play in response to structures of domination. What needs to be explored then, is the dense and complex subjectivities of one's habitus and the mediating forces that affect the way one digests structures of domination. Hence, although I do not consider race and gender and their roles in the thick fabric of habitus, or the ways in which race and gender might resist or reinterpret these structures of domination, this book acts as a contribution to the ways in which the variable of individualism is differently digested into the subjectivities of parents and teachers of different social classes.

Habitus and the Naturalization of Class-Based Individualisms

The body, a social product which is the only tangible manifestation of the "person" is commonly perceived as the most natural expression of innermost nature.

—Pierre Bourdieu, 1984:192

At the beginning of this book I asked a few questions about how class-based styles of individualism might be part of the child's habitus, and thus in some ways contribute to the reproduction of social inequality. How do class-based individualistic styles come to seem completely natural and "god-given," the only way to live and be? Bourdieu notes that habitus takes root in individuals in large part from early socialization experiences in which external social conditions (e.g., how wealth is distributed) are internalized. But there is very little in his work on the way in which class-based *individualisms* are part of this process. Hopefully, this book has helped the reader see the subtle ways in which class-based individualistic styles are a large part of the early socialization experiences where habitus begins to take root.

Each style of individualism I explored contained within it visions of the child's self as needing to be hard or soft, projective or protective. Seemingly natural conceptions of the world, self, life possibilities, and realities are taught, and these styles of individualism are a core part of each person's habitus. The child becomes disposed toward one orientation or another, toward ways of handling the self that involve dispositions such as protective caution or confident expansion. Both at home and in preschools, different kinds of class-based individualism are socialized as "natural" ways of being and responding to the world. Soft individualism becomes the "of course it's this way" filter through which the child views reality. Upper-middle-class emphases on self-expression of feelings are thus presented to the child as just the way things are, the way they ought to be, the way they must be, thereby masking and disguising the ways in which it is only one of many ways to behave and think about the self.

The concept of misrecognition is useful here insofar as it points to the ways in which the basic grammar of one's life (e.g., male domination, openness vs. protectiveness, one's place in the hierarchy, one's right to express oneself) is perhaps initially seen as so natural that it is not questioned at all, let alone seen as a social construction as opposed to a god-given truth. As Wacquant writes of Bourdieu's concept of misrecognition, "Things become seen as natural and necessary, rather than as the historically contingent fallouts of a given balance of power between classes, 'ethnic' groups or genders" (Bourdieu and Wacquant, 1992:14).

In speaking of male gender domination among the Kabyle of Algeria, Bourdieu writes,

[M]ale order is so deeply grounded as to need no justification: it imposes itself as self evident, universal. . . . the dominated, that is, women, apply to every object of the (natural and social) world and in particular to the relation of domination in which they are ensnared, as well as to the persons through which this relation realizes itself, unthought schemata of thought which are the product of the embodiment of this relation of power in the form of paired couples (high/low, large/small, inside/outside, straight/crooked, etc.), and which therefore lead them to construct this relation from the standpoint of the dominant, i.e. as natural. The case of gender domination shows better than any other that *symbolic violence accomplishes itself through an act of cognition and of misrecognition that lies beyond—or beneath—the controls of consciousness and will,* in the obscurities of the schemata of habitus that are at once gendered and gendering. (Bourdieu and Wacquant, 1992:171–172)

Especially among toddlers and young children, hard and soft, projective and protective dispositions take root with little resistance. Three- and four-year-olds lack the cognitive ability or the experience and savvy that enable one possibly to change dispositions or trajectories later on in life. As one could imagine, preschoolers often do not have the critical skills or varied life experience students in high school or college have that would enable them to contest or critique the dominant depiction of reality socialized by parents and teachers. Hence, unlike Willis (1977), who stresses the reactionary role of the working-class teenage lads against their class position, I did not encounter much visible resistance on the part of the preschoolers. Most children attend a preschool that is taught by teachers from their own social class, and this is the only reality they know. Because of preschoolers' lack of exposure to multiple realities, their initial exposure comes to take on an of course, god-given, natural cast. Ironically, one would think New York children in particular would be exposed to all sorts of varying realities, and yet, just as Parkside children only knew of New York through the upper east and west sides and the Soho-fied parts of downtown, so did Kelley kids stick to their own tight neighborhood outside of the city. Park Avenue was as far from Queens as from Montana or California.

And yet, it is important to note that just because individualisms take root so easily in preschoolers does not mean they can never be changed. These hard or soft dispositions do not turn us into preprogrammed robots with fixed schedules and futures. I have chosen to use the terms "style," or "orientation" rather than "type," insofar as these terms suggest a fluidity and agility to what is initially learned. (They also suggest that more than one style or orientation can exist beside another, whereas "types" seems to have the connotation of precluding other types.) But how do these individualisms work into one's core, the deepest habitus of the child, and start to feel natural?

Class-Based Individualistic Styles as Part of the Child's Habitus

It follows that the body is the most indisputable materialization of class taste, which it manifests in several ways. It does this first in the seemingly most natural features of the body, the dimensions (volume, height, weight) and shapes (round or square, stiff or supple, straight or curved) of its visible forms, which express in countless ways a whole relation to the body, i.e. a way of treating it, caring for it, feeding it, maintaining it, which reveals the deepest dispositions of the habitus.

—*Pierre Bourdieu, 1984:190*

Hard and soft, projective and protective core values are encoded in body habitus. Such deep internalization of "natural" tendencies is acquired not only through explicit teachings of rules and structural exercises but also through unconscious, informal modes of socialization. Perhaps what struck me most was the way in which "lessons" in hard or soft individualistic styles were not simply pamphlets handed out to children but were always accompanied by corresponding hard and soft tones of voice, facial expressions, body gestures, ways of walking, bodily proximity, and clothing style. (Again, all of these are things that Americans often mistakenly attribute as personal rather than class-learned attributes.) Or, within the various ways parents and teachers spoke, consider the types of metaphors used when speaking about the child and her future. Describing the child's self as a flower (Parkside) has a much different effect on the child than describing him as a fullback or Superman (Kelley). Describing life as a tough mountain to climb vs. a canvas upon which the child can spread her wings or a sky with no limits also enters the child's psyche indirectly and subtly, bringing its wake of protective caution or joyous abandon. It is this kind of exposure to various body styles and linguistic metaphors that begins to establish the child's own *naturalized* conception of her future place in the world.

One of the key differences I found between hard and soft individualism was the extent to which parents and teachers felt they must save face and voice in front of the child. Recall the way in Parkside preschools, the tendency was for teachers to present what they considered to be a very kind, gentle, accepting tone of voice and a loving, open, receptive facial expression. Given the constraints of a classroom filled with many young children, this was hard to muster when one's patience was low, and yet the "lowest" verbal response ever reached was one of disappointment or inattentive flatness (sometimes followed with an apology), during which the teacher was busily engrossed in something else. Emotions such as anger, frustration, disgust, or hatred were never shown in the bodies of the teachers in front of the children, whereas they were often shown to me, backstage. During my field work in Parkside I remember feeling completely exhausted at the end of a day of participant observation because I felt I also had to mimic the facial and voice posturing the teachers were modeling. I was keenly aware that I had to be acceptable to the teachers present if I were going to be allowed to observe the classrooms, and hence, I tried to act as they did in front of the children. Spending an entire day covering up annoyance, boredom, frustration, or anger with some of the children takes a great deal of energy. Saving voice, face, and body can be both consciously exhausting and unconsciously natural. Hence, backstage times (lunchbreaks, after school) could sometimes be quite spicy and full of complaint. I literally witnessed a visible "letting down" of face, voice, and body. I was reminded of Arlie Hochschild's discussions of "emotion work" and emotional labor among flight attendants.

When one child shied away from picking up a hermit crab that was on show for the day, the teacher quickly assured her that she didn't need to touch it. As she said this, the teacher facially postured a look of sincerity and concern, as if to reassure the child that she was not just saying this, she meant it too. Dress and clothing style were also child-tropic. Teachers at Parkside preschools were much more apt to wear more stereotypically feminine, obviously child-oriented colorful dresses and slacks that had animals on them or balloons or geometric shapes in bright colors. Bodily proximity was much closer than in Queens preschools. It was considered kind to squat down to the level of the child when speaking to her, and it was common to see these women holding children on their laps, hugging them, or asking them to come sit on their laps. Sometimes two or three would be crawling over the lap of one teacher, vying for the best position, the teacher trying to accommodate the needs for touch and affection of all three at once. Children all called the teachers by their first names. In this way, the Parkside child "learns a world" through body, voice, facial expression, and touch, experiencing school as more of a soft canvas that is open and receptive and filled with relatively little hierarchy.

Contrast this with the tendency of Kelley teachers to wear clothing that was less stereotypically feminine—practical gym suits or other relaxed-type sports clothing. These teachers were always addressed by children as "Miss so and so," never by their first name. Nor were children hugged much or invited to come sit on their laps. The children did not come to school to be babied and mothered but to grow up, become big kids, and prepare themselves for kindergarten and first grade. Perhaps most notable was that compared to the Parkside teachers, there was also a relative lack of concern about saving voice, face, and body in front of the child. Facial expressions and tone of voice associated with negative emotions were nonchalantly woven in and out of everyday conversations and interactions between teacher and child. When a teacher was disappointed, disgusted, impatient, bored, irritated, annoyed, or angry with the children, this was not necessarily hidden underneath a gentle and sympathetic face and voice. Nor was this seen as hurting the child, stunting his self-esteem or self-confidence. It was just the way life is, replete with ups and downs, frustrations and angers. Why posture a fairytale expression if this doesn't correspond with the world the child lives in and comes to know? I remember Miss D posturing boredom and frustration while waiting for a child to finish a project. This was shown through using a sterner face and louder voice than was used in Parkside preschools. Of course, this did not mean these teachers cared any less for the children than Parkside teachers or parents. This behavior was not seen as crushing the child's self-esteem. I came to see that lack of concern over saving face, voice, and body were both a model of the teacher's conception of the child's self as harder, as well as a model for how the teacher wanted the child to become. This behavior reflected the "harder" conception of self as well as actively toughened the child up "from baby to big first grader."

In all of the schools, individualistic styles, then, were not served on a plate, away from the body, giving the child the appearance of one among many options. Each style was held in the body, as a certain cultural capital, absorbed by speech and gesture, tone of voice, and turn of the head. This cultural capital, as Bourdieu reminds us, is a disguised form of economic capital, and in this way it "conceals the fact that it originates in material forms of capital which are also, in the last analysis, the source of its effects" (1977:183). Life trajectories of possibility and openness vs. hesitance and caution, of hardness vs. softness, were thus taught through and absorbed by the whole bodies of parents, teachers, and children. Such individualisms hence pass more easily from teacher or parent to child, insofar as they are accompanied by the naturalness and taken-for-grantedness of the whole weight of body, voice and facial expression. Of all ways cultural capital and individualistic styles passed from teacher to child, this seemed the most subtle and yet perhaps the most powerful.

Dissonance between Hard and Soft Individualisms

But what happens when home styles of class-based individualism do not match school styles of class-based individualism? In particular, what happens, as it did in one preschool I observed, when working-class preschoolers confront the psychologized expressive individualism of upper-middle-class pedagogy? In my research in one Queenston preschool where upper-middle-class soft individualism was taught to working-class children and parents I began to realize that it is here that the possibility of mislabeling a child's cultural capital and known style of individualism is at its greatest. Bourdieu writes of the ways in which most schools are dominated by upper-middle-class pedagogy,

> The teacher, who, while appearing to make judgments on "innate gifts," is in fact measuring by reference to the ethos of the cultivated elite. . . . The culture of the elite is so near to that of the school that children from the lower middle class can only acquire with great effort something which is given to the children of the cultivated classes—style, taste, wit—in short, those attitudes and aptitudes which seem natural in members of the cultivated classes and naturally expected of them precisely because (in the ethnological sense) they are the *culture* of that class. (Bourdieu, 1966:39)

Cultural production theorists interested in the ways in which teachers subconsciously process subtle class and cultural messages (such as dress, accent, play styles, attention spans, eye contact, tone of voice, response to hierarchy) and use them to measure their students' abilities often note the ways in which class hegemony exists in the public classroom. Wendy Luttrell, in her book *Schoolsmart and Motherwise: Working-Class Women's Identity and Schooling* (1997), describes the types of degradation and disdain (what Bourdieu and Passeron [1977] refer to as "symbolic violence") that schools seeped in upper-middle-class pedagogy inflict on students from clashing working-class backgrounds. Working-class women doubted their own value, voice, and abilities. "Their stories stress the formative, painful, and enduring effects of this school denial and self-doubt" (1997:114). But she also states that the women found creative ways to survive the schools' degradation and disdain. Women coped differently with the school's symbolic violence. Some women responded with silence and self-imposed invisibility, while others spoke up against teachers or developed an attitude toward authority" (1997:114).

The Queenston preschool I observed was dominated by a soft psychologized individualism despite its working-class parents and children. Nowhere was this more evident than in Mrs. Costado's struggles with getting the parents of Queenston preschoolers involved in their child's learning. What was supposedly going to entice them to come join the fun, however, was a psychological pedagogy of self-expression that conflicted with and made no sense in relation to their own class habitus. What was most ironic about the posters on parenting tips, the ABC's of helping your child, and family affirmatives lists were the ways in which they sugar coated the rather grim realities most parents were confronting on a daily basis. Most parents were exhausted and overworked, and were struggling with having to raise a child as a single parent, fighting a drug or alcohol addiction, working with welfare, or worn down by poverty.

For the rather angelic discourse of soft psychologized individualism to come in and recommend that a working-class mother take a hot bath instead of yelling at her child it must assume certain things: that she has enough time to take a bath, she has a bath that works, she has enough hot water, she has someone who will take care of her children while she takes a bath, and she feels she deserves a bath. After taking a bath, for this same poster to recommend that you tell your child how proud of them you are also presumes you are comfortable with such open compliments and self-expression, that you believe children should receive this as much as possible, that you believe children will benefit from this, and that you are calm and rested enough to speak in a gentle tone of voice. Hence, when a mother says, "I'm sick of her," and Mrs. Costado replies, "No, you're not," the mother's reality is in some ways being denied. Class is dismissed in favor of the sugar coating of soft psychologized individualism. Posters recommending social learning objectives of the teachers are written in a formal language quite foreign to most Queenston parents.

While my research did not focus on the ways in which working-class children responded to the soft individualism of certain teachers, the dissonance between the two styles was indeed noticed. In a few of the Head Start programs I visited while doing preliminary research, for example, I could clearly see the collision of two cultures, which often manifested itself in the lower-working-class children simply becoming silent, as if mystified by the fairylike teacher who moved around the classroom with a constant glow and smile, showering praise upon them. How these parents and children felt about this disjuncture (slighted, baffled, bemused, intimidated) was not the focus of my research at the time, but the obvious dissonance I observed leads one to question to what extent the converging of these two hard and soft realities feels jarring, uncomfortable, or even traumatic.

Other social theorists have noticed this dissonance as well. For example, nowhere is the agony of having to choose between the cultures of home/family and school better depicted than in Philippe Bourgois's *In Search of Respect: Selling Crack in Spanish Harlem.*

Bourgois describes the trauma of first contact with the public school system from the perspective of a new immigrant Puerto Rican mother and her second-generation son. Bourgois writes, "It is in school that the full force of middle-class society's definitions of appropriate capital and symbolic violence comes crashing down on a working-class Puerto Rican child" (177). Bourgois tells of the child's experiences as a six-year-old working-class Puerto Rican child in kindergarten.

> In his kindergarten homeroom, Primo inherited the instantaneous onus of his mother's identity as former rural plantation worker, and now new-immigrant inner-city sweatshop employee. Her functional illiteracy and her inability to communicate with the educational bureaucracy condemned Primo to appear uncooperative and slow-witted to his teachers. Perhaps right away he had to protect himself by resisting his teachers lest they unconsciously insult or hurt him should he make the mistake of trying to please them—and inevitably failing. Despite his anxious mother's admonishments that he respect his teacher and do well in school, success in the classroom would have betrayed his love for her. (176)

Primo's mother was quite insulted when her New York City–born toddler refused to answer her in Spanish, and this form of delinquency was only made worse in kindergarten. How does a child choose between parental cultural capital and school culture? In what ways does choosing one necessitate losing the other? What, then, can act as a bridge from the working-class and minority backgrounds to schools where upper-middle-class teachings of psychologized self-expression dominate? Peggy Miller writes that certain practices, such as show and tell and sharing time, are based on the pedagogical concept that personal storytelling can act as a bridge from home to school. (See Miller and Mehler, 1994.) Both her studies and those of others point to the common practice of storytelling in a wide range of working-class families. (See Wiley, Rose, Burger, and Miller, 1998; Heath, 1986; Miller, 1994; Miller and Sperry, 1988; Sperry and Sperry, 1996.) She writes, "by 3 years of age, telling stories of personal experience seems to be second nature to many working-class children" (Wiley, Rose, Burger, and Miller, 1998:844). And yet, while this research might suggest that storytelling in preschools might have a positive effect in easing the transition from working-class and minority home to school, other research points to the ways in which the storytelling around show and tell that is practiced in middle-class preschools is incompatible with working-class backgrounds. (See Michaels, 1991, and also Wiley, Rose, Burger, and Miller, 1998.)

Privileging Self-Expression the Upper-Middle-Class Way

Tobin (1995) states that many preschool activities such as show and tell emphasize the middle-class ideal of self-expression. Many of the teachers he cites positively coax and couch the child's unfolding narrative in a safe space in the same way Parkside mothers were careful to help the delicate petals of the flower unfold to their fullest expression. This kind of gentle coaxing and encouragement of a narrative is a far cry from the more oppositional teasing meant to toughen and densify the self in Queenston or Kelley. Children used to having to talk back and defend their statements and stories would find little need for this behavior in Parkside preschools. Tobin, in his article "The Irony of Self Expression" (1995), also points out how self-expression is so central to contemporary middle-class American cultural beliefs and practices that "it can be difficult for us to see them as anything other than natural and desirable" (1995:233). As a point of contrast, he describes Japanese approaches to dealing with children's expressions of feelings in which more emphasis is given to intuiting feelings than to expressing them. Nor is it always appropriate for Japanese children to express personal feelings in a large group setting. He also cites Ballenger, in her article "Because You Like Us: The Language of Control" (1992), who writes of her experiences at a Boston day care center where most of the staff was Haitian. Rather than the "how do you feel, tell me about your feelings" approach she was used to she found a shame-based approach to misbehavior. Hence, one of Tobin's main points is that " . . . popular pedagogies based on self-expression need to be critically examined and modified for use with African-American, Hispanic-American, Native-American, and Asian-American students" (1995:247).

Among other things, Tobin also argues that the pedagogy of self-expression is insensitive to class differences within the United States. He writes, "Although less often and openly discussed, social class differences in self-expression within American society are as profound and significant as ethnic and cultural differences" (1995:248). He cites Lisa Delpit (1996), who suggests, for example, that by conceptualizing self-expression as *natural* behavior, as part of one's true/real self, rather than as something learned and taught, the whole process middle-class children go through to learn this type of self-expression becomes ungraspable and mysterious to African-American children. How will these African American children then enter upper-middle-class jobs and power?

Peggy Miller's work on emotional socialization and class also points to these differences (1982; Miller and Sperry, 1987; Miller and Sperry, 1988). Working-class Baltimore adults and children share their feelings and express emotion without bathing them in a psychologized discourse of emotion words. Rather, they use action-oriented words, saying "I kicked the table" instead of "I was angry." Tobin writes of Miller's south Baltimore research:

> Moral fiber and intelligence in south Baltimore, as in many other American communities, are measured in part by one's ability to stand up to unjustified attacks on yourself and your friends. A child with a good character is one who is neither a sissy (someone who expresses hurt feelings when she should not) nor spoiled (someone who asserts her desire when she should not). In south Baltimore, self-expression has less to do with providing a running metanarration

on your thoughts and feelings than with being a fearless, formidable street-corner (or sandbox) debater and a witty and engaging back stoop storyteller. (1995:249)

Class Dismissed: The Myth of Naturalism/ Authenticity in Parkside Psychologized Individualism

How could the assumptions behind soft individualism contribute to a denial of social class? It seems important to examine, on a philosophical level, the way the notion of a natural, real, true self, found among some of the more extreme Parkside parents oriented toward pop psychology, denies the class construction of the child's self. The opening up of the child's self, which is so important in soft projective individualism, is for some parents simultaneously an exploration of the child's supposedly *true, unique, and natural* self. This process of exploration is often surrounded by discourses of naturalism rather than discourses of inequality and social class. The naturalist and individualist strains that run throughout the most extreme forms of the psychologized Parkside folk model of the self sometimes locate the "real" self as a natural entity separate and prior to class culture ("nature" is never associated with the group or class, or with culture or the public), whose false or public "outer layers" can be wiped off. In fact, class, along with culture, is seen as that epiphenomenal layer that must be wiped off in order to get at the true self. Hence, a child working diligently on an art project is not doing so from a place of upper-middle-class sentiments but rather from a natural talent and creativity unique to herself and only herself. In this way, class is subtly and indirectly dismissed by promoting a notion of a true/real self that is, among other things, supposedly free from the trappings of class. Hence, by denying that the deepest parts of the self, one's feelings, subjectivity, one's sacred ground of emotional being, can be constructed and influenced by class environments and worldviews, discourses around class are either ignored or denied. Habitus, and all its complexities, gets lost in a psychologized discourse of natural feelings, true talents, and real personalities. For Bourdieu (1984:275) the real self would then serve as a "thinly disguised expression(s) of a sort of dream of social flying, a desperate effort to defy the gravity of the social field."

When a Parkside parent says of her child, almost proudly, "Yep, she's stubborn, she's quirky" or "she doesn't take no for an answer" but feels that "this will work well for her in the long run," class is dismissed and naturalistic hyperindividualism applauded. The myth of naturalness allows upper-middle-class parents to see their children's success as stemming from "natural" sources, such as personality, talent, drive, hard work, rather than class-based sources. It denies the full extent that social grooming, habitus, and cultural capital play in determining a child's success in the playing field. A willingness to try new things, risk taking, self determination, optimism, precociousness, sense of humor, feistiness, and perseverance are labeled as character traits rather than typical behavior generated by a certain class habitus.

A pamphlet from the Child Care Resource Center describes how to identify various types of temperaments:

> Children are born with their own unique way of responding to the world. Your child's temperament describes how he will react to the world around him. It is a set of traits he was born with and will have for the rest of his life. It is not a reflection of your skills as a parent. A very active child will always be very active; His inner signals demand it.

Beneath this statement are listed various types of temperaments, and yet none of them are described as being the result of the child's class habitus, or the result of the type of behavior that is discouraged or allowed and encouraged in a soft or hard individualistic upbringing. Each is described as a biological unique trait that must be adapted to by the parent. The degree to which the child's sense of life possibility, level of optimism or pessimism, caution or abandon, self-expression, or reserve could be a result of poverty, class-based styles of individualism, or other aspects of social class is not addressed. Below are the biological traits the child was born with, that (this article posits) will be with him the rest of his life. These traits shape the child's temperament. At the bottom of this list is a note in a box, saying: "Remember you can't change your child's temperament. But you can learn about it and shape your parenting style around it to create a healthy, loving relationship with your child."

The article exhorts: You can't change your child's temperament. It is a part of him like the color of his eyes. Instead, you can change how you react to his behavior. For example, if your child seems "high" on the activity level, expecting him to sit through a movie or play quietly for more than five minutes is something he just can't do. So don't expect it of him. If you really want to take his sister to a movie, set up a play day with him at a friend's house.

As Bourdieu says, habitus is experienced as necessary, natural, inevitable, or as an obvious "choice" rather than a product of one's social environment. It is "necessity internalized and converted into a disposition" (1984:170) and often this is seen as a biological disposition. For example, in what Bourdieu calls "charismatic ideology," the notion of artistic talent as a gift of nature disguises the fact that it is a social privilege. Taste, vocational sense, or biological destiny of the true self are rarely associated with social class. He writes, "In general, children and their families make their own choices by reference to the constraints which determine them. Even when the choices seem to them to follow simply from taste or vocational sense, they nevertheless indicate the roundabout effects of objective conditions" (Bourdieu, 1966:34).

But as DeMott (1990:13) states, "The end of the myth of classlessness requires the beginning of awareness that details of *feeling*, and of knowledge differ vastly from class to class, and that the differences are not abstract." By engaging in a liberationist, naturalist conception of the child's identity, parents and teachers reject a categorizing, defining, and limiting of the self by society. In them we might find, as Bourdieu (1984:261) so perceptively writes in *Distinction:*

> a rejection of everything in themselves that is finite, definite, final, in a word, petit bourgeois, that is, a refusal to be pinned down in a particular site in social space . . . they see themselves as unclassifiable, "excluded," "dropped out," "marginal," anything rather than categorized, assigned to a class, a determi-

Traits	High	Low
Activity Level	always running, jumping, moving	is often sitting quietly
Regularity	has a set internal schedule for eating, sleeping, and other daily habits	unpredictable daily habits
Approach/ Withdrawal	jumps right into new situations	holds back, clings in new situations
Adaptability	quickly gets used to new people, new schedules and routines	takes a long time to get used to new people, routines, ideas
Sensory Threshold	is not bothered by loud noises, lots of people, new smells, or certain fabrics	dislikes loud noises, strong smells, clothing that feels irritating
Mood	always has a smile or laugh, views people and things in a positive way	is usually cranky or finds fault with everything
Intensity of Reaction	when upset, everyone knows it; when happy, bubbles over	rarely shows intense feelings
Distractibility	quick to notice everything going on around him, especially little things	stubborn, hard to get to change mind
Persistence/ Attention Span	never seems to give up, sticks with a difficult task	gets frustrated, gives up on task quickly

nate place in social space. And yet all their practices . . . speak of classification, but in the mode of denial.

We can begin, then, to answer the question: What role does the inherent naturalism of psychologized individualism have in maintaining social inequality, if only indirectly, by viewing class as that which is part of the *outer* layers of self that must be sloughed off to get to the natural individual core? Or, further, by viewing the true, core, natural part of the self as innately classless?

The reader might ask here, What are the ways soft psychologized individualism could possibly benefit children? Aside from the more obvious ways of helping children learn the cultural capital necessary to climb the social ladder, what are some of the more subtle ways in which a psychologized individualistic emphasis on feelings might be good for children living in this economically divided country? Below is one possibility.

Parkside Feelings: Empathy, Compassions, Imagining the Other

Parkside children are taught how to recognize, categorize, and express various feelings. We have seen this manifested in the classroom through Feeling Books, designated areas of the room a child could go when feeling overwhelmed or creative, and play areas meant for acting out feelings from home through role playing and dress up. Parkside parents and teachers spoke of the importance of mirroring their child's feelings.

Parkside preschool discipline is also highly oriented toward feelings, insofar as each child is asked to imagine how the other person feels in the situation: "Can you tell me how you would feel if someone hit you with a ball?" During story time, children sitting in a circle are asked to imagine how they think a bunny rabbit would feel when he loses his best friend or is lost in the field. Hence, children are asked not only to get to know their own emotional terrain but also that of others. Egos are described as delicate and selves are soft, fragile. In the bumping against each other that is inevitable in preschool social interaction, children learn that other children's selves can be hurt. Feelings can be crushed, wounded, and pain can go unrecognized if the child isn't careful.

Perhaps what impressed me the most about Parkside preschools and parents was their tremendous emphasis on empathy training and imagining how the deep interiors of others actually *felt*. Alongside individualism, children practiced a sort of phenomenology of *others'* emotions in the classroom, especially when someone's feelings were hurt. I was reminded of Lebra's (1976:38) description of the socialization of *omoiyari* (a rough equivalent of empathy) among Japanese children. Omoiyari "refers to the ability and willingness to feel what others are feeling, to vicariously experience the pleasure or pain that they are undergoing, and to help them satisfy their wishes." Lebra noted that in contrast to American mothers, Japanese mothers were found to appeal more to feelings in disciplining their children. Clancy has also noted that Japanese mothers, in giving directives, strongly emphasized sensitivity to the feelings of others (1986: 232). She states that in fact, in her research, 45 percent of all the rationales given by Japanese mothers for their directives were based on appeals to empathy. A certain degree of this was also common among Parkside teachers, where the rationales that almost always piggybacked directives were often about the importance of not hurting another child's feelings. Rather than hierarchical statements such as, "Do this because I'm the teacher and I told you so," you might hear, "You know, James, that really makes me feel nervous when you walk on the ledge, and I hate to feel nervous, so could you please get down from there?" Similarly, praise was given for a child who empathized with another. "That's very nice of you, Danny, to ask Rose to join us. It's not very fun to feel all alone during circle time, is it?"

What implications does this have, then, for challenging social inequality? At the most indirect level, empathy could promote a greater sense of connection between children and identification with the other. It allows the child to entertain the idea that the unique feelings of each self can still be grasped and understood, that in fact, each child has felt those same feelings at some point. This kind of other-oriented identification provides a much-needed common ground between the otherwise individualized, separated selves of Parkside children. For one moment, uniqueness takes a back seat, and common identification with a particular human feeling is imagined. If a Parkside teacher continually says to a child, "You have no idea how she feels and you never will," a sense of connection and help is unrealistic. Empathic conversations between children are shut down. This kind of empathy training encourages a certain responsibility in the child—to attempt to understand what *another* feels. Responsibility lies in both the speaker and the listener, for the one to express and the other to lean closer, imagine, and identify with the feeling. Hence, there is a great deal of potential here for the child to develop a subtlety of feeling for other people from different backgrounds.

And what of the disjuncture felt between what the teacher says and what the child feels, between saving face, voice, and body vs. letting one's frustration or anger show? In fostering open expression not all feelings are always accepted as legitimate, as when a child writes in her Feeling Book, "I feel happy when I kick the dog and my mother isn't looking" and the teacher gently suggests "we" describe another feeling. Socializing children to believe that everyone is their friend and that everyone is innately good and steering them toward the more positive spectrum of feelings is perhaps more apt to lead children to a position of compassion for those one does not understand or know. Ultimately, practices tinged with the irony of self-expression could also foster a strong belief in the inherent goodness of human beings, a stance that lends itself more toward compassion and forgiveness than to anger, alienation, and dismissal. If a Parkside child leans out of a taxi cab and sees a homeless woman dragging her bags along Park Avenue, a belief in her inherent goodness may be more apt to make him wish that woman had a bed for the night.

Furthermore, in preschool books written by soft psychologized individualists, one often finds that trees, animals, ducks, rocks, and flowers all have feelings, and nothing is too strange to identify with. Why not, then, include humans, especially the poor, in this circle of empathy and imagination? Why not extend the child's curiosity and sense of identification toward those from different socioeconomic backgrounds? Why not include social class or poverty in the circle of animation? Alongside stories of the hungry whale, the sad flower, why not continue widening the child's field of felt animation by leaning them toward the lives of other humans from different social classes? Establishing even an imperfect visceral bridge between rich and poor at least offers the child a common ground with which she can identify. It becomes easy then, simply to widen the circle of whom the child could empathize with. Other people, then, extend beyond the child's own immediate social milieu, as when a Parkside mother says to her daughter upon seeing a homeless woman pushing her cart across the street, "It probably doesn't feel good to have no home, does it? Can you imagine having no home?" Empathy here is established on a visceral level, which seems far more effective for preschoolers than saying, "Did you know that 1 percent of Americans own 98 percent of the nation's wealth?" Even if the child cannot imagine the complexity of feelings the homeless woman has, at least she can grab on to some sort of baseline of pain. This is a start, a place to begin. Without an invitation into another's feelings, the child might never wander in, given the incredible emphasis on privacy, independence, autonomy, and uniqueness that also surrounds them. A child who is taught to imagine how another feels, to try to identify with others, begins an exercise of extension and connection, a ritual of widening the self in a world animated by feeling.

Hence, I end this book with a number of questions—questions that could not have arisen without first exploring the incredible subtlety and nuance among varying individualistic styles and their relationship to social class.

In this culture of varied individualisms, if one individualism gains a certain hegemonic dominance in schools, how could this both increase and lessen social inequality?

What happens when in certain settings, one style of individualism is naturalized to all social classes?

How is hard individualism interpreted by those with a predominantly soft individualistic style?

How can we understand the various ways in which working-class and minority children might find this home-to-school transition difficult, as well as helpful or adaptive?

What are the pros and cons of using psychologized individualism in the most dominant educational programs?

If there is indeed a spread of psychologized soft individualism across the classrooms of America, how might naturalizing the culture and personality styles of one group of Americans (socialization of soft, psychologized individualism for example) actually lead to a series of inequities (lower grades and lack of encouragement, to name just a few) in which children from lower-class and minority ethnic backgrounds are left behind?

Appendix A

Sample Letter for Parents

October 15, 1993

Dear Parents of 4S,

As some of you may remember, I am working on my doctorate in psychological anthropology at Harvard University and have been doing some observing at Brick. I am interested in studying how different cultures socialize their children, especially how American preschools differ from those in Asian cultures. Part of my research also involves interviewing American parents and teachers on questions such as what you hope your child will learn as a result of going to preschool, what you feel the role of preschool should be, what is your favorite characteristic of your child, what rights should your child have, how important is free choice, praise or privacy for the child, etc. The interview should take a half hour to forty-five minutes at the most. I would like to interview each parent separately at whatever times are convenient for each of you. I am able to meet you at your homes or at the Brick Church School. I have a very flexible schedule that would allow me to meet you at most any time, weekdays or weekends. Also, since I live across the street from Brick, I would be able to meet for an interview with very little notice. I am hoping to start interviewing as soon as possible, but am open to speaking with some of you in the next couple months if that is more convenient.

Finally, I would also like to remind you that neither the name of the school, your names or the names of your children will be used in my dissertation.

Thank you for your cooperation this far in my project. I hope to hear from you.

Sincerely,

Adrie S. Kusserow

Name(s):
Phone Number(s):
I agree to be interviewed ____
I do not agree to be interviewed ____

Appendix B

Interview Questions

General Questions

1. Why did you send your child to preschool?
2. What are the most important things for children to learn in preschool? [show them list]
   Perseverance
   Cooperation and how to be a member of a group
   Sympathy/empathy/concern for others
   Creativity
   Beginning reading and math skills
   Self-reliance
   Self-confidence
   Art/music/dance
   Communication skills
   Physical skills
   Good health, hygiene, and grooming habits
   Gentleness
3. What are the most important characteristics of a good preschool teacher?
4. What are some of the characteristics or qualities you most want your child to develop? Why?
5. What are some of the characteristics you least want your child to develop? Why?
6. Tell me a story about a time you were proud of your child.
7. What are some of your favorite characteristics of your children?
8. What is one of your favorite things to do with your child and why?
9. What qualities or characteristics make a child "go bad" or get into trouble today?
10. What qualities will it take for your child to get a good job or successful (whatever that means to you) career today?
11. If you had to pick a public figure/celebrity that lived now or in the past, whose qualities you would like your child to have, who would that be?
12. What do you want your child to learn about feelings and emotions?
13. On a spectrum ranging from individualistic to collectivist/group oriented, how would you characterize our society? [Explain more fully in interview, ask them to rate our society, themselves, and their children on a scale from 0–10.] Is this how you would characterize yourself? Why are you this particular number? What number would you want for your child?
14. Pick three characteristics you'd like your child to have.
    Cooperative

Independent
Sympathetic/understanding of others
Self-reliant
Gets along well with others/Good in a group
Self-confident
Selfless/thinks of others frequently
Unique/creative

Praise

1. How important do you feel it is to praise your child?
2. What would happen if you didn't praise your child?

Creativity/Art

1. How important is it that the preschool foster an encouragement of the child's creativity? Why or why not? What does creativity do for the child?
2. Are there other things more important for the child to be developing?

Free Choice

1. How important to you is it that your child be given choices as to whom to play with, what activities to do, what paints to use, whom to sit with at lunch? What is free choice doing for the child?
2. How do you think no free choice would affect a child?
3. Beyond food, shelter, and love, what rights does your child have, if any?

Privacy

1. What does the word "privacy" mean to you?
2. Do you think it is important for your child to have privacy? Why or why not?
3. What would happen if your child didn't get privacy?
4. Is it more important for your child to learn to be alone or with a group, or are both equally important?

Discipline

1. Is there anything about how your parents raised you that you want to do with your child or would want to change?
2. What are some of the ways you discipline your child?
3. When your child misbehaves, why do you think s/he does this?
   Do you give him or her an explanation when you discipline them?
4. Describe someone you know and like very well.

Notes

Introduction

1. Lest the reader become confused by what I mean by *self*, I am always referring to a parent's conception of the child's self. This includes what Spiro (1993:114) describes as "the self-representation or the mental representation of the attributes of one's own person as they are known, both consciously and unconsciously, to the person herself or himself."
   During my interviews, parents spoke about their own conception of the child's self as they saw it, as well as how they hoped it would develop. None of these descriptions is a "true" reflection of the phenomenological experience of the children's selves. As such, these conceptions include aspects of one's culturally constituted *milieu* and *habitus*, which may or may not reflect the phenomenological realities of the child's self.

Chapter One

1. This does raise the important question, however, when it comes to American individualism; namely, do differences in social class and economic standing outweigh the influence of race and gender? Would race and gender *substantially* change the trajectories implied in each of these varying kinds of hard and soft individualism? Would a black woman from Queenston share the same general hard individualism of her white neighbors? Again, these are important questions that should be researched, but ones I decided not to focus on in my book. (See MacLeod, 1995.)
2. Shweder (and Much, 1991) argues that perhaps Western individualism has its origins in the institution of privacy, "that privacy promotes a passion or need for autonomy, which, for the sake of our sense of personal integrity, requires privacy" (1991:153). (See Trilling, 1972, p. 24.) In my questions I attempted to tease out the degree to which upper-middle and lower-class parents and teachers placed a value on privacy and the practices of privacy (seen in alone time, not opening others' mail, the child having a separate room, knocking before entering the child's room) and solitude.

Chapter Two

1. For examples of this, see Elvin, 1985; Lin, 1988; Mines, 1988; McHugh, 1988; Rosenberger, 1989; Kleinman and Kleinman, 1985; Ewing, 1990; Waters, 1990; Stephenson, 1991; Stairs, 1992; Oxfeld, 1992; Murray, 1993; Spiro,

1993; Derne 1992; Holland and Kipnis, 1994; Conklin and Morgan, 1996; Lamb 1997; Rosenberger, 1992, 1989.
2. See Riesman, Glazer, and Denney, 1950; Varenne, 1977; Hochschild, 1979; Gilligan, 1982; Lykes, 1985; Wilkinson, 1988; Hewitt, 1989; Sampson, 1988.
3. See Sennett, 1976; MacIntyre, 1984; Turner, 1976; Trilling, 1972; Berger et al., 1973.
4. This sort of unpacking can be accomplished through an approach to self that Csordas (1994) refers to as "cultural phenomenology," whereby theories of the self always remain tethered to the phenomenological and embodied experience of the specific cultural phenomena under study. If too often the self is described without reference to any concrete phenomenological base, Csordas, in his detailed account of symbolic healing among Catholic Charismatics in North America, points to the need for more of a balance between the methodological twins of phenomenology and semiotics (1994:ix). (For other phenomenological approaches in anthropology see also Desjarlais, 1992, 1997; Good, 1992; Jackson, 1996; Kapferer, 1997; Kleinman and Kleinman, 1985).
5. See Kohn, 1969; Hochschild, 1979; Richman, Miller, and Solomon, 1988; D. F. Miller, 1989; Lareau, 1989; Lubeck, 1985; Cook-Gumperz, 1979.
6. Social psychologists such as Triandis et al. (1985) and Kagitcibasi (1987) also focus on the coexistence of individual and group loyalties and the problems with placing them in bipolar positions.

Bibliography

Abbott, Susan. 1992. "Holding On and Pushing Away: Comparative Perspectives on an Eastern Kentucky Child-Rearing Practice." *Ethos* 20:33–66.

Abu-Lughod, Lila. 1986. *Veiled Sentiments: Honor and Poetry in a Bedouin Society*. Berkeley: University of California Press.

Apple, M. 1982. *Cultural and Economic Reproduction in Education: Essays on Class, Ideology, and the State*. London: Routledge and Kegan Paul.

Aretxaga, Begonia. 1994. "Dirty Protest: Symbolic Overdetermination and Gender in Northern Ireland Ethnic Violence." *Ethos* 23:123–148.

Ballenger, Cynthia. 1992. "Because You Like Us: The Language of Control." *Harvard Educational Review* 62:199–210.

Becker, Ann. 1992. *Body Image in Fiji*. Philadelphia: University of Pennsylvania Press.

Beiser, Morton. 1985. "A Study of Depression among Traditional Africans, Urban North Americans, and Southeast Asian Refugees." In *Culture and Depression*, edited by Arthur Kleinman and Byron Good. Berkeley: University of California Press, pp. 272–299.

Bellah, Robert N., Richard Madsen, William Sullivan, Ann Swidler, and Steven Tipton. 1985. *Habits of the Heart: Individualism and Commitment in American Life*. New York: Harper & Row.

Berger, Peter L., Brigitte Berger, and Hansfried Kellner. 1973. *The Homeless Mind: Modernization and Consciousness*. New York: Random House.

Bernstein, Basil. 1971 *Class, Codes and Control: Theoretical Studies Toward a Sociology of Language*. London: Routledge and Kegan Paul.

Bock, Philip. 1988. "The Importance of Erving Goffman to Psychological Anthropology." *Ethos* 16:3–20.

Bourdieu, Pierre. 1990. *The Logic of Practice*. Cambridge: Polity Press.

———. 1984. *Distinction: A Social Critique on the Judgment of Taste*. London: Routledge and Kegan Paul.

———. 1977a. "Cultural Reproduction and Social Reproduction." In *Power and Ideology in Education*, edited by Jerome Karabel and A. H. Halsey. New York: Oxford University Press.

———. 1977b. *Outline of a Theory of Practice*. Cambridge: Cambridge University Press.

———. 1966. "The School as a Conservative Force: Scholastic and Cultural Inequalities." In *Contemporary Research in the Sociology of Education*, edited by John Eggleston. London: Methuen, pp 32–46

Bourdieu, Pierre, and J. Passeron. 1977. *Reproduction in Education, Society and Culture*. London: Sage.

Bourdieu, Pierre and L. Wacquant. 1992. *An Invitation to Reflexive Sociology*. Cambridge: Polity Press.

Bourgois, Philippe. 1996. *In Search of Respect: Selling Crack in El Barrio*. Cambridge: Cambridge University Press.

Bowles, S., and H. Gintis. 1976. *Schooling in Capitalist America*. London: Routledge and Kegan Paul.

Bowles, S., and H. Gintis. 1972. "I.Q. in the U.S. Class Structure." *Social Policy* 3:65–69.

Brodwin, Paul. 1993. "Private Bodies and Social Orders: A Critical Anthropology of Embodiment." Paper presented to the Center for Twentieth-Century Studies, University of Wisconsin-Milwaukee.

Butler, Judith. 1990. "Gender Trouble: Feminist Theory, and Psychoanalytic Discourse." *Gender Trouble: Feminism and the Subversion of Identity.* New York: Routledge, Chapman & Hall, Inc.

———.1989. *Carnegie Hill: An Architectural Guide.* New York: Carnegie Hill Neighbors, Inc.

———. 1987. *Subjects of Desire: Hegelian Reflections in Twentieth-Century France.* New York: Columbia University Press.

Carrithers, M., S. Collins, and S. Lukes, eds. 1985. *The Category of the Person: Anthropology, Philosophy, History.* Cambridge: Cambridge University Press.

Carroll, R. 1987. *Cultural Misunderstandings: The French-American Experience.* Chicago: University of Chicago Press.

Clancy, Patricia. "The Acquisition of Communicative Style among Japanese." In *Language Socialization Across Cultures,* edited by Bambi Schieffelin and Elinor Ochs. Cambridge: Cambridge University Press, 1986, pp. 213–250.

Collins, R. 1971. "Functional Conflict Theories of Educational Stratification." *American Sociological Review* 36:1002–1019.

Conklin, Beth A., and Lynn M. Morgan. 1996. "Babies, Bodies and the Production of Personhood in North America and a Native Amazonian Society." *Ethos* 24:657–694.

Cook-Gumperz, J. 1979. *Social Control and Socialization.* London: Routledge and Kegan Paul.

Csordas, Thomas. 1994. *The Sacred Self: A Cultural Phenomenology of Charismatic Healing.* Berkeley: University of California Press.

Curran, P. 1989. *Grace before Meals: Food Ritual and Body Discipline in Convent Culture.* Urbana: University of Illinois Press.

Danforth, Loring M. 1989. *Firewalking and Religious Healing: The Anastenaria of Greece and the American Firewalking Movement.* Princeton, NJ: Princeton University Press.

Delpit, Lisa. 1996. *Other People's Children: Cultural Conflict in the Classroom.* New York: New Press.

DeMott, Benjamin. 1990. *The Imperial Middle: Why Americans Can't Think Straight about Class.* New York: William Morrow and Company, Inc.

Derne, Steve. 1992. "Beyond Institutional and Impulsive Conceptions of Self: Family Structure and the Socially Anchored Real Self." *Ethos* 20:259–288.

Desjarlais, Robert. 1997. *Shelter Blues: Sanity and Selfhood among the Homeless.* Philadelphia: University of Pennsylvania Press.

———. 1992. *Body and Emotion: The Aesthetics of Illness and Healing in the Nepal Himalayas.* Philadelphia: University of Pennsylvania Press.

Dilthey, Wilhelm. 1958. *Die Geistige Welt. Einleitung in die Philosophie des Lebens.* Gesammelte Schriften, vol. 6. Stuttgart: B.G. Teubner Verlagsgesellschaft.

Dumont, Louis. 1965. "The Functional Equivalents of the Individual in Caste Society." *Contributions to Indian Sociology* 7:85–99.

Ehrenreich, Barbara. 1989. *Fear of Falling: The Inner Life of the Middle Class.* New York: Pantheon Books.

The Encyclopedia of New York City. 1995. New Haven: Yale University Press.

Elvin, M. 1985. "Between Heaven and Earth: Conceptions of Self in China." In *The Category of the Person,* edited by M. Carrithers, S. Collins, and S. Lukes. Cambridge, England: Cambridge University Press, pp. 156–189.

Erchak, Gerald Michael. 1992. *The Anthropology of Self and Behavior.* New Brunswick, NJ: Rutgers University Press.

Ewing, Katherine. 1990. "The Illusion of Wholeness: Culture, Self, and the Experience of Inconsistency." *Ethos* 18:251–279.

Fischer, Michael M.J. 1986. "Ethnicity and the Post-Modern Arts of Memory." In *Writing Culture: The Poetics and Politics of Ethnography,* edited by James Clifford and George E. Marcus. Berkeley: University of California Press.

Foley, D. E. 1990. *Learning Capitalist Culture: Deep in the Heart of Tejas.* Philadelphia: University of Pennsylvania Press.

Foucault, Michel. 1983. "On the Geneology of Ethics: An Overview of Work in Progress." In *Beyond Structuralism and Hermeneutics,* edited by H. Dreyfus and P. Rabinow. Chicago: University of Chicago Press, pp. 229–252.

Friedenberg, Edgar. 1959. *The Vanishing Adolescent.* Boston: Beacon Press.

Gaines, Atwood. 1992. *Ethnopsychiatry: The Cultural Construction of Professional and Folk Psychiatry.* Albany: State University of New York Press.

Gans, Herbert. 1988. *Middle American Individualism: The Future of Liberal Democracy.* New York: The Free Press.

Geertz, Clifford. 1984. "From the Native's Point of View: On the Nature of Anthropological Understanding." In *Culture Theory: Essays in Mind, Self and Emotion,* edited by Richard A. Shweder and Robert A. LeVine. Cambridge: Cambridge University Press, pp. 123–136.

———. 1973. *The Interpretation of Culture.* New York: Basic Books.

Gilligan, Carol. 1982. *In a Different Voice: Psychological Theory and Women's Development.* Cambridge: Harvard University Press.

Gilligan, Carol, T. Hanmer, and N. Lyons, eds. 1990. *Making Connections: The Relational Worlds of Adolescent Girls at Emma Willard School.* Cambridge: Harvard University Press.

Giroux, Henry. 1983. *Theory and Resistance in Education.* London: Heinemann Educational Books.

Goffman, Erving. 1959. *The Presentation of Self in Everyday Life.* New York: Doubleday.

Good, Byron. 1992. "A Body in Pain." In *Pain as Human Experience: An Anthropological Perspective,* edited by Mary-Jo Delvecchio-Good, Paul Brodwin, Byron Good, and Arthur Kleinman. Berkeley: University of California Press.

Good, Mary-Jo Delvecchio and Byron J. Good. 1988. "Ritual, the State, and the Transformation of Emotional Discourse in Iranian Society." *Culture, Medicine and Psychiatry* 12:43–63.

Gordon, Deborah, and Margaret Locke. 1988. "Tenacious Assumptions in Western Medicine." In *Biomedicine Examined.* Kluwer Academic Publishers.

Hallowell, Irving. 1955. *Culture and Experience.* Philadelphia: University of Pennsylvania Press.

Heath, Shirley Brice. 1986. "What No Bedtime Story Means: Narrative Skills at Home and School." In *Language Socialization across Cultures,* edited by B. Schieffelin and E. Ochs. Cambridge: Cambridge University Press, pp. 97–127.

Heelas, Paul, and Andrew Lock, eds. 1981. *Indigenous Psychologies: The Anthropology of Self.* London: Academic Press.

Hendry, Joy. 1986. *Becoming Japanese: The World of the Preschool Child.* Honolulu, Hawaii: University of Hawaii Press.

Hewitt, John P. 1989. *Dilemmas of the American Self.* Philadelphia: Temple University Press.

Hochschild, Arlie. 1979. "Emotion Work, Feeling Rules, and Social Structure." *American Journal of Sociology* 85(3):551–575.

Hofstede, G. 1980. *Culture's Consequences.* Beverly Hills, CA: Sage.

Hollan, David. 1992. "Cross-cultural Differences in the Self." *Journal of Anthropological Research* 48:283–300.

Holland, Dorothy, and Andrew Kipnis. 1994. "Metaphors for Embarrassment and Stories of Exposure: The Not-So-Egocentric Self in American Culture." *Ethos* 22(3):316–342.

Holland, Dorothy, and Naomi Quinn, eds. 1987. *Cultural Models in Language and Thought.* Cambridge: Cambridge University Press.

Hollingshead, A. B. 1958. *Social Class and Mental Illness.* New York: John Wiley & Sons, Inc.

———. 1949. *Elmtown's Youth.* New York: Wiley and Sons.

Hsu, Francis L. K. 1983. *Rugged Individualism Reconsidered: Essays in Psychological Anthropology.* Knoxville, TN: The University of Tennessee Press.

Hui, C. H. 1984. "Individualism-Collectivism: Theory, Measurement and Its Relation to Reward Allocation." Ph.D. diss., University of Illinois.

Jackson, Michael, ed. 1996. *Things as They Are: New Directions in Phenomenological Anthropology.* Bloomington: Indiana University Press.

James, Muriel, and Dorothy Jongeward. 1971. *Born to Win.* Center City, MN: Hazelden.

Johnson, F. 1985. "The Western Concept of Self." In *Culture and Self,* edited by A. Marsella, G. DeVos, and A. Hsu, London: Tavistock, pp. 57–82.

Kan, Sergei. 1987. "Memory Eternal: Orthodox Christianity and the Tlingit Mortuary Complex." *Arctic Anthropology* 24:32–55.

Kapferer, Bruce. 1997. *The Feast of the Sorcerer: Practices of Consciousness and Power.* Chicago: University of Chicago Press.

Kashima, Yoshihisa. 1987. "Conceptions of Person: Implications in Individualism/ Collectivism Research." In *Growth and Progress in Cross-Cultural Psychology,* edited by Cigdem Kagitcibasi. Lisse: Swets & Zeitlinger B.V.

Keesing, Roger. 1982. *Kwaio Religion.* New York: Columbia University Press.

Kleinman, Arthur. 1986. *Social Origins of Distress and Disease: Neurasthenia and Pain in Modern China.* New Haven: Yale University Press.

Kleinman, Arthur, and Joan Kleinman. 1985. "Somatization: The Interconnections in Chinese Society among Culture, Depressive Experiences, and Meanings of Pain." In *Culture and Depression,* edited by Arthur Kleinman and Byron Good. Berkeley: University of California Press, pp. 429–491.

Kohn, Melvin. 1969. *Class and Conformity: A Study in Values.* Homewood, IL: The Dorsey Press.

———. 1963a. "Social Class and Parent-Child Relationships: An Interpretation." *American Journal of Sociology* 68:471–480.

———. 1963b. "Social Class and the Exercise of Parental Authority." In *Personality and Social Systems,* edited by N. Smelser and W. Smelser. New York: Wiley, pp. 297–323.

Kohn, Melvin, and Carmi Schooler. 1983. *Work and Personality: An Inquiry into the Impact of Social Stratification.* Norwood, NJ: Ablex Publishing Corporation.

Kohut, H. 1985. *Self Psychology and the Humanities.* New York: W. W. Norton.

———. 1977. *The Restoration of the Self.* New York: International Universities Press.

Kondo, Dorinne. 1990. *Crafting Selves: Power, Gender, and Discourses of Identity in a Japanese Workplace.* Chicago: University of Chicago Press.

Kuhn, M. H., and T. S. McPartland. 1954. "An Empirical Investigation of Self-Attitudes." *American Sociological Review* 19:68–76.

Kusserow, Adrie. 1999a. "De-Homogenizing American Individualism: Socializing Hard and Soft Individualism in Manhattan and Queens." *Ethos* 27:210–234.

———. 1999b. "Crossing the Great Divide: Anthropological Theories of Western Self." *Journal of Anthropological Research* 55:541–562.

Lamb, S. 1997. "The Making and Unmaking of Persons: Notes on Aging and Gender in North India." *Ethos* 25:279–302.

Lareau, Annette. 1989. *Home Advantage: Social Class and Parental Intervention in Elementary Education.* London: The Falmer Press.

Lasch, Christopher. 1979. *Culture of Narcissism: American Life in an Age of Diminishing Expectations.* New York: W.W. Norton & Company.

Lebra, Takie. 1976. *Japanese Patterns of Behavior.* Honolulu: University of Hawaii Press.

LeVine, Robert A. 1990. "Infant Environments in Psychoanalysis: A Cross-Cultural View." In *Cultural Psychology: Essays in Comparative Human Development,* edited by J. Stigler, R. Shweder and G. Herdt. Cambridge: Cambridge University Press, pp. 454–477.

———. 1983. "Fertility and Child Development: An Anthropological Approach." In *Child Development and International Development: Research-Policy Interfaces,* edited by D. Wagner. San Fransisco: Jossey-Brass.

———. 1982. *Culture, Behavior and Personality: An Introduction to the Comparative Study of Psychosocial Adaptation.* New York: Aldine Publishing Company.

Levine, Robert A., et al. 1994. *Childcare and Culture: Lessons from Africa.* New York: Cambridge University Press.

LeVine, Robert A., Patrice Miller, and Mary Maxwell West, eds. 1988. *Parental Behavior in Diverse Societies.* San Fransisco: Jossey-Bass, Inc.

Levy, Robert. 1990. *Mesocosm: Hinduism and the Organization of a Traditional Newar City in Nepal.* Berkeley: University of California Press.

———. 1973. *Tahitians: Mind and Experience in the Society Islands.* Chicago: University of Chicago Press.

Lewis, Catherine C. 1989. "From Indulgence to Internalization: Social Control in the Early School Years." *Journal of Japanese Studies* 15(1):139–157.

Lifton, Robert J. 1970. *Boundaries: Psychological Man in Revolution.* New York: Vintage.

Lin, N., 1988. "Chinese Family Structure and Chinese Society." Bulletin of Institute of Ethnology. Academia Sinica 65:59–129.

Lindholm, Charles. 1997. "Does the Sociocentric Self Exist? Reflections on Markus and Kitayama's 'Culture of Self.'" *Journal of Anthropological Research* 53:405–422.

———. 1990. *Charisma.* Oxford, England: Basil Blackwell.

———. 1988. "Lovers and Leaders: A Comparison of Social and Psychological Models of Romance and Charisma." *Social Science Information* 27(1):3–45.

———. 1982. *Generosity and Jealousy: The Swat Pukhtun of Northern Pakistan.* New York: Columbia University Press.

Lubeck, Sally. 1985. *Sandbox Society: Early Education in Black and White America.* Philadelphia: Falmer Press.

Luttrell, Wendy. 1997. *Schoolsmart and Motherwise: Working-Class Women's Identity and Schooling.* Routledge: New York.

Lutz, Catherine. 1988. *Unnatural Emotions: Everyday Sentiments on a Micronesian Atoll and Their Challenge to Western Theory.* Chicago: University of Chicago Press.

Lutz, Catherine, and Lila Abu-Lughod, eds. 1990. *Language and the Politics of Emotion.* Cambridge: Cambridge University Press.

Lykes, M. B. 1985. "Gender and Individualist vs. Collectivist Bases for Notions about the Self." *Journal of Personality* 53:356–383.

MacIntyre, Alasdair. 1984. *After Virtue: A Study in Moral Theory.* Notre Dame, IN: University of Notre Dame Press.

MacLeod, Jay. 1995. *Ain't No Makin' It: Aspirations and Attainment in a Low-Income Neighborhood.* Boulder: Westview Press.

———. 1987. *Ain't No Makin' It: Leveled Aspirations in a Low-Income Neighborhood.* Boulder: Westview Press.

Marcus, George E., and Michael M. J. Fischer. 1986. *Anthropology as Cultural Critique.* Chicago: University of Chicago.

Markus, Hazel, and Shinobu Kitayama. 1991. "Culture and the Self: Implications for Cognition, Emotion, and Motivation." *Psychological Review* 98:224–253.

Marriott, McKim. 1976. "Interpreting Indian Society: A Monistic Alternative to Dumont's Dualism." *Journal of Asian Studies* 36(3):189–195.

Marsella, Anthony, George DeVos, and Francis Hsu, eds. 1985. *Culture and Self.* London: Tavistock.

Martin, Emily. 1987. *The Woman in the Body: A Cultural Analysis of Reproduction.* Boston: Beacon Press.

McCreery, John L. 1977. "Potential and Effective Meaning in Therapeutic Ritual." *Culture, Medicine and Psychiatry* 2:53–70.

McHugh, Ernestine. 1988. "Concepts of the Person among the Gurungs of Nepal." *American Ethnologist* 15:75–87.

Mead, Margaret. 1949. *Coming of Age in Samoa.* New York: New American Library.

Michaels, S. 1991. "The Dismantling of Narrative." In *Developing Narrative Structure*, edited by A. McCabe and C. Peterson. Hillsdale, NJ: Erlbaum, pp. 303–351.

Miller, Darla Ferris. 1989. *First Steps toward Cultural Difference: Socialization in Infant/Toddler Day Care.* Washington, D.C.: Child Welfare League of America.

Miller, Peggy J. 1996. "Instantiating Culture through Discourse Practices: Some Personal Reflections in Socialization and How to Study It." In *Ethnography and Human Development: Context and Meaning in Social Inquiry*, edited by R. Jessor, A. Colby, and R. A. Shweder. Chicago: University of Chicago Press.

———. 1994. "Narrative Practices: Their Role in Socialization and Self-Construction." In *The Remembered Self: Construction and Accuracy in the Self Narrative*, edited by U. Neisser and R. Fivush. Cambridge: Cambridge University Press, pp.158–179.

———. 1990. "Narrative Practices and the Social Construction of Self in Childhood." *American Ethnologist* 17:292–311.

———. 1986. "Teasing as Language Socialization and Verbal Play in a White, Working-class Community." In *Language Socialization across Cultures*, edited by B. B. Schieffelin and E. Ochs. Cambridge: Cambridge University Press, pp.199–212.

———. 1984. "Culture and the Development of Everyday Social Explanation." *Journal of Personality and Social Psychology* 46:961–978.

————. 1982. "Culture and the Development of Social Explanation." Ph.D. diss. University of Chicago.

Miller, P. J. and R. Mehler 1994. "Personal Storytelling, Socialization, and Self Construction at Home and in Kindergarten." In *The Need for Story: Cultural Diversity in Classroom and Community*, edited by A. Hass-Dyson and C. Genish. Urbana, IL: National Council of Teachers of English, pp. 38–54.

Miller, P. J. and Barbara Byhouwer Moore. 1989. "Narrative Conjunctions of Caregiver and Child: A Comparative Perspective on Socialization Through Stories." *Ethos* 17:428–449.

Miller, P. J. and L. L. Sperry. 1988. "Early Talk about the Past: The Origins of Conversational Stories of Personal Experience." *Journal of Child Language* 15: 293–315.

————. 1987. "The Socialization of Anger and Aggression." *The Merrill-Palmer Quarterly* 33:1–31.

Mines, M., 1988. "Conceptualizing the Person: Hierarchical Society and Individual Autonomy in India." *American Anthropologist* 90:568–579.

Moffat, Michael. 1992. "Ethnographic Writing about American Culture." *Annual Review of Anthropology* 21:205–229.

————.1989. *Coming of Age in New Jersey: College and American Culture*. New Brunswick, NJ: Rutgers University Press.

Murphy, Robert. 1990. *The Body Silent*. New York: W.W. Norton.

Murray, D. W. 1993. "What Is the Western Concept of the Self? On Forgetting David Hume." *Ethos* 21:3–23.

Myers, Fred. 1979. "Emotions and the Self: A Theory of Personhood and Political Order among the Pintupi Aborigines." *Ethos* 9: 343–370.

Obeyesekere, Gananath. 1981. *Medusa's Hair: An Essay on Personal Symbols and Religious Experience*. Chicago: University of Chicago Press.

Oxfeld, E. 1992. "Individualism, Holism and the Market Mentality: Notes on the Recollections of a Chinese Entrepreneur." *Cultural Anthropology* 7:267–300.

Peak, Lois. 1991. *Learning to Go to School in Japan: The Transition from Home to Preschool Life*. Berkeley: University of California Press.

————. 1989. "Learning to Become Part of the Group: The Japanese Child's Transition to Preschool Life."*Journal of Japanese Studies* 15 (1):93–123.

Potter, D. M. 1973. *History and American Society: Essays of David M. Potter*, edited by D. E. Fehrenbacher. New York: Oxford University Press.

Quinn, N. 1982. "'Commitment' in American Marriage: A Cultural Analysis." *American Ethnologist* 9:775–798.

Richman, Amy L., P. Miller, and M. Solomon. 1988. "The Socialization of Infants in Suburban Boston." In *Parental Behavior in Diverse Societies*, edited by R. LeVine, P. Miller, and M. West, San Francisco: Jossey-Brass, pp. 65–75.

Riesman, David. 1964. *Individualism Reconsidered*. New York: Free Press.

Riesman, David, with Nathan Glazer and Reuel Denney. 1950. *The Lonely Crowd: A Study of the Changing American Character*. New Haven: Yale University Press.

Rogoff, B. 1990. *Apprenticeship in Thinking: Cognitive Development in Social Context*. New York: Oxford University Press.

Rosaldo, Michelle. 1984. "Toward an Anthropology of Self and Feeling." In *Culture Theory: Essays on Mind, Self, and Emotion*, edited by R. Shweder and R. A. LeVine. New York: Cambridge University Press, pp. 137–157.

Rosenberger, Nancy. 1992. *Japanese Sense of Self*. Cambridge: Cambridge University Press.

———. 1989. "Dialectic Balance in the Polar Model of Self: The Japan Case." *Ethos* 17(4):88–113.

Rotenberg, M. 1977. "Alienating Individualism and Reciprocal Individualism: A Cross-cultural Conceptualization." *Journal of Humanistic Psychology* 17:3–17.

Said, Edward. 1978. *Orientalism.* New York: Vintage Books.

Sampson, Edward E. 1988. "The Debate on Individualism: Indigenous Psychologies of the Individual and Their Role in Personal and Societal Functioning." *American Psychologist* 43(1):15–22.

Schachter, S., and J. E. Singer. 1962. "Cognitive, Social and Physiological Determinants of Emotional State." *Psychological Review* 69:379–399.

Scheper-Hughes. 1979. *Saints, Scholars and Schizophrenics: Mental Illness in Rural Ireland.* Berkeley: University of California Press.

Schieffelin, Bambi and Elinor Ochs. 1984. "Language Acquisition and Socialization: Three Developmental Stories and Their Implications." In *Culture Theory: Essays on Mind, Self and Emotion,* edited by Richard Shweder and Robert LeVine. Cambridge: Cambridge University Press, pp. 276–322.

Seitz, Sharon. 1996. *The Other Islands of New York City: A Historical Companion.* Backcountry Publications.

Sennet, Richard. 1976. *The Fall of Public Man.* New York: W.W. Norton & Company.

Sennet, Richard and Jonathan Cobb. 1972. *The Hidden Injuries of Class.* New York: Vintage Books.

Seyfried, Vincent F. 1982. *Queens: A Pictorial History.* New York: Donning Co.

Shokeid, M. 1988. *Children of Circumstances: Israeli Emigrants in New York.* Ithaca, NY: Cornell University Press.

Shweder, Richard. 1985. "Menstrual Pollution, Soul Loss and the Comparative Study of Emotions." In *Culture and Depression,* edited by Arthur Kleinman and Byron Good. Berkeley: University of California Press, pp. 182–216.

Shweder, Richard and Edmund J. Bourne. 1984. "Does the Concept of the Person Vary Cross-Culturally?" In *Culture Theory: Essays on Mind, Self and Emotion,* edited by R. Shweder and R. LeVine. New York: Cambridge University Press.

Shweder, Richard, Manamohan Mahapatra, and Joan Miller. 1990. "Culture and Moral Development." In *Cultural Psychology: Essays on Comparative Human Development.* New York: Cambridge University Press.

Shweder, Richard, with Joan G. Miller. 1991. "The Social Construction of the Person: How Is It Possible?" In *Thinking through Cultures: Expeditions in Cultural Psychology.* Cambridge, MA: Harvard University Press.

Shweder, Richard, with Nancy C. Much. 1991. "Determinations of Meaning: Discourse and Moral Socialization." In *Thinking through Cultures: Expeditions in Cultural Psychology.* Cambridge, MA: Harvard University Press.

Slater, Philip. 1970. *The Pursuit of Loneliness: American Culture at the Breaking Point.* Boston: Beacon Press.

Sontag, Susan. 1978. *Illness as Metaphor.* New York: Farrar, Straus & Giroux.

Sourcebook of Zip Code Demographics. 2002. New York: ESRI Press.

Sperry, L. L. and D. E. Sperry. 1996. "The Early Development of Narrative Skills." *Cognitive Development* 11:443–465.

Spiro, Melford. 1993. "Is the Western Conception of the Self 'Peculiar' within the Context of the World Cultures?" *Ethos* 21(2):107–153.

Stairs, Arlene. 1992. "Self-Image, World-Image: Speculations on Identity from Experiences with Inuit." *Ethos* 20:116–126.

Stephenson, Peter H. 1991. "Going to McDonald's in Leiden: Reflections on the Concept of Self in Society in the Netherlands." *Ethos* 17:226–247.

Stevenson, Harold and Shin-Ying Lee. 1990. *Contexts of Achievement: A Study of American, Chinese and Japanese Children. Monographs of the Society for Research in Child Development.* Chicago: University of Chicago Press.

Stigler, James W., and Michelle Perry. 1990. "Mathematics Learning in Japanese, Chinese and American classrooms." In *Cultural Psychology: Essays in Comparative Human Development,* edited by J. Stigler, R. Shweder, and G. Herdt. Cambridge: Cambridge University Press, pp. 328–356.

Strauss, Claudia. 2000. "The Culture Concept and the Individualism-Collectivism Debate: Dominant and Alternative Attributions for Class in America." In *Culture Thought and Development,* edited by Larry Nucci, Geoffrey Saxe, and Elliot Turiel. Mahwah, NJ: Lawrence Erlbaum Associates.

Strauss, Claudia and Naomi Quinn. 1997. *A Cognitive Theory of Cultural Meaning.* Cambridge: Cambridge University Press.

Stromberg, Peter G. 1991. "Symbols into Experience: A Case Study in the Generation of Commitment." *Ethos* 19:102–126.

———. 1990. "The Impression Point: Synthesis of Symbol and Self." *Ethos* 18:56–74.

———. 1981. "Consensus and Variation in the Interpretation of Symbolism: A Swedish Example." *American Ethnologist* 8:544–559.

Taylor, Charles. 1989. *Sources of the Self: The Making of the Modern Identity.* Cambridge: Harvard University Press.

Tipton, Steven. 1982. *Getting Saved From the Sixties: Moral Meaning in Conversion and Cultural Change.* Berkeley: University of California Press.

Tobin, Joseph. 1995. "The Irony of Self-Expression." *American Journal of Education* 103: 233–258.

Tobin, Joseph, David Wu, and Dana Davidson. 1989. *Preschool in Three Cultures: Japan, China, and the United States.* New Haven: Yale University Press.

Tocqueville, Alexis De. 1969. Democracy in America. Garden City, NY: Doubleday. (Original Publication 1835.)

Triandis, Harry C. 1989. "The Self and Social Behavior in Differing Cultural Contexts." *Psychological Review* 96(3):506–520.

———. 1987. "Individualism and Social Psychological Theory." In *Growth and Progress in Cross-Cultural Psychology,* edited by Cigdem Kagitcibasi. Berwyn: Swets North America, Inc.

———. 1983. *Allocentric vs. Idiocentric Social Behavior: A Major Cultural Difference between Hispanics and Mainstream.* Champaign, IL: Department of Psychology, University of Illinois.

Triandis, Harry, C., Kwok Leung, Marcelo J. Villareal, and Felicia L. Clack. 1985. "Allocentric versus Idiocentric Tendencies: Convergent and Discriminant Validation." *Journal of Research in Personality* 19:395–415.

Trilling, Lionel. 1972. *Sincerity and Authenticity.* Cambridge, MA: Harvard University Press.

Tuan, Yi-Fu. 1982. *Segmented Worlds and Self: Group Life and Individual Consciousness.* Minneapolis: University of Minnesota Press.

Turner, Ralph. 1976. "The Real Self: From Institution to Impulse." *American Journal of Sociology* 81:989–1016.

Varenne, Herve. 1977. *Americans Together: Structured Diversity in a Midwestern Town.* New York: Teachers College Press.

Waterman, Alan S. 1981. "Individualism and Interdependence." *American Psychologist* 36(7):762–773.

Waters, Mary. 1990. *Ethnic Options: Choosing Identities in America.* Berkeley: University of California Press.

Weber, Max. 1949. *The Methodology of the Social Sciences.* Trans. and edited by Edward A. Shils and Henry A. Finch. New York: Free Press.

Wellencamp, Jane C., and Douglas Hollan. 1981. "The Influence of American Concepts of the Self on the Experience of Bereavement." Paper presented at the Kroeber Anthropological Society, spring 1981, Berkeley, California.

White, Geoffrey, and John Kirkpatrick, eds. 1985. *Person, Self and Experience: Exploring Pacific Ethnopsychologies.* Berkeley: University of California Press.

White, M. 1987. *The Japanese Educational Challenge: A Commitment to Children.* New York: Free Press.

Whiting, John. 1966. *Field Guide for a Study of Socialization.* New York: John Wiley and Sons, Inc.

Whiting, John, and B. Whiting. 1975. *Children of Six Cultures.* Cambridge, MA: Harvard University Press.

Whittaker, Elvi. 1992. "The Birth of the Anthropological Self." *Ethos* 20:191–219.

Wiley, A., A. Rose, L. Burger, and P. J. Miller. 1998. "Constructing Autonomous Selves through Narrative Practices: A Comparative Study of Working-class and Middle-class Families." *Child Development* 69(3): 833–847.

Wilkinson, Rupert. 1988. *The Pursuit of American Character.* New York: Harper & Row.

Willis, Paul. 1977. *Learning to Labor.* Aldershot: Gower.

Yanigasako, Sylvia. 1985. *Transforming the Past: Tradition and Kinship among Japanese Americans.* Stanford, CA: Stanford University Press.

Index